m

NEW YORK CITY

Yellow cabs on Fifth Avenue, with Saint Patrick's Cathedral in the background, ©Tips Images

MICHELIN

| **Editorial Director** | Cynthia Clayton Ochterbeck |

mustsees New York City

Editor	Jonathan P. Gilbert
Principal Writer	Anne-Marie Scott
Production Manager	Natasha G. George
Cartography	Peter Wrenn
Photo Editor	Alison Coupe, Yoshimi Kanazawa
Photo Research	Jenni Rainford
Proofreaders	Alison Coupe, Rachel Mills
Layout	Alison Rayner, Natasha G. George
Cover & Interior Design	Chris Bell

Contact Us:

Michelin Maps and Guides
One Parkway South
Greenville, SC 29615
USA
www.michelintravel.com
michelin.guides@us.michelin.com

Michelin Maps and Guides
Hannay House
39 Clarendon Road
Watford, Herts WD17 1JA
UK
☏(01923) 205 240
www.ViaMichelin.com
travelpubsales@uk.michelin.com

Special Sales:

For information regarding bulk sales, customized
editions and premium sales, please contact
our Customer Service Departments:

USA	1-800-432-6277
UK	(01923) 205 240
Canada	1-800-361-8236

Michelin Apa Publications Ltd

A joint venture between Michelin and Langenscheidt

58 Borough High Street, London SE1 1XF, United Kingdom

© 2009 Michelin Apa Publications Ltd
ISBN 978-1-906261-60-3
Printed: December 2008
Printed and bound: Himmer, Germany

Note to the reader:
While every effort is made to ensure that all information printed in this guide is correct and
up-to-date, Michelin Apa Publications Ltd. accepts no liability for any direct, indirect or
consequential losses howsoever caused so far as such can be excluded by law. Admission
prices listed for sights in this guide are for a single adult, unless otherwise specified.

Welcome to New York City

New York Skyline

Brigitta L. House/Avalon Travel

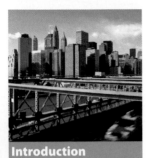

Introduction

**New York City:
All that Glitters** 21

Must See

p.74

p88

TABLE OF CONTENTS

★★★ ATTRACTIONS

Unmissable attractions awarded three stars in this guide include:

Statue of Liberty p 51

©PhotoDisc

Hudson River Valley p 110

©Maureen Plainfield/Dreamstime.com

Metropolitan Museum of Art
p 60

Brigtta L. House/Michelin

Central Park p 84

©Terraxplorer/iStockphoto.com

Brooklyn Bridge   p 46

©Jeremy Edwards/iStockphoto.com

Fifth Avenue   p 148

©Oliver Malms/iStockphoto.com

Museum of Modern Art   p 60

The Museum of Modern Art/©2005 Timothy Hursley

Bronx Zoo   p 124

©Sharon Kennedy/iStockphoto.com

Empire State Building   p 47

©Christopher Walker/Fotolia.com

★★★ ATTRACTIONS

Unmissable sights in and around New York City

For more than 75 years people have used the Michelin stars to take the guesswork out of travel. Our star-rating system helps you make the best decision on where to go, what to do, and what to see.

★★★	Absolutely Must See
★★	Really Must See
★	Must See
No Star	See

ACTIVITIES

**Unmissable Bars,
Shows, Cycle Rides
Shopping and more**

STAR ATTRACTIONS

CALENDAR OF EVENTS

Listed below is a selection of New York City's most popular annual events. Please note that dates may vary from year to year. For more detailed information, contact NYC & Co. *(212-484-1200 or 800-692-8474; www.nycvisit.com).*

January

Chinese New Year Celebrations
Chinatown
www.explorechinatown.com

Winter Antiques Show
Park Avenue Armory
718-292-7392
www.winterantiquesshow.com

February

Westminster Dog Show
Madison Square Garden
212-465-6741
www.westminsterkennel
club.org

March

St. Patrick's Day Parade, Fifth Ave.
44th to 86th Sts.
www.saintpatricksday
parade.com

April

Cherry Blossom Festival
Brooklyn Botanic Garden
718-623-7200
www.bbg.org

Easter Sunday Parade, Fifth Ave.
57th St. to 49th St.

New York International Auto Show
Jacob K. Javits Center
718-746-5300
www.autoshowny.com

May

TriBeCa Film Festival
TriBeCa
212-941-2400
www.tribecafilmfestival.org

June

JVC Jazz Festival New York
Various locations
www.festivalproductions.net

LGBT Pride Week
Various locations
212-807-7433
www.nycpride.org

Mermaid Parade
Coney Island
718-372-5159
www.coneyislandusa.com

March: St Patrick's Day Parade

©Kelly McCarthy/Creative Commons

©NYC&Co.

Mermaid Parade

Museum Mile Festival
212-606-2296
www.museummilefestival.org
**National Puerto Rican
Day Parade**
Fifth Ave.
718-401-0404
www.nationalpuerto
ricandayparade.org
SummerStage in Central Park
Jun–Aug at Rumsey Playfield
212-360-2777
www.summerstage.org

July
Midsummer-Night Swing
Lincoln Center
212-721-6500
www.lincolncenter.org
Macy's Fireworks Celebration
East River from 23rd to 42nd Sts.
212-494-4495

August
Mostly Mozart Festival
Lincoln Center
212-721-6500
www.lincolncenter.org
Harlem Jazz & Music Festival
Harlem
www.harlemdiscover.com

US Open Tennis Tournament
USTA National Tennis Center,
Queens
718-760-6200
www.usta.com

September
Feast of San Gennaro
Little Italy
212-768-9320
www.sangennaro.org
New York Film Festival
Lincoln Center
212-875-5050
www.filmlinc.com

October
**Columbus Day Parade,
Fifth Ave.**
47th to 79th Sts.
212-249-9923
www.columbuscitizensfd.org
Halloween Parade
Greenwich Village
www.halloween-nyc.com

November
**Macy's Thanksgiving
Day Parade**
Central Park West to
Herald Square
212-494-4495
New York City Marathon
Verrazano-Narrows Bridge to
Central Park
212-860-4455
www.ingnycmarathon.org

December
**Christmas Tree
Lighting Ceremony**
Rockefeller Center
212-632-3975
New Year's Eve Ball Drop
Times Square
www.timessquarenyc.org

PRACTICAL INFORMATION

WHEN TO GO

New York takes on a different character during each of its four distinct seasons.

The crisp, cool days of **fall** bring the debut of the city's renowned cultural season; be sure to reserve theater, opera and concert tickets well in advance. Fall is a lovely time for strolling in parks and window-shopping along streets festooned with brilliantly colored trees.

Holiday decorations, performances and festivities abound in early **winter**, a premium (and pricey) time to visit. Things calm down a bit in January and February; many hotels offer low-season discounts and midwinter can be a great time to land tickets to blockbuster Broadway shows.

Weather in the brief **spring** ranges from balmy to rainy to frigid. In May the city's parks and gardens burst into bloom, drawing New Yorkers outdoors to enjoy mild temperatures and sunny days.

Although hot and muggy, **summer** in the city offers its own particular charms. Many New Yorkers head out of town in July and August, leaving a calmer, less crowded city. It's easier to snag a table at popular restaurants, and free cultural festivals, concerts, films and theater performances abound, many of them outdoors in shady parks and green spaces.

KNOW BEFORE YOU GO

Useful Websites

www.nycvisit.com - The official tourism bureau (see below) website is packed with up-to-the-minute information on events, hotels, restaurants, shopping and more.

www.nytimes.com - The online version of the New York Times maintains a travel guide with news and information on hotels, restaurants, events and shows.

http://nymag.com - The online version of New York Magazine; check here for news, events, fashion and shopping information.

http://newyork.citysearch.com - Users can access a directory of services and reviews of restaurants, nightclubs, spas, hotels and more.

www.in-newyork.com - The website of IN New York magazine features event calendars, shopping, nightlife, sightseeing, etc.

NYC & Company

New York City's official tourism bureau has a wealth of information about sightseeing, accommodations, recreation and events:

NYC & Company - 810 Seventh Ave., New York, NY 10019; 212-484-1200; www.nycvisit.com
To receive a visitor information packet, call 800-692-8474. Visitor information counselors can be reached at 212-484-1222.

New York City Average Seasonal Temperatures (recorded at Central Park)				
	Jan	Apr	July	Oct
Avg. high	38°F/3°C	61°F/16°C	85°F/29°C	66°F/19°C
Avg. low	26°F/-3°C	44°F/7°C	70°F/20°C	50°F/10°C

Visitor Centers

Visitor centers are generally open every day, including holidays, during business hours. Neighborhood kiosks, which have both neighborhood-specific and citywide information, may be closed in inclement weather. For updates, check online at www.nycvisit.com.

Midtown – NYC & Company's main visitor center is located at 810 Seventh Ave. between W. 52nd & 53rd Sts.

Times Square – Large center at 1560 Broadway, between W. 46th & 47th Sts.

Financial District – Information center at Federal Hall National Memorial, 26 Wall St.

Chinatown – Kiosk in the triangle formed by Canal, Walker & Baxter Sts.

City Hall Park – Kiosk on the Broadway sidewalk at Park Row.

International Visitors

Visitors from outside the US can obtain information from the multilingual staff at NYC & Co. (*www.nycvisit.com*) or from the US embassy or consulate in their country of residence (many foreign countries also maintain consulates in New York City). For a complete list of American consulates and embassies abroad, visit the U.S. Embassy website at: *http://usembassy.state.gov/*.

Entry Requirements – Travelers entering the United States under the Visa Waiver Program (VWP) must present a machine-readable passport; otherwise, a US visa is required. Citizens of VWP countries are permitted to enter the US for general business or tourist purposes for a maximum of 90 days without needing a visa. For a list of countries participating in the VWP, contact the US consulate in your country of residence or consult the official Visa Services website (*http://travel.state.gov*).

Citizens of nonparticipating countries must have a passport and a visitor's visa.

All travelers (including infants and children) entering the US from countries participating in the Western Hemisphere Travel Initiative (Canada, Mexico, Central and South America, Bermuda and the Caribbean) must carry a passport if traveling by air. Starting June 1, 2009, US citizens entering the US from WHTI countries by any means must present a passport, passport card or other WHTI-compliant document. For information on entry requirements, see *http://travel. state.gov* or contact the US consulate in your country of residence.

US Customs – All articles brought into the US must be declared at the time of entry. Prohibited items include plant material, firearms and ammunition, meat or poultry products. For information, contact the U.S. Customs Service (*877-227-5511; www.cbp.gov*).

Accessibility

Federal law requires that businesses (including hotels and restaurants) provide access for the disabled, devices for the hearing impaired, and designated parking spaces. For further information, contact the Society for Accessible Travel and Hospitality (SATH), 347 Fifth Ave., Suite 605, New York, NY 10016 (*212-447-7284; www.sath.org*).

All national parks have facilities for the disabled, and offer free or discounted passes.

PRACTICAL INFORMATION

For details, contact the National Park Service (*Office of Public Inquiries, 1849 C St NW, Rm 1013, Washington, DC 20240; 202-208-4747; www.nps.gov*).

Passengers who will need assistance with train or bus travel should give advance notice to Amtrak (*800-872-7245 or 800-523-6590/TDD*) or Greyhound (*800-752-4841 or 800-345-3109/TDD*). Make reservations for hand-controlled rental cars in advance with the rental-car company.

GETTING THERE

By Air

New York City is served by three airports: two in the borough of Queens and one in New Jersey. They are all run by the Port Authority of New York and New Jersey. In all three airports, ground transportation and information booths are located on the baggage-claim level.

John F. Kennedy International Airport (JFK) –

In Queens, 15 miles southeast of Midtown Manhattan (*718-244-4444; www.panynj.gov*).

LaGuardia Airport (LGA) –

In Queens, eight miles northeast of Midtown Manhattan (*718-533-3400; www.panynj.gov*).

Newark Liberty International Airport (EWR) –

In Newark, NJ, 16 miles southwest of Midtown Manhattan (*973-961-6000; www.panynj.gov*).

Airport Transfers

New York City's major airports are served by various transfer services. For a description of all options, call the Port Authorty's recorded information line at 800-247-7433.

The Grid

Manhattan's streets are in a grid pattern (except Greenwich Village and the Financial District).

Streets run east–west and avenues run north–south. Fifth Avenue is the dividing line between east and west addresses. **Downtown** is south; **Uptown**, north. "Downtown" also refers to the area below 34th Street. **Midtown** stretches from 34th to 59th Street; Uptown is the area north of that. Most Manhattan streets are one-way.

Taxi service is available outside each terminal. Passengers at Kennedy and LaGuardia airports should wait in line and allow a uniformed dispatcher to hail the next available cab. Avoid solicitations from unauthorized drivers. Fares to Manhattan: from JFK, $45 flat rate to any point in Manhattan (tolls not included); from LGA, $20–$30 (average metered rate) plus tolls; from EWR, $50–$75 (average metered rate) plus tolls. A 50¢ surcharge is added to all metered fares nightly 8pm–6am; there is a $1 peak-time surcharge weekdays 4pm–8pm.

Air Train Newark (*888-397-4636; www.airtrainnewark.com*) links Newark airport with the New Jersey Transit and Amtrak networks. **Air Train JFK** (*877-535-2478; www.panynj.com/airtrain*) links JFK's eight terminals to PATH subway and bus lines to New York City and Long Island. LaGuardia Airport is accessible via the **M60 bus**. **Super Shuttle** (*212-258-3826; www.supershuttle.com*) offers service between airports and to and from Manhattan by van 24 hours daily (*$16–$21*). The **New York**

Airport Service (*212-875-8200; www.nyairportservice.com*) express bus runs between Kennedy and LaGuardia airports and Midtown Manhattan's major transit hubs and hotels (*fare and schedule information available online*). **Olympia Trails Airport Express Bus** (*877-863-9275; www.coachusa.com*) runs from Newark airport to Penn Station, Grand Central Terminal and the Port Authority Bus Terminal (*fare and schedule information available online*).

By Train
Daily service to New York's **Penn Station** (*W. 32nd St. & Seventh Ave.*) is provided by Amtrak (*800-872-7245; www.amtrak.com*) and the commuter lines of the Long Island Railroad (*718-217-5477*) and New Jersey Transit (*973-275-5555; www.njtransit.com*). **Grand Central Terminal** (*E. 42nd St. & Park Ave.*) is served by Metro-North (*212-532-4900 or 800-638-7646*) trains from Manhattan to New Haven, Connecticut; Wassaic, New York; and Poughkeepsie, New York. PATH (*800-234-7284; www.panynj. gov/path*) lines connect Manhattan with cities in New Jersey.

By Bus
The **Port Authority Bus Terminal** (*W. 42nd St. & Eighth Ave; 212-564-8484*) is the city's main bus terminal and is used by both long-distance and commuter carriers. For schedules, routes and fares for trips throughout the US, contact Greyhound (*800-231-2222; www.greyhound.com*).
For service in the Northeast, contact Peter Pan (*800-343-9999; www.peterpanbus.com*).

By Car
New York City is situated at the crossroads of **I-95** (north-south) and **I-80** (east-west). Four tunnels and six major bridges lead into Manhattan from all directions; most of them have tolls.

Driving in the US – Visitors bearing valid driver's licenses issued by their country of residence are not required to obtain an International Driver's License. Drivers must carry vehicle registration and/or rental contract, and proof of automobile insurance at all times. Gasoline is sold by the gallon. Vehicles in the US are driven on the right-hand side of the road. Distances are posted in miles.

GETTING AROUND

On Foot
New York is a very walkable city. There are 20 blocks per mile running north–south and six blocks per mile running east–west. Fifth Avenue marks the division between east and west; address numbers get larger as you move away from Fifth Avenue in either direction. It's a good idea to get the cross street of any address you're trying to locate.

By Public Transportation
The Metropolitan Transportation Authority (MTA) oversees an extensive network of subways, buses and commuter trains throughout the area. Contact MTA's Travel Information Center (*718-330-1234; www.mta.nyc.ny.us*) for route, schedule and fare information. The **MetroCard** automated fare card can be used on all systems; discount passes are available.

Subway – *For New York City subway map, see inside back cover.*

City Buses – New York City Transit buses generally operate daily 5:30am–2am. Buses on some major routes run 24 hours a day. Route maps are posted at bus stops; citywide bus maps are available at visitor centers. Fares (*$2*) can be deducted from a MetroCard or paid in exact change (*coins only*).

By Taxi

www.nyc.gov/html/tlc.

Only yellow taxi cabs with roof medallions showing the taxi number are authorized to pick up passengers on the street (numbers are illuminated on available cabs). Taxi stands can be found at many hotels and transportation hubs; otherwise hail one at the curb. The fare starts at $2.50, then increases 40¢ each 1/5mi or 60 seconds of wait time. Tolls not included. A single fare covers all passengers in the cab.

By Car

It's best to avoid driving in New York City, but if you must, stay off the roads during rush hours (*weekdays between 7am–9am and 4pm–6pm*). Use of seat belts is required, and child safety seats are mandatory for children under 4 years of age (seats are available from rental-car agencies).

In the state of New York it is illegal to drive with a mobile phone in your hand. Street parking can be difficult to come by; if you do find a space, read signs carefully, as parking tickets often run $100 or more. Garage parking costs around $6–$15 per hour.

Hotel and motel chains in New York City		
Property	**Contact**	**Web site**
Best Western	800-528-1234	www.bestwestern.com
Comfort, Clarion & Quality Inns	800-228-5150	www.choicehotels.com
Fairmont	877-441-1414	www.fairmont.com
Four Seasons	212-758-5700	www.fourseasons.com
Helmsley	800-221-4982	www.helmsleyhotels.com
Hilton	800-445-8667	www.hilton.com
Holiday Inn	800-465-4329	www.holiday-inn.com
Hyatt	800-233-1234	www.hyatt.com
ITT Sheraton	800-325-3535	www.sheraton.com
Marriott	800-228-9290	www.marriott.com
Radisson	888-201-1718	www.ritzcarlton.com
Ritz-Carlton	800-241-3333	www.ramada.com
W Hotels	877-946-8357	www.whotels.com
Westin	888-625-5144	www.westin.com

Important Phone Numbers	
Emergency (24hrs)	911
Police *(non-emergency, Mon–Fri 9am–6pm)*	311 or 646-610-5000
NY Hotel Urgent Medical Services	212-737-1212
Dental emergencies – NYU College of Dentistry Jan Linhart D.D.S., P.C. (24hrs)	212-998-9458 212-682-5180
Poison Control Center (24hrs)	212-764-7667
24-hour Pharmacy: Duane Reade, 3 locations in Manhattan Rite Aid, 5 locations in Manhattan	 212-265-2101 800-748-3243
CVS, 8 locations in Manhattan	800-746-7287

BASIC INFORMATION

Accommodations

For a list of suggested accommodations, see Must Stay.
CRS Hotels – *800-555-7555; www.crshotels.com*
Quikbook – *800-407-3351; www.quikbook.com*
B&B Network of New York – *212-645-8134; www.bedandbreakfastnetny.com*
Affordable New York City – *212-533-4001; www.affordable newyorkcity.com*
Manhattan Getaways – *212-956-2010; www.manhattangetaways.com*
City Lights Bed and Breakfast – *212-737-7049 ; www.citylightsbed andbreakfast.com*
Hostels – *www.hostels.com* – A no-frills, inexpensive alternative to hotels, hostels are a great choice for budget travelers. Prices average $25–$75 per night.

Business Hours

Most retail stores and specialty shops open Mon–Sat 10am–6pm, Sun noon–6pm. Banks are generally open Mon–Fri 9am–3:30pm; some offer Saturday service 9am–noon.

Communications

Telephone - Area codes must be used for local calls in New York City. Dial 1 + area code + seven-digit number.
Manhattan: 212, 646, 917
Bronx, Brooklyn, Queens, Staten Island: 347, 718, 917
Internet Access - Free access is available at all branches of the New York Public Library. Many hotels offer free internet access to their guests. You can also link to the net (for a fee) at internet cafes. WiFi (wireless internet) hotspots abound in the city.

Discounts

CityPass - 888-330-5008. www.citypass.com. You can save up to 50 percent on admission fees by purchasing a CityPass booklet *($74 adults, $54 youth ages 12-17)*, which includes tickets to the American Museum of Natural History, Circle Line Harbor Cruise or Statue of Liberty, Empire State Building Observatory, Guggenheim Museum, the Metropolitan

Museum of Art and the Museum of Modern Art. Buy online or at any participating attraction.

Senior Citizens - Many hotels, attractions and restaurants offer discounts to visitors age 62 or older (proof of age may be required). The **AARP**, formerly the American Association of Retired Persons, offers discounts to its members (*601 E St. NW, Washington, DC 20049; 888-687-2277; www.aarp. org*). Passengers age 60 and older receive a 50% discount on public transportation fares; applications for half-fare MetroCards are available at 718-243-4999.

Electricity
Voltage in the US is 110 volts AC, 60 Hz. Foreign-made appliances may need AC adapters (available at specialty travel and electronics stores) and North American flat-blade plugs.

New York City's Professional Sports Teams				
Sport/Team	**Season**	**Venue**	**Info/Tickets**	**Web site**
Baseball/ New York Mets (NL)	Apr-Oct	Shea Stadium	718-507-6387	www.mets.com
Baseball/ New York Yankees (AL)	Apr-Oct	Yankee Stadium	718-293-4300 212-307-1212	www.yankees.com
Football/ New York Giants (NFC)	Sept-Dec	Meadowlands (Giants Stadium)	201-935-8111 201-935-8222	www.giants.com
Football/ New York Jets (AFC)	Sept-Dec	Meadowlands	516-560-8200	www.newyork jets.com
Men's Basketball/ New York Knicks (NBA)	Oct-Apr	Madison Square Garden	212-465-5867 212-307-7171	www.nyknicks.com
Women's Basketball/ New York Liberty (WNBA)	May-Aug	Madison Square Garden	212-564-9622 877-962-2849	www.nyliberty.com
Hockey/ New York Rangers (NHL)	Oct-Apr	Madison Square Garden	212-465-6000 212-307-7171	www.newyork rangers.com
Soccer/ New York Red Bulls (MLS)	Mar-Oct	Giants Stadium	201-583-7000 212-307-7171	www.newyork redbulls.com

MUST KNOW

Measurement Equivalents									
Degrees Fahrenheit 95°	86°	77°	68°	59°	50°	41°	32°	23°	14°
Degrees Celsius	35°	30°	25°	20°	15°	10°	5°	0°	-5°	-10°
1 inch = 2.5 centimeters	1 foot = 30.5 centimeters								
1 mile = 1.6 kilometers	1 pound = 0.4 kilograms								
1 quart = 0.9 liters	1 gallon = 3.8 liters								

Media

Newspapers and Magazines -
In addition to the New York Times
(see box), dailies include the Daily
News (www.nydailynews.com), the
New York Post (www.nypost.com)
and Newsday (www.newsday.com).
The business daily Wall Street Jour-
nal (www.wsj.com) is published
Mon–Sat.

Money

Cash, Cards and Cheques -
Automated Teller Machines (ATMs)
are located at banks, airports,
grocery stores and shopping malls.
Most banks, stores, restaurants and
hotels accept travelers' checks with
picture identification. To report
a **lost or stolen card**: American
Express (800-528-4800); Diners Club
(800-234-6377); MasterCard (800-
307-7309); or Visa (800-336-8472).
Currency Exchange - Visitors
can exchange currency at the
international terminal of all three
airports. Travelex (212-679-4365)
offers currency exchange at its
four Manhattan locations.

Restaurants

*For a list of suggested
accommodations, see Must Eat.*
Reservation websites - Dinner
Broker offers discounts for reserv-
ing tables at off-peak dining hours
through its website (www.dinner
broker.com). For regular online
reservations, Open Table (www.
opentable.com) is a good bet.

Smoking

Smoking is prohibited throughout
the state of New York in bars,
restaurants, clubs and workplaces.

Taxes and Tipping

Prices displayed in the US do not
include sales tax (8.375% in New
York City), which is not reimburs-
able. It is customary to give a small
gift of money – a **tip** – for services
rendered to waiters (15-20% of
bill), porters ($1 per bag), chamber
maids ($2 per day) and cab drivers
(15% of fare).

In The News

The city's leading daily newspaper, the New York Times (www.nytimes.com) has
comprehensive listings of film, theater, art galleries, museum exhibitions and
special events in its two-part Weekend section (Fri), and in the Arts & Leisure
section (Sun). Local weeklies, including the New Yorker, Time Out New York, and the
Village Voice also have listing sections. They're available at newsstands throughout
the city.

PRACTICAL INFORMATION

NEW YORK CITY

The City That Never Sleeps. The Big Apple. No matter what you call it, New York packs a staggering world into just 320 square miles. With more than eight million residents at last count, this glittering city is by far the most populous in the US; a global melting pot that acts as a cultural magnet and an economic powerhouse.

Manhattan with Brooklyn Bridge in the foreground

©Matt Tilghman/iStockphoto.com

It's not for nothing that New Yorkers have a reputation for being swaggering and brash; theirs is one great city. It's also a relatively young one. European settlement began in earnest here in 1625, when the Dutch East India Company established the Nieuw Amsterdam trading post at the southern tip of Manhattan Island. That name, which comes from an Algonquian term meaning "island of hills," suggests that the natives ventured farther into the island's rolling northern reaches than the colonists, who for the better part of 200 years remained on flat land near the shore, behind a defensive wall (today's Wall Street).

The transfer of authority from Dutch to British hands in 1664 – and the new name, after the Duke of York – didn't faze early New Yorkers, most of whom had little allegiance to either crown; they were here to make money. Manhattan was perfectly suited to global trade, thanks to the safe environment provided by the snug arrangement of other land masses around its large harbor. As port activity grew, so did colonist friction with British democracy, which granted British subjects 'virtual representation' in parliament by MPs elected by landowners, famously interpreted as "taxation without representation." When war broke out, the British took over the prize colonial city almost immediately and occupied it until independence.

After briefly serving as the United States' capital, New York established the financial institutions that led the new nation into the Industrial Age. In 1792 brokers met under a buttonwood tree at Wall and Williams streets and founded the forerunner to the New York Stock Exchange. In 1811 Manhattan's gridiron plan was laid out, and the exploding population spread northward into the brushy reaches above present-day downtown. When the 363-mile Erie Canal linked the city with the Great Lakes in 1825, New York became the nation's preeminent port and ship-building capital. The city's leading businessmen leveraged this advantage skillfully, investing their profits in new building projects. New York's population doubled every 20 years, fed by waves of European immigrants, who would help build the city not just with their hands but with their ideas. The dynamism and density of New York City pushed the decision to build farther into the sky than had ever been done before. In the second half of the 20C, the city solidified its international position in industry, commerce and finance, and its skyline, bristling with skyscrapers, reflected that prosperity.

New York's growth has not been without setbacks. A cholera epidemic in 1832 killed 4,000 citizens. A fire in 1845 leveled 300 buildings. In 1975 the city defaulted into bankruptcy. Finally, the September 11, 2001, terror-ist attack took 2,979 lives and felled one of the city's proudest landmarks, the twin towers of the World Trade Center. But, New York City has proved remarkably resilient to such tragedies. Ambi-tious plans to rebuild downtown Manhattan into a model 21C city are well on their way to fruition. These plans have their critics, but in New York, that's all part of the process. The results speak for themselves.

©Jeff Greenberg/NYC&Co.

Broadway at night

NEIGHBORHOODS

New York is a lively place in part because it is a city of neighborhoods, each with its own character, yet always in flux. From block to block, you never know what you'll come upon. Walking is the best way to find out; that's why so many visitors leave New York complaining about sore legs. We have listed Manhattan neighborhoods South to North.

Financial District

The district occupies the southern tip of Manhattan below Vesey and Fulton Sts. There is a visitor information center at Federal Hall National Memorial, 26 Wall St. 4 or 5 train to Fulton St. See map opposite.

Considered by some the financial center of the world, the neighborhood, anchored by **Wall Street★★**, teems by day with traders, brokers, office workers and tourists. Imposing banking buildings loom overhead, including the granddaddy of them all, the **Federal Reserve Bank of New York★★** *(33 Liberty St.; 212-720-6130)*, with its excellent History of Money exhibit. Signs of recovery from the 2001 terrorist attack are apparent everywhere, and rebuilding continues at the **World Trade Center Site★★** *(see Historic Sites)*.

Chinatown★★

The heart of the district is bounded by Canal, Worth & Baxter Sts. and the Bowery. A staffed visitor information booth (open year-round Sun–Fri 10am–6pm, Sat 10am–7pm) is located in the triangle formed by Canal, Walker & Baxter Sts. www.explorechinatown.com. N, Q, R, W, 6, J, M or Z train to Canal St. See map p. 26.

Dim Sum

A visit to Chinatown just isn't complete without a visit to one of its renowned dim sum palaces. Among your best bets is **Vegetarian Dim Sum House** at 24 Pell Street *(212-577-7176)*, which serves meat-free versions of the standards. For gourmet dim sum, try **Dim Sum Go Go** *(5 E. Broadway; see Must Eat)*.

Chinatown

©Jeff Greenberg/NYC&Co

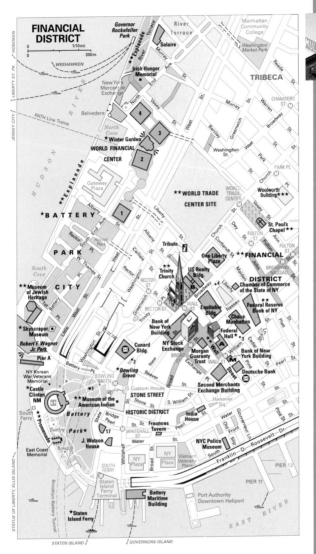

FINANCIAL DISTRICT

Governor Rockefeller Park

River Terrace

Manhattan Community College

Solaire

Washington Market Park

1/10mi

200m

WEEHAWKEN

Irish Hunger Memorial

TRIBECA

New York Mercantile Exchange

Reade St.

CHAMBERS ST.

Warren St.

PATH Line Trains

Belvedere

Murray St.

Broadway

North Cove

Barclay St.

Greenwich St.

West St.

Winter Garden

PARK PL.

WORLD FINANCIAL CENTER

Washington St.

Park Pl.

Church St.

Woolworth Building ★★★

Gateway Plaza

★ BATTERY

WORLD TRADE CENTER SITE

Vesey St.

St. Paul's Chapel ★★

Albany St.

★★ WORLD TRADE CENTER SITE

Day St.

FULTON ST.

FULTON ST.

PARK

Liberty St.

Cortlandt St.

★★ FINANCIAL

Tribute

One Liberty Plaza

BROADWAY-NASSAU

South Cove

Carlisle

Rector St.

★★ Trinity Church

US Realty Bldg.

DISTRICT

Chamber of Commerce of the State of NY

★★ Museum of Jewish Heritage

CITY

RECTOR ST.

WALL ST.

Federal Reserve Bank of NY

Equitable Bldg.

Nassau St.

Pine St.

★ Skyscraper Museum

Bank of New York Building

NY Stock Exchange

Chase Manhattan

Robert F. Wagner Jr. Park

Cunard Bldg.

BROAD

Federal Hall ★★★

William St.

Bank of New York Building

Pier A

Morgan Guaranty Trust

WALL ST.

Pearl St.

NY Korean War Veterans Memorial

BOWLING GREEN

Beaver St.

Deutsche Bank

★ Castle Clinton NM

Second Merchants Exchange Building

Hanover Sq.

★★ Museum of the American Indian

STONE STREET

S. William St.

India House

Governeur Ln.

Front St.

Battery

US Custom House

HISTORIC DISTRICT

Stone St.

Water St.

Bridge St.

Pearl St.

NYC Police Museum

Old Slip

South Ferry

J. Watson House

Fraunces Tavern

Whitehall St.

Water St.

Vietnam Veterans Plaza

Franklin D. Roosevelt Dr.

PIER 13

East Coast Memorial

SOUTH FERRY

NY Plaza

NY Plaza

Broad St.

PIER 11

Staten Island Ferry Terminal

Battery Maritime Building

Port Authority Downtown Heliport

EAST RIVER

★ Staten Island Ferry

STATEN ISLAND

GOVERNORS ISLAND

JERSEY CITY / LIBERTY ST. PK. / HOBOKEN

HUDSON RIVER

Esplanade

STATUE OF LIBERTY, ELLIS ISLAND

Brooklyn-Battery Tunnel

Sprawling Chinatown is a veritable city within a city. The narrow streets are lined with colorful shops stocking everything from lychee to lipstick, while storefront restaurants serve up all manner of Asian cuisine. The first Chinese to settle in New York were men who came via the western states, where they had worked in the California

23

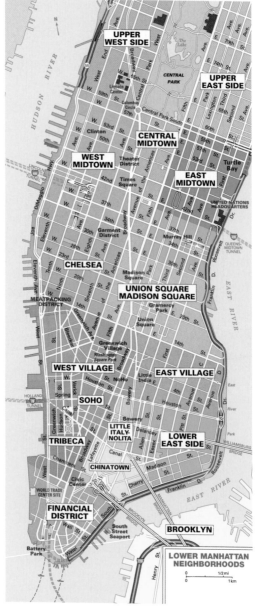

LOWER MANHATTAN NEIGHBORHOODS

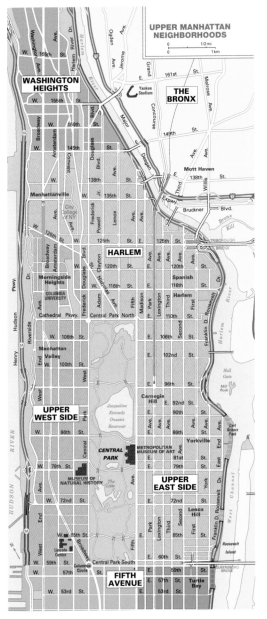

UPPER MANHATTAN NEIGHBORHOODS

0   1/2 mi
0   1 km

WASHINGTON HEIGHTS

Yankee Stadium

THE BRONX

Mott Haven

Manhattanville

City College of NY

HARLEM

Spanish Harlem

Morningside Heights

COLUMBIA UNIVERSITY

Manhattan Valley

Carnegie Hill

Jacqueline Kennedy Onassis Reservoir

UPPER WEST SIDE

CENTRAL PARK

Yorkville

METROPOLITAN MUSEUM OF ART

The Lake

MUSEUM OF NATURAL HISTORY

UPPER EAST SIDE

Lenox Hill

Lincoln Center

Columbus Circle

Roosevelt Island

FIFTH AVENUE

Turtle Bay

25

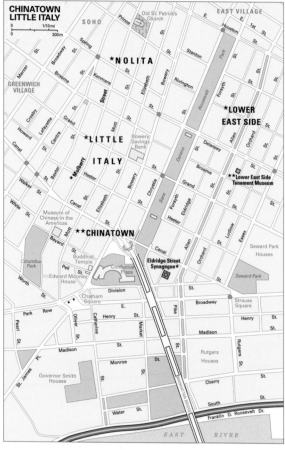

CHINATOWN
LITTLE ITALY

goldfields or on the transcontinental railroad. The majority had no intention of staying; they merely wished to make their fortunes and return to comfortable lives in China. Ultimately though, many formed families or were joined by relatives from back home. Today Chinatown is one of New York's most densely populated neighborhoods, and it continues to grow past its old boundaries

into Little Italy and the formerly Jewish Lower East Side. Crowded on weekends, the area bursts its seams at Chinese New Year (first full moon after January 19), when dragons dance in the streets accompanied by banner-carrying attendants and fireworks.

Shopping – **Mulberry** and **Mott streets** are lined with shops piled high with displays of bamboo plants, tea sets, silk dresses,

Best of Little Italy

Tile floors, tin ceilings, and ice-cream parlor chairs make **Caffe Roma** *(385 Broome St. at Mulberry St.; 212-226-8413)* one of the most appealing of Little Italy's cafes. For a festive dinner, try the cheap-but-good **La Mela** *(167 Mulberry St., between Broome & Grand Sts.; 212-431-9493)*, open every night past midnight. **Ferrara** *(195 Grand St., between Mott & Mulberry Sts.; 212-226-6150)* is the place for housemade cannoli, tiramisu, and Italian pastry. For lunch, head to **Alleva Dairy** *(188 Grand St. at Mulberry St.; 212-226-7990)* and order a prosciutto, mozzarella, and roasted-pepper sandwich, the deli's specialty. Established in 1905, **Lombardi's** *(32 Spring St., between Mott & Mulberry Sts.; 212-941-7994)* dishes up thin-crust pies baked in coal-fired ovens. Expect a wait on weekend nights.

Chinese lanterns, fans and the like. Canal Street between Broadway and Mulberry Street is world-famous for being crammed full of tiny stalls selling knock-off designer goods, especially handbags and scarves.

Little Italy★

Bounded by Canal, Houston and Lafayette Sts. & the Bowery. N, Q, R, W, 6, J, M or Z train to Canal St. See map opposite.

Little Italy is one of the tastiest corners of the city, with cafes for cappuccino and cannoli; grocery stores full of fresh pasta, salamis, olives and cheeses; and friendly and inexpensive red-sauce joints. The area took on its Italian character between the 1880s and the 1920s, when thousands of migrants left epidemics and poverty in Sicily and southern Italy, to come to the US. Mostly arriving through Ellis Island, they formed one of the city's tightest-knit communities. Though today the neighborhood is being pinched by Chinatown to the east and SoHo to the west, a sense of place still prevails.

Mulberry Street – Sometimes called the Via San Gennaro, Mulberry Street is Little Italy's main drag. It becomes a vast alfresco restaurant during the popular

Little Italy

©NYC&Co.

NEIGHBORHOODS

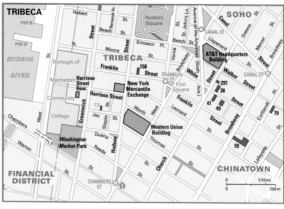

TRIBECA • SOHO • TRIBECA • HUDSON RIVER • FINANCIAL DISTRICT • CHINATOWN

Feast of San Gennaro in mid-September, and is closed to traffic on weekends between May and October.

Nolita★ – This newly trendy area stretches from Broome to Houston streets on **Mulberry**, **Mott** and Elizabeth streets. Part of Little Italy, it was named by real-estate developers who in the 1990s wanted to distinguish it from the old neighborhood. The tactic worked. Today Nolita is bursting with cafes and boutiques, relatively few of which are Italian in character.

TriBeCa★

1 train to Franklin St.
www.tribeca.org. See map above.

Far less crowded and commercial than its neighbor SoHo, the wedge-shaped district named for its shape and location (TRIangle BElow CAnal) is an intriguing district of warehouses, art spaces, luxury co-ops, and chic restaurants such as **Chanterelle** (*2 Harrison St.*), **Nobu** (*105 Hudson St.*) and

Robert De Niro's **Tribeca Grill** (*375 Greenwich St.*). Interior design galleries line the block of Franklin Street between Varick and Hudson; you'll find art and performance spaces along the bricked stretch of White Street east of Broadway.

SoHo★

Bounded by Sullivan,
West Houston, Lafayette &
Canal Sts. R or W train to Prince St,
or C or E train to Spring St.
See map opposite.

Home to dozens of artists and galleries in the 1980s, SoHo – short for South of Houston (pronounced HOW-stun) – has more recently become one of New York's most popular shopping districts. Visitors throng the neighborhood on weekends, making even walking down the sidewalk difficult – especially given the profusion of sidewalk tables piled with purses and jewelry, sunglasses, scarves and the like. Weekdays are slightly more manageable. Though most of its art galleries have decamped

for Chelsea, some excellent ones remain. Two to keep in mind are the **Drawing Center** (35 Wooster St.), which champions drawings both historical and contemporary, and **Deitch Projects** (76 Grand St.), which sponsors playful avant-garde mixed-media exhibits and performances.

Lower East Side★

Bounded by Houston, Canal and Clinton Sts. and the Bowery. Visitor center: 72 Orchard St (open Mon–Fri 9am–5pm, weekends 10am–4pm; 212-226-9010; www. lowereastsideny.com). F train to Delancey St.; B or D train to Grand St. See map p. 30.

Despite being one of New York's hippest 'hoods,' the Lower East Side has, for the most part, a refreshing lack of attitude and an astounding amount of local pride. "Come one, come all" has been its message to visitors since the 1880s, when it became the quintessential American melting pot. Though today's immigrants tend to be

young artists, history lives on at the **Lower East Side Tenement Museum★★** (see Museums) and in the neighborhood's many famous ethnic eateries.

Eldridge Street Synagogue★ – *12 Eldridge St., between Canal & Division Sts. Open year-round Sun, Tue–Thu 11am–4pm. Closed Jewish & national holidays. Guided tours (call for times & prices). 212-219-0888. www.eldridgestreet.org.*

A Nosher's Paradise

The Lower East Side was the original nosher's paradise, and for those in the know, it remains so. Since opening in 1914, **Russ & Daughters** (179 E. Houston St.; 212-475-4880) has been winning awards for its Caspian Sea caviar. For a tart accompaniment, go to **Guss' Lower East Side Pickles** (85 Orchard St.; 917-701-4000), founded in 1910. Need your sugar fix? Stop in at **Sweet Life** (63 Hester St.;212-598-0092), the Lower East Side's preeminent candy shop since 1982.

NEIGHBORHOODS

29

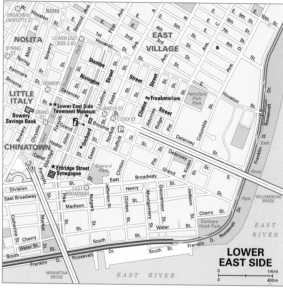

Completed in 1887, Eldridge Street was the first synagogue built by Eastern European Jews.
The recently renovated building boasts a striking rose window set against an ornate Moorish facade.

Greenwich Village

Greenwich Village★★

Bounded by Houston & W. 14th Sts., between Broadway and the Hudson River. A, B, C, D, E, F or V train to W. 4th St.; 1 train to Christopher St. See map opposite.

New York's historic bohemia centers on Washington Square *(see Parks)* and extends west to the Hudson in a beguiling tangle of streets lined with trees and town houses. Started as an Algonquin Indian settlement called *Sapokani-kan*, the site gave rise to a British village in 1696.
Artists and intellectuals, including Edgar Allan Poe, began arriving in the 1840s. The trickle turned into a flood in the early 1900s, and the 1960s saw figures such as Bob Dylan putting down roots here. Since then the struggling-artist

MUST SEE

©Jean-Marie Lanlo/Fotolia.com

30

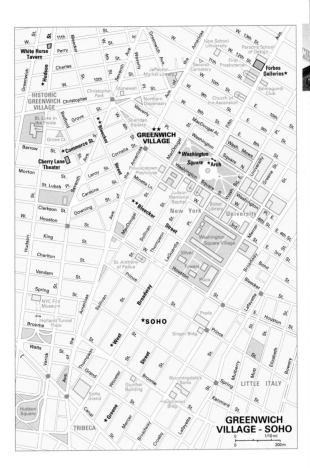

GREENWICH
VILLAGE - SOHO

crowd has moved to the edgier East Village, but Greenwich Village retains a charm all its own.

Bleecker Street★★ – A stroll up Bleecker Street will show you the full range of Village life. The intersection of Bleecker and MacDougal Streets is the epicenter of New York University's student district. Venture northwest (the street runs at an angle to Manhattan's grid) and you'll find a profusion of Italian bakeries and delis between Sixth and Seventh avenues. Keep going, and you'll enter the quaintest part of the village. Most of the row houses here were built between 1820 and 1855. End your stroll at **Magnolia Bakery** *(no. 401; 212-462-2572)* and sample of one of their thickly frosted cupcakes, which enjoy a cult following.

Chelsea★★

West of Sixth Ave., between W. 14th & W. 30th Sts. 1, C or E train to 23rd St.; M23 bus to Tenth Ave. See map below.

Beautifully refurbished brownstones and a thriving arts scene have made Chelsea a desirable address in recent years, especially in the gay community.

It was named after the London neighborhood in the mid-18C, but most of its housing stock dates to the 19C.

Today Chelsea is *the* place in New York for gallery hopping.

Rubin Museum of Art★★ and **Chelsea Art Museum★** – *See Museums.*

Chelsea Historic District★ – *W. 20th, 21st & 22nd Sts., between Ninth & Tenth Aves.* Here stand some of

Apartment in Chelsea

©Nicole K.Cioe/iStockphoto.com

Chelsea's loveliest brownstones. Note especially the Greek Revival **Cushman Row** (*406–418 W. 20th St.*), dating from 1840.

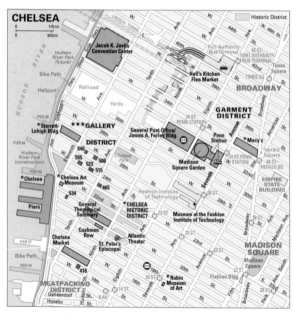

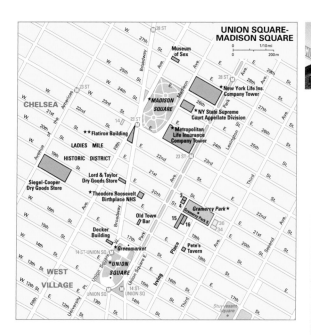

UNION SQUARE-
MADISON SQUARE

0   1/10mi
0   200m

Gallery Hopping in Chelsea★

Chelsea's many galleries are
concentrated between 20th and
30th streets west of Tenth Avenue.
Three not to miss: **Matthew
Marks** (523 W. 24th St.; 212-243-
0200; www.matthewmarks.com);
Gagosian (555 W. 24th St.;
212-741-1111; www.gagosian.
com); and **Gladstone Gallery**
(515 W. 24th St.; 212-206-9300; www.
gladstonegallery.com). For a list of
shows and opening receptions, as
well as a map, pick up a free **Gallery Guide** at any major gallery.

Union Square★/
Madison Square★

*L, N, Q, R, W, 4, 5 or 6 trains to
Union Square. See map above.*

Handsome brick and cast-iron
retail buildings line Broadway, Fifth
and Sixth Avenues. The shopping
corridors are linked by residential
enclaves and pretty parks, including busy Union Square, site of the
Union Square Greenmarket★
(see Parks). A few blocks east lies
the posh **Gramercy Park★**
neighborhood, with its welter of
popular cafes. One of downtown's
loveliest public spaces, **Madison
Square★** boasts three iconic
towers; the **Flatiron Building★★**,
the **Metropolitan Life Insurance
Co. Tower★** and the 40-story
**New York Life Insurance Co.
Tower★** *(see Landmarks)*.

NEIGHBORHOODS

Midtown

From 34th St. to 59th St. between the Hudson and East Rivers. For maps to Central and East Midtown, see Landmarks.

Towering skyscrapers, flashing neon, gargantuan department stores, world-class art and architecture–Midtown Manhattan is the nexus of New York shopping and entertainment. Its cache of familiar icons includes the **Empire State Building★★★**, **Grand Central Terminal★★★**, **Rockefeller Center★★★**, the **Chrysler Building★★★** and the **United Nations★★★**. *See Landmarks.*

Broadway

From 40th to 50th Sts. Any train to 42nd St.-Times Square. See map below.

New York's (and the nation's) live theater and entertainment capital grew out of the vaudeville houses that sprang up around **Times Square★★** *(see Musts for Fun)* in the early 20C. Today electronic signs and marquees flash and scroll on every facade, creating a round-the-clock glow for shoppers and theatergoers along Broadway, West 43rd St. and **West 42nd Street★★** *(between Broadway and Eighth St.).*

Upper East Side★★

From E. 59th St. to E. 97th St., between Central Park & the East River. N, R or W train to Fifth Ave-59th St. See maps on inside front cover and under Walking Tours.

Although Millionaires' Row – Fifth Avenue – is now Museum Mile, the Upper East Side is still the wealthiest neighborhood in the city. In

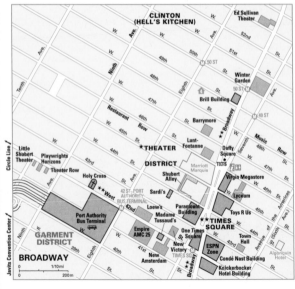

Upper West Side Highlights

- **American Museum of Natural History**★★★ –
  Central Park West between W. 77nd & W. 81st Sts. See Museums.
- **New-York Historical Society**★★ –
  170 Central Park West. See Museums.
- **Cathedral of St. John the Divine**★★ –
  Amsterdam Ave. at W. 112th St. See Historic Sites.
- **Lincoln Center**★★ –
  Broadway between W. 62nd & W. 65th Sts. See Performing Arts.

the late 19C, rich industrialists including Andrew Carnegie and Henry Clay Frick began building mansions on the large lots along Fifth Avenue, abutting the park. The ladies who lunch followed, moving into luxury apartment buildings along Park Avenue and town houses on the side streets.
Fifth Avenue★★★ – You'll find more cultural capital on this strip than on virtually any street in the world. Three not to miss: the **Frick Collection**★★★ *(at E. 70th St.)*, the **Metropolitan Museum of Art**★★★ *(at E. 82nd St.)* and the **Guggenheim Museum**★★ *(at E. 89th St.). See Museums.*

Madison Avenue★★ – *See Must Shop.* Chock-a-block with exclusive boutiques, Madison Avenue is also home to the **Whitney Museum**★★ *(at E. 75th St.; see Museums)* and the **Carlyle Hotel**★ *(at E. 76th St.; see Nightlife)*, famous for its cabaret acts.

Upper West Side★★

From Columbus Circle to W. 125th St., between Central Park and the Hudson River. Any train to Columbus Circle/59th St. See map p. 36.

The Upper West Side remains an enclave of literate liberals and performing artists drawn to the area's world-famous cultural venues, parks and tidy brownstones. Development has been relatively recent. In the late 19C, much of the area was still populated by stray goats. When New York's first luxury apartment house was erected on West 72nd Street and Central Park West in 1884, it was considered so

NEIGHBORHOODS

Brigitta L. House/Michelin

Upper West Side

35

UPPER WEST SIDE

0   1/2 mi
0   500 m

HUDSON RIVER

Symphony Space
Joan of Arc Statue
Soldiers' and Sailors' Monument
Zabar's
Eleanor Roosevelt Monument
Beacon Theater
★★★ AMERICAN MUSEUM OF NATURAL HISTORY
★★ New-York Historical Society
Ansonia
San Remo
The Dakota
Juilliard School
★★ LINCOLN CENTER
Hotel des Artistes
Guggenheim Bandshell
★★★ CENTRAL PARK
Damrosch Park
Tavern on the Green
Century
★ Time Warner Center
Trump International Hotel and Tower
Columbus Circle
CENTRAL MIDTOWN

Jacqueline Kennedy Onassis Reservoir

METROPOLITAN MUSEUM OF ART
The Lake
UPPER EAST SIDE
Children's Zoo
Wildlife Center
The Pond
HUNTER COLLEGE

far away from the heart of the city that it was dubbed the **Dakota** (Henry Hardenbergh's Gothic pile has since become famous as the site of John Lennon's murder). Noel Coward, Babe Ruth, Dustin Hoffman, and Jerry Seinfeld are just some of the famous residents who have called this neighborhood home over the years.

Distinguished **Columbia University★** lying between Morningside Park and **Riverside Park★**, was designed by Frederick Law Olmstead. Graced by majestic elms and threaded by curving **Riverside Drive★**, Riverside Park boasts beautiful views over the Hudson River.

Harlem★

Bounded by 110th & 135th Sts. between Madison Ave. & Frederick Douglass Blvd. (Eighth Ave.). A, B, C, D, 2 or 3 train to 125th St. See map on inside front cover. Because Harlem is so large, we recommend taking a tour.

🎫 **Harlem Spirituals, Inc.** *(reservations required; 212-391-0900; www.harlemspirituals. com) offers an evening tour that includes soul food and jazz; a Sunday visit with a gospel and soul-food brunch; and a Wednesday-morning gospel visit.*

The **Municipal Art Society** *also conducts tours of the neighborhood on an occasional basis, as well as private tours by appointment (212-935-3960; www.mas.org).*

Though only a fraction of the city's African Americans live in Harlem today, the neighborhood continues to nurture its history as a fulcrum of black culture. The neighborhood dates back to 1658 but was mostly rural until the railroad and elevated trains linked it to the rest of the city in the 19C. By the early 1890s Harlem was one of New York's most fashionable enclaves. The Harlem Renaissance came in the 1920s when black musicians (Count Basie, Duke Ellington) and writers (Zora Neale Hurston, Langston Hughes) electrified the world with their originality. Recent investment has brought new life into this quarter. Former president Bill Clinton, for instance, established his offices on 125th Street, and the famous **Apollo Theater** *(see Performing Arts)* just completed a $12 million face lift. The **Schomburg Center for Research in Black Culture★** *(515 Malcolm X Blvd./Lenox Ave., at W. 135th St.; exhibition hall open year-round Mon–Wed noon–8pm, Thu–Sat 10am–6pm, Sun 1–5pm; closed major holidays; 212-491-2200; www.schomburgcenter.org)* is a branch of the New York Public Library system and contains one of the world's largest archives relating to black heritage, with excellent temporary exhibits on African American history.

The **Studio Museum in Harlem★** *(144 W. 125th St. See Museums)* is also worth a look..

Washington Heights

North of 145th St. between Hudson and Harlem Rivers. See map p. 25.

Manhattan's hilly northern reaches were the site of Fort Washington, a Revolutionary War outpost. The **George Washington Bridge★★** spans the Hudson River from here to New Jersey. A treasure of medieval art and architcture, **The Cloisters★★★** *(see Museums)* crown a hill in lovely Fort Tryon Park. Worth a look is the **Hispanic Society of America★** *(613 155th St. 1 train to 157th St.; open Tue–Sat 10am–4:30pm, Sun 1–4pm; 212-926-1234; www.hispanicsociety.org)*, a small museum with world-class portraits by El Greco, Goya, Ribera and Velázquez.

Brownstones in Harlem

©Thomas Pozzo di Borgo/Bigstockphoto.com

NEIGHBORHOODS

SKYSCRAPERS

Looking around you in New York isn't enough: you have to look up to notice some of the city's finest features. From the Woolworth Building's copper crown to the Sony Tower's "Chippendale" roofline, some surprises lurk up there in the clouds. For the full scoop on New York's changing skyline, stop by the new **Skyscraper Museum★** in Battery Park City *(212-968-1961; www.skyscraper.org).*

Chrysler Building★★★

405 Lexington Ave. at E. 42nd St.
4, 5, 6 or 7 train to Grand Central
Terminal. See map opposite.

When you have money, you can do anything; or so Walter P. Chrysler must have thought when he commissioned architect William Van Alen to design the world's tallest building. One of the first large buildings to use metal extensively on its exterior, the 77-story Art Deco landmark pays sparkling homage to the car. It was briefly the world's tallest building in 1930, after its architect secretly ordered a 185-foot spire attached to its crown, edging out the Bank of Manhattan, which was two feet taller. Alas, the distinction lasted only a few months; the Empire State Building blew both buildings away when it opened in 1931. Stylistically the Chrysler Building has stood the test of time: the six semi-circular arches of its stainless-steel pinnacle, patterned after a 1930 Chrysler radiator cap, glim-

Chrysler Building

Brigitta L. House/Michelin

mer majestically during the day and are dramatically lit at night. An Art Deco masterpiece faced in red African marble, onyx and amber, the **lobby** sports a ceiling mural by Edward Trumbull and ornate elevator doors decorated with inlaid woods.

They Don't Call It the Chrysler Building For Nothing

The Chrysler building is crawling with automotive decorations throughout its architecture. If you can crane your neck back far enough, you should be able to see the following elements:

- Aluminum trim
- Metal hubcaps
- Gargoyles in the form of radiator caps
- Car fenders
- Stylized racing cars
- Silver hood ornaments

MUST SEE

NBC Studio Tour

Ever wonder what goes on behind that glowing screen you call a TV? Here's your chance to find out. Tours *(70min)* lead guests through the network's "golden days" in radio, around the sets of NBC Nightly News and NBC Sports, and past technology used in weather broadcasting *(for tour information, call 212-664-7174 or log on to www.nbcuniversalstore.com; children under six not permitted)*. Another option is to attend a live taping of **Late Nite with Conan O'Brien** or **Saturday Night Live**, both headquartered in studios at the GE Building. Your best bet is to get tickets well in advance, but there are also some same-day standby tickets available. *Children under 16 are not permitted. For more information, call 212-664-3056.*

GE Building
★★★

30 Rockefeller Plaza. B, D, F or V train to 47th-50th Sts./Rockefeller Center. See map p. 50.

This lithe 70-story skyscraper, originally called the RCA Building, is the Rockefeller Center's tallest and finest structure. It was finished in 1933, and John D. moved the Rockefeller family offices into the building shortly thereafter. Its strong vertical lines, softened with staggered setbacks in the upper stories, are considered a triumph of Art Deco design. To see them without breaking your neck, go to the Channel Gardens on the other side of the skating rink and look up, up, up.

39

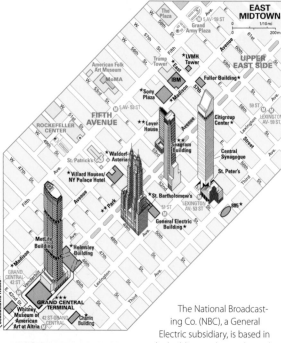

The National Broadcasting Co. (NBC), a General Electric subsidiary, is based in the building, and several popular **television shows** were headquartered in studios here, including *The Tonight Show*, *Jeopardy!*, *Late Night with David Letterman* and *The Today Show*. You can see the production facilities by attending a taping of a current show, or by taking the NBC Studios Tour (see p. 39).

Observation Deck★★

212-698-2000. Open daily 8am–midnight. $20.

Reopened in late 2005 after a $75 million renovation, Top of the Rock contains exhibits on the history of the building as well as an open-air platform on the 70th floor with spectacular 360-degree views of the city.

G.E. Building

© Jeff Greenberg/NYC&Co.

MUST SEE

Rainbow Grill

212-632-5100. Open daily 5–11:30pm. Jacket required; no jeans or sneakers.

You'll get some of the best **views★** in the city from this 65th-floor watering hole and restaurant, a New York institution.

Lobby

The murals by Spanish artist Jose Maria Sert are actually the second set to adorn these walls. The first, by the Mexican artist Diego Rivera, were destroyed for their anti-capitalist themes. Rivera re-created them in Mexico City, adding a likeness of John D. Rockefeller drinking a martini with a few "painted ladies."

Woolworth Building★★★

223 Broadway at Barclay St. R or W train to City Hall. See map p. 23.

This 1913 skyscraper was financed by F.W. Woolworth, an Upstate New York native who made his fortune with a nationwide chain of five-and-dime stores. Woolworth paid $13.5 million in cash for the building (it remained in the hands of the same owner for 85 years). The original plans called for a 625ft structure, but after the caissons were sunk, Woolworth insisted that his headquarters top the 700ft Metropolitan Life Insurance Tower. Architect Cass Gilbert (who also designed the Supreme Court building in the nation's capital) happily revised his plans, designing a structure measuring 792 feet and one inch.

The Gothic masterpiece reigned as the tallest building in the world

Woolworth Building

Brigitta L. House/Michelin

from 1913 until 1930, when it was bypassed by no. 40 Wall Street (now the Trump Building). Today the building remains one of New York's 20 tallest buildings.

On its opening day in April 1913, President Woodrow Wilson pressed a button in Washington, DC, turning on 80,000 interior bulbs and exterior floodlights to the appreciative *oohs* and *ahs* of thousands of spectators.

The building was quickly dubbed the "Cathedral of Commerce" thanks to its ecclesiastical references. The granite and limestone base of the structure shoots upward 27 stories without setbacks, then gives way to a 27-story tower ornamented with gargoyles, pinnacles, flying buttresses and finials, all elements of European Gothic architecture.

The top is crowned by a copper pyramidal roof. The spectacular lobby *(closed to the public)* rises three stories to a stained-glass, barrel-vaulted ceiling, and is decorated with Byzantine-style mosaics and frescoes.

LANDMARKS

Flatiron Building

©Jeff Greenberg/NYC&Co.

Flatiron Building★★

175 Fifth Ave. at 23rd St. N, R or W train to 23rd St. See map p. 33.

Even if you've never been to New York City, you've likely seen this building before – it's a popular backdrop on television shows and movies. When you see it from the north side, you'll see how it got its name: only 6 feet wide at its sharp corner, the Flatiron Building rises 22 stories straight up from the sidewalk, like an extremely tall iron. Other New Yorkers think it looks more like a grand ship, with its prow pointed up Fifth Avenue.

Always a Great Notion

Daniel Burnham had the right idea when he said: "Make no little plans; they have no magic to stir men's blood and probably will themselves not be realized. Make big plans; aim high in hope and work, remembering that a noble, logical diagram once recorded will not die."

Famed Chicago architect Daniel H. Burnham designed the building, which was originally called the Fuller Building after its original owner, the Fuller Construction Company, to make maximum use of the sliver of land it occupies. Though it wasn't the first skyscraper made with a steel skeleton, it was a dramatic example of the kind of robustness steel could provide. Locals were skeptical, calling the slim structure "Burnham's Folly" during construction, in the expectation that it would be toppled by a strong wind. Such was not the case, and within a few years of its completion in 1902 the Flatiron Building was one of the most popular picture-postcard subjects in the country.

The intricately wrought limestone and terra-cotta facade resembles that of an Italian palazzo, with an enormous cornice that makes the building appear to loom over the street. By contrast, most of the skyscrapers of that era were tapered near the top in order to accentuate their height and allow light to filter down to the lower stories.

Enter the Flatiron Building's lobby to see a display of historical photos, then cross 23rd Street to charming Madison Square Park and snap one of your own.

MUST SEE

Citigroup Center★

153 E. 53rd St. at Lexington Ave. E or V train to Lexington Ave.-53rd St. See map p. 40.

This 915-foot aluminum and glass-sheathed tower (1978) is best known for its roof, which slopes at a 45-degree angle and is visible in most pictures of the New York City skyline. The building is pretty spectacular viewed from below as well. The tower stands on four colossal pillars – each nine stories, or 115 feet, high and 22 feet square – set at the center of each side, rather than at the corners of the building. Under one of these cantilevered corners nestles St. Peter's Church, which sold its land to Citicorp on the condition that a new church building would be integrated within the complex. Though it looks tiny from the outside, the chapel, with its 80-foot ceiling and generous sidewall and roof lighting, feels surprisingly spacious.

The Rest of the Best: Skyscrapers

Bold letters in brackets refer to the map on the inside front cover.

Lever House★★ [A]

390 Park Ave.

Designed by Skidmore, Owings, and Merrill in 1952, a 21-story vertical slab of sheer, blue-green glass and stainless steel seems to hover asymmetrically above a 2-story horizontal base. It sparked the building boom that replaced Park Avenue's sedate stone apartment buildings with "glass box" corporate headquarters.

Lever House

R.Corbel/Michelin

Seagram Building★★ [B]

375 Park Ave.

The 38-story Seagram Building, designed in 1958 by Mies van der Rohe and Philip Johnson, is considered one of the finest International-style skyscrapers in New York. Its facade of vertical bronze I-beams separating large glass windows served as a model for office towers worldwide. The building houses **The Four Seasons** *(see red-tabbed MICHELIN GUIDE section)*, an opulent restaurant with lavish travertine, marble and wood interiors also designed by Mies van der Rohe and Philip Johnson.

Sony Plaza★ (former AT&T Headquarters) [C]

550 Madison Ave. at E. 55th St.

New Yorkers call it the "Chippendale building" for its roofline, which looks like the top of a Colonial armoire; architecture buffs have dubbed it the first post-Modern skyscraper (1984, Philip Johnson and John Burgee). Inside is the high-tech Sony Wonder Lab *(see Musts for Kids)*.

43

Bloomberg Tower [D]

731 Lexington Ave. at E. 58th St.

Headquarters of Mayor Mike's media empire, this elegant 54-story glass tower (2004, Cesar Pelli & Assoc.) has received high marks for its light, graceful form and soaring atrium, a glass-hung public space called the Beacon Court. The tower's upper stories, topped with a flat roof, glow white at night.

CBS Building [E]

51 W. 52nd St. at Sixth Ave.

Known as the Black Rock, the 38-story CBS Building is the only high-rise building designed by Finnish-born architect Eero Saarinen.

Daily News Building★

220 E. 42nd St., between Second & Third Aves.

Vertical "stripes," (white brick piers alternating with patterned red and black brick spandrels) make the 1930 Daily News Building look taller than its 37 stories. The lobby is famed for its huge revolving globe – 12 feet in diameter – and the clock that gives readings in 17 time zones.

53rd at Third★

Between E. 53rd & 54th Sts.

It should be obvious at a glance why people call this otherwise nameless skyscraper the "lipstick building." Rising in tiers from tall columns, the elliptical tower of reddish-brown and pink stone and glass was designed by post-Modernists Philip Johnson and John Burgee and completed in 1986.

Metropolitan Life Insurance Company Tower★

Madison Ave. between E. 23rd and E. 24th St.

This square Renaissance Revival tower (1909, Le Brun and Sons), which looks like a brightly lit castle at night, is known for its gargantuan four-sided clock, whose hour hands weigh 700 pounds apiece.

Trump Tower [F]

725 Fifth Ave. at E. 56th St.

Rising 58 stories, this dark glass-sheathed tower has myriad tiny

Trump World Tower

Jeff Gynane/BigStockPhoto.com

setbacks, many topped with trees and shrubs, giving the appearance of a hanging garden. Its six-story, pink-marble atrium features an 80-foot waterfall.

Trump World Tower

845 United Nations Plaza. See map p. 39.

Looming over the U.N. complex, Donald Trump's 2001 contribution to the New York skyline is a slender, 72-story bronze-colored glass box, the tallest residential building in the world.

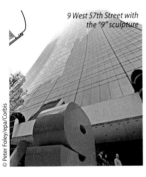
9 West 57th Street with the "9" sculpture

© Peter Foley/epa/Corbis

General Electric Building★

570 Lexington Ave. at E. 51st St. See map p. 40.

Not to be confused with the GE Building in Rockefeller Center *(see p. 39)*, this marvelous 51-story Art Deco tower (1931) bears playful references to its original tenant. Look for rays, flashes, lightning bolts, and the intriguing metal clock bearing the GE logo.

Chanin Building★

122 E. 42nd St. at Lexington Ave.

A prime example of the Art Deco style, this 56-story building (1929, Irwin Chanin) features a buttressed crown that was originally illuminated at night. A terra-cotta frieze of floral bas-reliefs by Edward Trumbull wraps the bottom four floors. Don't miss the intricately detailed lobby, especially the door frames, grilles and mailboxes.

New York Life Insurance Company Tower★

51 Madison Ave. between E. 26th and E. 27th Sts. See map p. 33

Woolworth Building architect Cass Gilbert designed this 40-story Gothic Revival tower (1928); its pyramidal crown figures prominently on the nighttime skyline. The building stands on the site of the original Madison Square Garden, before the arena was rebuilt in the Garment District.

9 West 57th Street★

9 W. 57th St.

This striking 50-story high rise of dark glass and white travertine (1974, Skidmore, Owings & Merrill) swoops skyward from a broad base. The chunky red "9" sculpture on 57th Street is the work of graphic designer Ivan Chermayeff.

MetLife Building

200 Park Ave. at E. 45th St. See map p. 40.

Bauhaus architect Walter Gropius had a hand in the conception of this 59-story skyscraper (1963), which drew rumbles of protest because it blocked the view down Park Avenue.

ICONS

Statue of Liberty, Empire State Building, Brooklyn Bridge. Your little-town blues will melt away when you see these awesome icons of The Big Apple. Some of these buildings are lucky to still be here.
For years New Yorkers thought city land was too valuable for buildings to be "marked." That attitude changed after Pennsylvania Station was demolished in 1965, and the Landmarks Preservations Commission was formed as a result.

Brooklyn Bridge★★★

Extending southeast from City Hall Park (see Historic Sites), the bridge connects downtown Manhattan with Brooklyn. 4, 5 or 6 train to Brooklyn Bridge-City Hall.

With its great Gothic towers and its spider's web of cables, the Brooklyn Bridge is one of New York's best-known landmarks. Building it wasn't easy. German-born John Augustus Roebling got the commission to design it in 1869, but shortly after the plans were approved, one of his feet was crushed while he was taking measurements for the piers. Despite an amputation, gangrene set in and he died three weeks later. His son Washington Roebling took over the project, but he was injured too, getting the bends in an underwater expedition to build the foundations. Washington oversaw construction from his sickbed from that point on. Finally, in 1883 after 14 years of work, the link between Brooklyn and Manhattan was complete: and with what style – New York at last had a world-class monument. The Brooklyn Bridge ranked as the world's largest until 1903.

How the Brooklyn Bridge Measures Up

- **Height** – Its towers rise 276 feet; the maximum clearance above the water is 133 feet.
- **Length** – The bridge stretches 5,989 feet, with a center span of 1,595 feet between the two towers.
- **Strength** – Four huge cables, interlaced with a vast network of wire, support the steel span. Each 16-inch-thick cable is 3,515 feet long.

Hoofing it

A stroll across the Brooklyn Bridge is one of the most dramatic walks in the city, offering terrific views, especially at sunset. The pedestrian walkway begins near the Brooklyn

Brooklyn Bridge

Brigitta L. House/Michelin

Bridge-City Hall subway station in Manhattan, and near the High Street-Brooklyn Bridge station in Brooklyn. Allow about 30 minutes to cross the expanse.

Empire State Building ★★★

*Fifth Ave. & 34th St.
212-736-3100. www.esbnyc.com.
Open year-round daily 8am– 2am
(last elevator up at 1:15am).
$19 adults. Any train to 34th St. –
Herald Square.*

© Jeff Gynane/BigStockPhoto.com

Empire State Building

As robust as it is in reality, this 102-story Art Deco skyscraper looked like a mere toy in the 1933 film *King Kong*. Indeed, the image of the giant gorilla scaling the building with a doll-like, hysterical Fay Wray in his hand is burned into the minds of many.

Since then, the Empire State Building has become the quintessential New York landmark. Because of its massive footprint and its tapered upper stories, the building seems to play hide-and-seek. You can be standing right next to the Empire State Building and not know it's there, but twenty blocks, or even several miles away it totally dominates the skyline – especially at night, when its crown is lit.

Although construction started just weeks before the stock market crash of 1929, it wasn't slowed by the Depression; in fact, the building sometimes rose more than a story each day. In 1945 a B-25 bomber crashed into the 79th floor, killing the plane's crew and 14 people inside, but the robust structure was undamaged. Today the Empire State Building, including its three-story-high European marble lobby decked out with sleek Art Deco detailing and 73 elevator cars, appears much as it did when it was built.

View From The Top

To get to the 86th-floor **observatory★★★**, enter the Empire State Building from Fifth Avenue. Check the sign inside the entrance indicating the wait time and the visibility level. The highest visiblity level posted is 25 miles; on overcast days the view can be a mile or less. If you decide to proceed, take the escalator to the second floor and get in line. The lines tend to be the shortest first thing in the morning. Tickets can be purchased in advance through the building's website (www.esbnyc.com); note that even if you have a pre-purchased ticket or a City-Pass *(see p 17)*, you still have to wait in line twice: first for the security checkpoint and then for an elevator. Bags larger than an airline carry-on are not allowed, and there is no coat check, so pack lightly. Enjoy the view!

LANDMARKS

Grand Central Terminal

©Mario Savoia/iStockphoto.com

Grand Central Terminal★★★

Park Ave. at E. 42nd St.
www.grandcentralterminal.com.
4, 5, 6 or 7 train to Grand Central.

There's a reason that Grand Central Terminal is held up as the epitome of hustle and bustle (i.e. "It's like Grand Central station around here!"). This magical public space is crisscrossed by 150,000 commuters each workday. Railroad baron "Commodore" Cornelius Vanderbilt financed its $80 million construction by, quite literally, covering his tracks. In 1903 the city had banned steam locomotives to reduce air and noise pollution, and Vanderbilt had to either go electric or leave the city. He not only electrified his trains but, with the help of engineer William J. Wingus, routed them underground, freeing up a vast stretch of Park Avenue between East 42nd & East 59th streets for real estate development. When it opened in 1913, Grand Central Terminal was called "the gateway to the nation," but like many landmarks in New York, it was threatened with demolition in the 1960s.

Thanks to civic boosters, it was saved, and a $200 million restoration in the mid-1990s brought it back to its original splendor. To really soak up the vibe, grab a drink at the lavish Campbell Apartment *(see Nightlife)* or a meal at Grand Central Oyster Bar *(see Musts for Fun)*.

Facade – The recently spiffed-up 42nd Street facade, of Stony Creek

---

Isn't It Grand?

To take a self-guided tour of the station, go to the I LOVE NEW YORK information window and pick up a map. You can also print out a two-page walking-tour guide from the website. Free guided tours are offered Wednesdays and Fridays. The Wednesday tour is led by the Municipal Art Society *(212-935-3960)*: meet at the information booth in the center of the main concourse at 12:30pm. The Friday tour is led by the Grand Central Partnership *(212-883-2420)*: meet at the sculpture court of the Altria Building, corner of Park Avenue and 42nd Street at 12:30pm.

granite and Bedford limestone, has three grand arches flanked by Doric columns. On top is a 13-foot clock and Jules-Felix Coutain's 1914 sculpture depicting Mercury, supported by Minerva and Hercules.

Main Concourse – The vaulted turquoise ceiling, decorated with the constellations of the Zodiac, soars to a wondrous height of 12 stories.

Dining Concourse – This lower-level food court showcases locally owned restaurants. Here you'll find the best quick bites in the area, especially on weekends, when lunch spots for the office crowd are closed.

New York Transit Museum Gallery and Store – 212-878-0106; www.mta.info/museum. This annex of the main museum in Brooklyn Heights (see Best of the Boroughs) mounts changing exhibits on transportation history and sells transit-related merchandise, such as wallet-size subway maps.

New York Public Library★★★

476 Fifth Ave., between W. 40th & W. 42nd Sts. 917-275-6975. www.nypl.org. Open Mon–Sat 11am–6pm (Tue & Wed until 7:30pm), Sun 1pm–5pm. Closed major holidays. 7 train to 5th Ave.; B, D, F, or V train to 42nd St.

To escape the hubbub of Midtown on a warm day, there's nothing like sipping an iced coffee on the New York Public Library's well-worn steps. However, you have to go inside to really appreciate what the library has to offer – museum-quality exhibits and lavish interiors that you can explore for free.

New York Public Library
NYC&Co.

Carrère and Hastings designed this 1911 Beaux-Arts masterpiece. Its imposing Fifth Avenue entrance, made of white Vermont marble, is guarded by two photogenic lions, and its Sixth Avenue back-yard is none other than Bryant Park. Eleven thousand visitors from around the globe enter the library daily to admire its architectural treasures and to pore over its 50 million circulation items, which make NYPL one of the greatest research institutions in the world.

Rose Main Reading Room – Nearly two city blocks long, the glorious third-floor reading room has 51ft-high ceilings covered with cerulean murals, rows of long oak tables dotted with brass reading lamps, and intricately carved woodwork.

DeWitt Wallace Periodical Room – Rich wood paneling and 13 murals by 20C artist Richard Haas decorate this cozy space on the first floor.

McGraw Rotunda – At the top of the main staircase you'll find a soaring rotunda adorned with murals depicting the recorded word.

Astor Hall – In this white-marble foyer, just inside the Fifth Avenue entrance, you'll find information booths staffed by friendly volunteers.

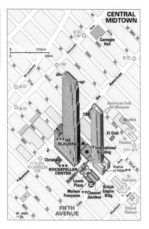

Rockefeller Center★★★

In Midtown, between Fifth & Seventh Aves., and W. 47th & W. 51st Sts. B, D, F or V train to 47th-50th Sts./Rockefeller Center.

A "city within a city," the coordinated urban complex of limestone buildings and gardens goes together like a sweater set from Saks Fifth Avenue, with all the proper accessories. Rockefeller Center didn't come into the world so cool and collected; in fact it was born of John D. Rockefeller's desperation to make good on an investment that looked for years like a sink hole for the family oil fortune. In 1928 Rockefeller signed a 24-year lease with Columbia University for the core 12 acres. He had grand plans for a colossal new venue to house the Metropolitan Opera, but after the October 1929 stock market crash, the Met pulled out and the university wouldn't budge on the terms of the rent. Rockefeller would pay that bill and shell out even more in the next 10 years to demolish 228 smaller buildings and put the initial cluster of 14 Art Deco structures in their place. An elegant ensemble of buildings – there are now 19 on 22 acres, linked by underground concourses – Rock Center combines high and low structures with open space, art, shops and restaurants.

GE Building★★★ – *30 Rockefeller Plaza. See Skyscrapers.*

Radio City Music Hall★★ – *1260 Ave. of the Americas. See Performing Arts.*

Rockefeller Center

Brigitta L. House/Michelin

A Piece of the Rock

If you visit Rockefeller Center between 7am and 10am weekdays, you can join the mob of placard-holding tourists who form the human backdrop of the *Today Show*, filmed at NBC's street-level studios *(Rockefeller Plaza & 49th St.)*. Better yet, you can enjoy a coffee across the plaza at Dean & Deluca and ponder American zeal to be on TV, no matter how silly you look.

MUST SEE

Ferries to the Statue of Liberty *($12 round-trip)* leave every 25 minutes from Battery Park in Manhattan between 8:30am and 4:30pm in summer; every 45 minutes between 9am and 3:30pm the rest of the year. Ferries leave every 45 minutes in summer from Liberty State Park in New Jersey. All ferries stop on both Liberty Island and Ellis Island. Buying ferry tickets online (at least two days in advance) allows you to avoid ticket lines and reserve a Monument Pass (the only way to enter the statue). Same-day tickets may be purchased at the ticket office inside Castle Clinton National Monument *(see Historic Sites)* in Battery Park; advance tickets may be picked up at the Will Call window. Ferries *(877-523-9849; www.statuecruises.com).* are boarded on a first-come, first-served basis.

Channel Gardens★★ – *Fifth Ave., between E. 49th & E. 50th Sts.*
These seasonal flowerbeds were named in 1936 by a clever journalist who observed that they separated the Maison Française (1933) and the British Empire Building (1932), just as the English Channel separates France and Great Britain. Benches around the perimeter provide a pefect place to relax.

Rockefeller Plaza – This pedestrian concourse slices north-south through the middle of the complex. In winter it hosts a 10-story-tall Christmas tree and, in the lower plaza, an ice rink where skaters glide and twirl before a gold-leaf statue of the god Prometheus. Non-skaters can enjoy hot chocolate or a drink at the cafe overlooking the rink. In summer the rink gives way to an open-air cafe.

Atlas★★ – Fronting the 41-story International Building, the monumental sculpture of the globe-toting god created by Lee Lawrie was picketed at its unveiling for its resemblance to Italian dictator Benito Mussolini.

Statue of Liberty★★★

Liberty Island. 212-363-3200. www.nps.gov/stli. Grounds open daily 9:30am–5pm (extended hours in summer). Closed Dec 25. For information on visiting, see above.

With a torch in her hand and broken shackles at her feet, the Statue of Liberty has been welcoming "huddled masses" to New York for more than a century.
In 1865 a French historian first thought of memorializing the

© Jeff Greenberg/NYC&Co.
Statue of Liberty

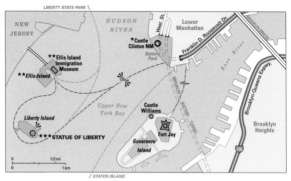

quest for freedom shared by France and the US. In 1874 the Alsatian sculptor Frédéric-Auguste Bartholdi set to work on his design. First he sculpted models of "Lady Liberty" in clay and plaster. Then, for the real thing, he applied 300 copper sheets to a 151 ft iron and steel skeleton made by French engineer Gustave Eiffel (who later created the Eiffel tower).

The statue was completed in 1884, then dismantled and packed into 220 shipping crates for her transatlantic voyage. She was unveiled on October 28, 1886, with President Grover Cleveland presiding over the foggy ceremony.

Monument – The pedestal and its observation deck are open only to visitors with Monument Passes (see p. 51). The original torch is located in the lobby. You can also take in the Statue of Liberty Exhibit, which features videos, oral histories and full-scale replicas of Lady Liberty's face and foot. Elevators ascend 10 stories to the top of the pedestal, where you can enjoy spectacular views of the tip of Manhattan, New York harbor and the statue itself.

Grounds – Ranger-guided tours of the island's grounds are offered free of charge at regularly scheduled times throughout the day (staff permitting). Check at the information center for daily program information.

Ellis Island Immigration Museum★★ – *See Museums.*

Visiting the U.N.

Enter the complex through the visitor entrance on First Ave. between 45th & 46th Sts. The General Assembly Building lobby, shops and post office can be visited year-round daily *(except major holidays)* 9am–5pm free of charge. Other parts of the UN complex may be visited by 45-min guided tour only, Monday through Friday 9:30am–4:45pm; $12.50 per person. A limited schedule may be in effect during the general debate *(mid-Sept–mid-Oct)*. Children under 5 years of age are not permitted on tours. For tours in languages other than English, call 212-963-7539 after 10am on the day you would like to visit. Lines are usually shortest in the morning.

United Nations Headquarters★★★

First Ave. between E. 42nd & E. 48th Sts. 212-963-8687. www.un.org. 4, 5, 6 or 7 train to Grand Central.
For tours, see sidebar opposite.
Closed major holidays.

The heady mission of the group that works in this complex of buildings and parks is to "preserve international peace and security, promote self-determination and equal rights, and encourage economic and social well being." The term "United Nations" was coined by Franklin D Roosevelt in 1941 to describe the countries allied against the Axis powers in WW II. Afterward, world leaders saw a need for a permanent peacekeeping force. The U.N. came into being in San Francisco on October 24, 1945, when a majority of its 51 founding members ratified its charter. John D. Rockefeller Jr. lured the group to New York with an $8.5 million gift, which was used to buy 18 acres on the East River. A team of 14 designers from around the world collaborated on the design of the complex, whose concept is credited to the French architect Le Corbusier, a pioneer of the International style. Today, the U.N. incorporates 191 countries.

United Nations headquarters

United Nations

General Assembly Building★★

Outside this long, low concrete structure that forms the heart of the U.N., member states' flags are arranged alphabetically from Afghanistan to Zimbabwe, just as their delegations are seated in the assembly hall. In the lobby is a dramatic 15-foot-by-12-foot stained-glass window by French artist Marc Chagall.

Secretariat Building★★

Not open to the public.

This tall, narrow, shimmering green-glass slab (1950) houses offices for 7,400 employees.

Conference Building

The five-story Conference Building contains meeting space for the U.N.'s three councils.

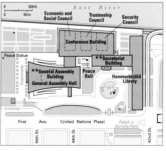

MUSEUMS

Culture vultures, welcome to New York City, home of the biggest, boldest museums in the US. History lurks in medieval cloisters – a gift of John D. Rockefeller – and modern tenements. As for art, let's talk world-class: the Met, MoMA, the Guggenheim, the Whitney. You could spend years wandering their halls and still not take it all in. Still, don't forget the little guys. What New York's smaller institutions lack in breadth, they often make up for in depth and atmosphere. Note that all of the museums listed in this section are located in Manhattan.

For museums in boroughs outside Manhattan, see BEST OF THE BOROUGHS.

American Museum of Natural History★★★

Central Park West between 77th & 81st Sts. 212-769-5100. www.amnh.org. Open year-round daily 10am–5:45pm. $15 (includes all exhibits); $24 includes exhibits and space show. Closed Thanksgiving Day & Dec 25. B, C train to 81st St.; 1 train to 79th St.

If you think of natural history museums as places with case after case of beetles pinned onto cork board, this place will make you think again. A famed research facility, the AMNH is working hard to make the natural world

as fascinating to today's young people as it was to those who never experienced television, air travel or the Internet. The cornerstone of the present facility was laid in 1874 by President Ulysses S. Grant. Theodore Roosevelt, an ardent naturalist, contributed a bat, a turtle, four bird eggs, twelve mice and the skull of a red squirrel. Today, only a small portion of the museum's more than 30 million artifacts and specimens, gathered from more than 1,000 globe-trotting expeditions, are on view at any given time. The following exhibits, several of which were recipients of major renovations in

American Museum of Natural History

American Museum of Natural History

recent years, are by far the most compelling you'll find here.

Fossil Halls★★ – *Fourth floor.* Bone up on your prehistory in these bright, modern galleries, which trace the course of vertebrate evolution with 600 specimens from the museum's million-piece vertebrate fossil collection, the world's largest. The two most popular halls contain 100 dinosaur skeletons, set in positions showing how the animals are thought to have carried themselves in the wild. Admire, among others, the whip-tailed *Apatosaurus*, the spiny-backed *Dimetrodon*, and the fearsome *Tyrannosaurus rex*, with its 4ft jaw and 6in teeth.

Rose Center for Earth and Space★★ – Stargazers, keep your eyes peeled: this dazzling space center, inaugurated in 2000, blends cutting-edge science with high-impact visuals to describe the mysteries of the cosmos.
A good place to start is with a **star show★★★** in the Hayden Sphere *(advance tickets and information: 212-769-5200 or www.amnh.org).* The digital program takes spectators on a virtual ride through the Milky Way Galaxy to the edge of the observable universe, using 3-D maps developed with the help of NASA. On the lower level, the glittering **Hall of the Universe★** has a video feed from the Hubble

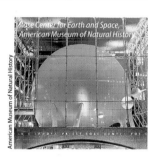

Rose Center for Earth and Space, American Museum of Natural History

American Museum of Natural History

Space Telescope; towering models of cosmic phenomena; and artifacts including the 15-ton Willamette Meteorite.

Hall of Ocean Life★ – *First floor.* Reopened in summer 2003 after a \$25 million renovation, this two-story hall showcases different ocean environments and denizens with dioramas and videos. The centerpiece is a 94ft model of a **blue whale** *(Balaenoptera musculus)* suspended in a dive position. The largest animal that ever lived, this phenomenal creature can grow to a weight of 400,000 pounds and swallow up to 17,000 gallons of water filled with shrimp-like krill in a single gulp.

Hall of African Mammals★ – *Second floor.* Encircling an impressive herd of African elephants on the alert, the dioramas here present zebras, antelopes, gorillas, lions and gazelles in their natural surroundings.

MUSEUMS

55

The Cloisters★★★

Fort Tryon Park, between W. 190th & W. 200th Sts. from Broadway to the Hudson River. 212-923-3700. www.metmuseum.org.
Open Mar–Oct Tue–Sun 9:30am–5:15pm. Rest of the year Tue–Sun 9:30am–4:45pm. Closed Mon & major holidays. $20 suggested donation. A train to 190th St.

©Mick Hale/Metropolitan Museum Art/NYC&Co.

The Cloisters

The Cloisters offers one of New York's most serene museum experiences. Built on a hilltop in a park overlooking the Hudson, the compound incorporates architectural treasures from Europe, including four cloisters (quadrangles surrounded by covered walkways, or arcades), to create what looks like a fortified monastery. Within are 5,000 pieces from the Metropolitan Museum's stellar collection of medieval art. The core of the collection was put together by the American sculptor George Grey Barnard (1863–1938) and was first presented to the public in 1914. In 1925 oil scion John D. Rockefeller donated 40 medieval sculptures to the Met, along with the money to buy Barnard's collection. Five years later he presented the city of New York with an estate he owned in northern Manhattan

(now Fort Tryon Park), provided that the north end of the property be reserved for the Cloisters. The site is lovely to visit on a nice day, when you can watch sunlight filter in through the many treasured stained-glass windows.

Frick Collection★★★

1 E. 70th St. between Fifth and Madison Aves. 212-288-0700. www.frick.org. Open year-round Tue–Sat 10am–6pm; Sun 11am–5pm. Closed Mon & major holidays. $15. 6 train to 68th St.

For a glimpse at the spoils of the Gilded Age, look no farther than the Frick, one of the world's most distinguished small museums. Pittsburgh steel and railroad tycoon Henry Clay Frick amassed this remarkable trove of paintings,

---

Highlights of The Cloisters

- **Cuxa Cloister★★**, from a 12C monastery in the French Pyrenees, is the largest in the complex, but is only one quarter the size of the original.
- **Fuentidueña Chapel★**, devoted to Spanish Romanesque art.
- The walkway of the **Saint-Guilhem Cloister★**, from Montpellier, France, contains a magnificent series of 12C–13C columns and capitals.
- **Campin Room★★** has the 15C **Annunciation Triptych** by Robert Campin.
- The 13C–14C **Bonnefont Cloister★★** has a medieval herb and flower garden.
- The **Gothic Chapel★★** is the setting for a collection of tomb effigies.
- The **treasury** displays the Cloisters' collection of smaller objects, including a walrus-ivory cross from the 12C, and magnificent **Book of Hours** manuscript.

MUST SEE

furnishings, sculpture and china over the course of four decades. In 1913 he commissioned Thomas Hastings to build a 40-room manse for his holdings; he took up residence here in 1914 and died five years later. Since the museum's opening in 1935, the building has been expanded twice and the collection has grown by a third.

Fragonard Room★★★ – Eleven decorative paintings by the 18C artist Jean-Honoré Fragonard, including four depicting the "progress of love," are complemented by exquisite 18C French furniture and Sèvres porcelain.

Living Hall★★ – Masterpieces by Holbein, Titian and El Greco share space with pieces by 17C cabinet-maker André-Charles Boulle.

West Gallery★★★ – Landscapes by Ruisdael and Corot, among others, hang alongside portraits by Rembrandt *(Self-Portrait)* and Velázquez *(Philip IV of Spain)* in the house's largest gallery.

Enamel Room★ – Piero della Francesca's image of St. John the Evangelist is the only large painting by Piero in the US. Note also the splendid Limoges painted enamels dating from the 16C–17C.

East Gallery – Works in this gallery rotate frequently, but you're still likely to see the four sumptuous full-length portraits by Whistler.

The Frick Collection

©John Bigelow Taylor/The Frick Collection

MUSEUMS

57

Metropolitan Museum of Art

©NYC&Co.

The Metropolitan Museum of Art★★★

Fifth Ave. at E. 82nd St. 212-535-7710. www.metmuseum.org. Open year-round Tue–Sun 9:30am–5:30pm (Fri & Sat until 9pm). Closed major holidays except holiday Mondays. Suggested contribution: $20 (includes same-day admission to The Cloisters). 4, 5 or 6 train to 86th St.

Art lovers from around the world flock to the Met, the biggest museum in the Western Hemisphere. The collection embraces three million objects tracing 5,000 years of human history, so you

can spend a day studying one period or get a primer on all of art history. The museum has humble origins: founded in 1870, it opened in a dancing academy. In 1880 it moved to its present location, but its signature Beaux-Arts facade, designed by Richard Morris Hunt, wasn't completed until 1902. Actually, it was never finished. Look atop the twinned columns – those chunky blocks were supposed to be carved. A master plan drawn up for the museum's centennial celebration in 1970 called for an ambitious expansion. Wings and courtyards built through the 1990s complemented the Met's traditional exhibition halls with space for, among other things, a massive Egyptian temple (Temple of Dendur) and the personal collection of a Wall Street mogul (Lehman Pavilion).

Best of The Met

American Wing★★★ – Spanning three centuries, the collection includes decorative arts from the Jacobean style through the work of Frank Lloyd Wright. Painting highlights include masterworks of the Hudson River school and high-

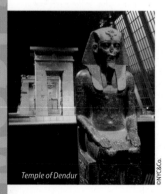

Temple of Dendur

©NYC&Co.

society portraits by John Singer Sargent. The sunlit Charles Engelhard Court displays Tiffany stained glass, sculpture and architectural fragments.

Ancient Art★★★ – The Egyptian wing is a perennial favorite, its 69,000 square feet of exhibition space ending in the glass-enclosed Temple of Dendur. On the other side of the Met, the newly renovated galleries for Greek and Roman art display statues, vases, bronzework and sarcophagi.

European Sculpture and Decorative Arts★★★ – This is one of the museum's largest departments, with more than 50,000 works from the Renaissance to the early 20C. Pieces are displayed in exquisitely re-created period rooms.

European Paintings★★★ – Paintings on the 2nd floor include works by Titian, Raphael, Tiepolo, El Greco, Velázquez, Thomas Gainsborough and others. The museum owns 20 paintings by Rembrandt.

19C European Paintings and Sculpture★★★ – These recently reconfigured and expanded galleries display one of the world's foremost collections of works spanning the 19C. It was a fertile century, and you'll see its evolution from the Neoclassicism of J.A.D. Ingres to the tempestuous work of Vincent Van Gogh.

Arts of Africa, Oceania and the Americas★★ – These spacious galleries full of stunning totem poles, masks, shields and sculpture are dedicated to Michael Rockefeller, the oil scion who died on an anthropological visit to New Guinea in 1961.

Lehman Collection★★ – Shown in rotating exhibits, the 3,000-work

MUSEUMS

collection is most famous for its 14C and 15C Italian paintings.

Medieval Art★★ – Complementing the collection at the Cloisters, 4,000 works of Byzantine silver, Romanesque and Gothic metalwork, stained glass and tapestries can be found in moody galleries, including a cryptlike space under the stairs of the Great Hall.

Costume Institute★ – A magnet for style mavens, the institute recently mounted a retrospective of designs by the House of Chanel.

Abby Aldrich Rockefeller Sculpture Garden and the David and Peggy Rockefeller Building

The Museum of Modern Art - ©2005 Timothy Hursley

Museum of Modern Art (MoMA)★★★

11 W. 53rd St., between Fifth & Sixth Aves. 212-708-9400. www.moma.org. Open year-round Wed–Mon 10:30am–5:30pm (Fri until 8pm). Closed Tue, Thanksgiving Day & Dec 25. $20 (free Fri after 4pm). E or V train to Fifth Ave.-53rd St.

MoMA dazzles visitors with its vast, open floor plan, delightful restaurants, and, of course, unparalleled collection of modern art – including some of the world's most famous paintings. The museum was founded in 1929 by three wealthy, forward-thinking women – Abby Aldrich Rockefeller, Lillie

P. Bliss, and Mary Quinn Sullivan. Over the next decade, founding director Alfred H. Barr Jr. shaped MoMA's philosophy, mounting shows of daring new paintings as well as photography, architecture and design, none of which were considered legitimate art forms at the time. Since then MoMA's holdings have grown to encompass almost 200,000 objects from the mid-19C to the present, organized in six collecting areas.

Painting and Sculpture★★★ – MoMA owns many of the most famous modern artworks in the world, including Van Gogh's *Starry Night*, Monet's *Waterlilies*, Picasso's *Les Demoiselles d'Avignon*, Salvador Dali's *Persistence of Memory*,

Dining at MoMA

MoMA's three eateries take an artful approach to museum food. **The Modern** is the fanciest of the three, presenting excellent contemporary cuisine in a sleek, Bauhaus-inspired dining room overlooking the sculpture garden *(reservations recommended: 212-333-1220)*. Open past museum hours due to its separate entrance on West 53rd Street, the Modern also has a more casual Bar Room and seasonal terrace. On the second floor of the museum, **Cafe 2** is a stylish rustic Italian diner, serving panini and handmade pastas. In a small space overlooking the sculpture garden, **Terrace 5** offers sumptuous gourmet desserts and "savory bites" like marinated olives, smoked salmon and artisanal cheese, along with cocktails, wine and espresso drinks. For kids, there's hot chocolate, chocolate milk and rootbeer floats.

MUST SEE

Andrew Wyeth's *Christina's World*, and Andy Warhol's *Campbell's Soup Cans*.

Architecture and Design★★ – Includes Frank Lloyd Wright and Mies van der Rohe models, Bauhaus furniture, Tiffany glass, Russian Constructivist posters.

Film and Media – 20,000 silent, experimental, animated, documentary and feature films and stills.

Photography★★ – 25,000 works surveying the history of photography.

Drawings★ – More than 7,000 works, from Dada to the Russian avant-garde.

Prints and Illustrated Books★ – Bibliographic arts and printmaking, including the graphic arts of Picasso.

American Folk Art Museum★★

[M4] *on the map on the inside front cover. 45 W. 53rd St. between Fifth & Sixth Aves. 212-265-1040. www.folkartmuseum.org. Open Tue–Sun 10:30am–5:30pm (Fri until 7:30pm). Closed Mon & major holidays. $9 (free Fri 5:30–7:30pm). E or V train to Fifth Ave.*

Defined as any work by an untrained artist, folk art can be as functional as a weather vane or as odd as a sculpture made from chicken bones. You'll find both at this provocative museum, housed in an ingenious, seven-story, metal-clad structure (2001, Tod Williams & Billie Tsien) hard against the Museum of Modern Art. Above the entrance, a column of glass panels is set at a sharp angle to the metal facade, like a half-open door letting in a long shaft of light. Inside, a narrow corridor opens into a vast atrium around which the museum's formidable collections are arrayed both on the walls and in specially designed niches in the stairwells.

The bilevel permanent exhibit, "Folk Art Revealed," comprising 150 works from the 6,000-piece permanent collection, challenges viewers to consider folk art's function and the persistence of certain themes. Patriotic symbols are a mainstay of

Augt Bandal/American Folk Art Museum

Child-Headed Whiplash-Tail Blengins. by Henry Darger

MUSEUMS

Cooper-Hewitt, National Design Museum

the form, ranging from a wooden gate painted with the American flag in 1876, to a red, white, and blue "freedom quilt" made by an African-American artist facing racism in the South in the 1960s. Other folk art is utilitarian yet beautiful: the massive wooden tooth that serves as a dentist's shingle, the ship's figurehead, the Shaker cupboard. You'll find your imagination intrigued perhaps most by the wildly idiosyncratic expressions that grow out of deprivation and mental illness, such as the romantic storybooks by recluse Henry Darger. A recent exhibit featured the haunting wooden portraits of Asa Ames, a little-known sculptor active in New York state in the mid-19C.

Cooper-Hewitt, National Design Museum★★

2 E. 91st St. at Fifth Ave. 212-849-8400. www.cooperhewitt. org. Open year-round Mon–Fri 10am–5pm (Fri until 9pm), Sat 10am–6pm, Sun noon–6pm. Closed major holidays. $15. 4, 5 or 6 train to 86th St.

Founded by Sarah, Eleanor and Amy Hewitt – granddaughters of industrialist Peter Cooper – this eclectic museum shows how artists across cultures and centuries have enhanced everyday objects. Visitors also get a de facto house tour, as the museum is situated in the sumptuous, 64-room mansion that once belonged to steel baron Andrew Carnegie. Be sure to at least step into the foyer, which is covered in magnificent woodwork. Interestingly, at the time of its completion in 1902, the house was surrounded by farms and shanties. By the time Carnegie died in 1919, Fifth Avenue was the city's smartest address.

Collection – An affiliate of the Smithsonian Institution, the Cooper-Hewitt owns more than 250,000 objects related to the art, craft and commerce of design. The prints and drawings collection is particularly robust, with works by 15C Italian master Andrea Mantegna, Americans Frederic Church and Winslow Homer, and Italian surrealist Giorgio de Chirico. Other highlights include an assortment of 18C and 19C birdcages, 10,000 wall coverings, 45 pieces of Roman-Syrian glass, and 1,000 embroidery samplers dating from the 17C to the 19C.

Visit – The vast majority of the museum's 9,000 square feet of gallery space is devoted to major temporary exhibitions. One recent show explored the Rococo movement and its revivals. The museum also mounts its "Selects" series of exhibitions of works drawn from the permanent collection, all guest curated by respected designers and design firms.

Ellis Island Immigration Museum★★

On Ellis Island in New York Harbor; for ferry information, see Landmarks/Statue of Liberty. 212-363-3200. www.ellisisland. com or www.nps.gov/elis. Open year-round daily 9:30am–5:15pm. Closed Dec 25.

Hate waiting in lines? Imagine being among the 5,000 newly

arrived immigrants who were processed here every day between 1900 and 1924. Today the grandly refurbished processing center takes visitors on a journey through that painstaking process and stands as a testament to what it means to start life over in a new land.

Ellis Island Immigration Museum

©Jeff Greenberg/NYC&Co.

MUSEUMS

Ellis Island stands in New York Harbor approximately halfway between lower Manhattan and the Statue of Liberty, and was a natural portal to the new world.

A whopping twelve million people took their first step on American soil here.

The island was declared part of the Statue of Liberty National Monument in 1965, and after a $156 million restoration program, the 200,000-square-foot Ellis Island Immigration Museum was opened in 1990. The French Renaissance building is the only one of the island's 33 structures accessible to the public.

First floor – Visitors coming off the ferry enter the baggage room, where immigrants were separated (sometimes forever) from their belongings.

Second floor – The sweeping Registry Room/Great Hall, capped with a vaulted ceiling of 28,000 interlocking tiles, was the site of initial inspections.

Third floor – Exhibits include keepsakes from immigrants and their families, and a dorm room re-creating the cramped conditions of life on the island.

Guggenheim Museum★★

1071 Fifth Ave., between E. 88th & E. 89th Sts. 212-423-3500. www.guggenheim.org. Open Fri–Wed 10am–5:45pm (Fri until 7:45pm). Closed Thanksgiving Day and Dec 25. $18. 4, 5 or 6 train to 86th St.

Frank Lloyd Wright's spiraling Modernist statement – one of the most original buildings in the US – is reason enough to check out the Guggenheim, also home to some fine modern and contemporary art. **Solomon R. Guggenheim** (1861–1949), heir to a vast mining fortune, started his collection with Old Masters, but in the early 20C shifted his focus to nonrepresentational art. In 1943 Frank Lloyd Wright was commissioned to design a permanent home for Guggenheim's collection. Wright was an outspoken critic of New York architecture, and the city returned the favor by blasting his design. The 1959 structure, an idiosyncratic composition based on a complex trigonometric spiral, clashed with the sedate brownstones of the Upper East

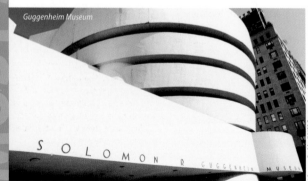

Guggenheim Museum

SOLOMON R GUGGENHEIM MUSEUM

©Susana Pashko/NYC&Co.

Side and was a nightmare to construct. Worse, its interior ramp and sloping walls made presenting and viewing art difficult, if not impossible. Wright considered it his crowning achievement. In 1992 a 10-story limestone annex was built behind the structure, with ramps leading from Wright's nautilus into more hospitable gallery spaces.

Collection – The Guggenheim Foundation owns about 6,000 paintings, sculptures and works on paper, though only about 100 are on display at any given time. Core holdings comprise 195 works by Wassily Kandinsky – the largest group of his works in the US – and more than 75 pieces by Klee, Chagall, Delaunay, Dubuffet and Mondrian. However, the only works permanently on display are selections from the **Thannhauser Collection**★ of late-19C and early-20C art, including paintings by Picasso, Cézanne, Degas, Manet, Pissarro, Toulouse-Lautrec and Van Gogh; Picasso is especially well represented with both early and late paintings. The rest of the museum is devoted to large-scale temporary shows, some taking up virtually the whole museum.

Lower East Side Tenement Museum★★

108 Orchard St. at Broome St. 212-982-8420. www.tenement.org. Open daily 11am–5pm. Visitor center open Mon and Wed–Fri 11am–6pm (Thu until 8:15pm); Sat & Sun 10:45am–6pm. Closed major holidays. Tenements may be visited by 1hr guided tour only (see Touring Tip p. 66). F train to Delancey St.

Lower Eastside Tenement Museum

Lower Eastside Tenement Museum

If Ellis Island recounts chapter one of the American immigrant experience, this remarkable museum recounts chapter two – out loud and in person. 🚶**Tour guides** interpret several generations of immigrant life at 97 Orchard Street, a five-story tenement building (now a National Historic Landmark) in the heart of what was once the most densely populated neighborhood in the US.

MUSEUMS

Between 1863 and 1935, some 7,000 people lived in this single structure alone. Guides use sociological data, keepsakes, anecdotes, photographs, newspaper clippings, architectural details and historical recordings to show how a few families got along.

Getting By: Immigrants Weathering Hard Times – This tour explores the apartments of the German-Jewish Gumpertz family in the 1870s and the Sicilian-Catholic Baldizzi family in the 1930s.

Piecing It Together: Immigrants in the Garment Industry – This tour features two Jewish families affiliated with the garment industry circa 1897 and 1918.

The Moores: An Irish Family in America – The tour introduces visitors to a family of Irish immigrants who lost a child while living here in 1869, and examines health-care choices in the 19C.

Confino Living History – Especially designed for families with kids, the tour explores the apartment once occupied by the Confinos, Sephardic Jews who emigrated to the US from Turkey in the 1900s. A guide acting as the family's sassy teenage daughter tells stories and answers questions. *See Musts for Kids.*

Morgan Library★★

225 Madison Ave. at 36th St. 212-685-0008. www.themorgan. org. Open Tue–Fri 10:30am–5pm (Fri until 9pm); Sat 10am–6pm; Sun 11am–6pm. $12. 6 train to 33rd St.

To see Beethoven's Violin Sonata No. 10 in G Major as it emerged from the composer's pen is to glimpse a mind furiously engaged at work. The Morgan has thousands of such one-of-a-kind masterpieces. The collection of

Morgan Library

Morgan Library/©2005 Todd Eberle

rare books, manuscripts, drawings, paintings, seals and letters grew out of the personal holdings of wealthy financier **John Pierpont Morgan** (1837–1913). In 1902 he commissioned the noted firm McKim, Mead, and White to build a home for his growing "library." The Italian Renaissance main building, constructed of Tennessee marble blocks, was completed in 1906 and opened to the public after Morgan's death in 1913. An annex was added in 1928. The third building on the site, the brownstone where Pierpont Morgan's son J.P. once lived, dates to 1852. A major expansion by Renzo Piano, completed in 2006, doubled the exhibition space and drew rave reviews for its unifying composition of glass and steel pavilions.

The Collection – Highlights include the country's largest and finest collection of Rembrandt etchings, three Gutenberg bibles and Henry David Thoreau's journal. Rotating exhibits might present drawings by Leonardo and Degas; original scores by Mahler and Schubert; and handwritten manuscripts by Dickens, Twain and Jane Austen.

Museum of the City of New York★★

1220 Fifth Ave. at E. 103rd St. 212-534-1672. www.mcny.org. Open year-round Tue–Sun 10am–5pm. Closed Mon & major holidays. $9. 6 train to 103rd St.

The Museum of the City of New York chronicles the Big Apple's growth from Dutch trading post to thriving metropolis with period rooms, galleries, and historical exhibits. Founded in 1923, the museum first resided at Gracie Mansion. It moved to the current location, a Georgian Revival building fronting Central Park, in 1929. Since then the collection has grown to encompass more than 1.5 million paintings, prints, photographs, costumes, toys (includes a series of exquisite **dollhouses**), rare books, manuscripts, sculptures and other artifacts.

Museum of Jewish Heritage★★

36 Battery Place. 646-437-4200. www.mjhnyc.org. Open year-round Sun–Thu 10am–5:45pm (Wed until 8pm), Fri 10am–5pm (3pm in winter). Closed Sat, Jewish holidays & Thanksgiving Day. $10 (free Wed 4pm–8pm). 4 or 5 train to Bowling Green.

Boasting magnificent views of the Statue of Liberty and Ellis Island, this "living memorial to the Holocaust" celebrates freedom while remembering the stories of those who struggled or died to achieve it. The main, ziggurat-shaped building holds the museum's core exhibition of 2,000 historic photographs, 800 historical and cultural artifacts and 24 original documentary films. The galleries in the adjoining Morgenthau Wing hold temporary exhibits.

Garden of Stones★ – In September 2003 English sculptor Andy Goldsworthy hollowed out eighteen boulders, filled them with soil, and planted a single dwarf oak in each. As each tree matures in the coming decades – it will take 50 years for them to reach maturity – it will merge with the stone, symbolizing life emerging from lifelessness.

MUSEUMS

Rotunda, National Museum of the American Indian

National Museum of the American Indian

National Museum of the American Indian★★

[M1] *on the map on the inside front cover. 1 Bowling Green. 212-514-3700. www.nmai.si.edu. Open year-round daily 10am–5pm (Thu until 8pm). Closed Dec 25. 4 or 5 train to Bowling Green.*

The little sister of a larger facility with the same name in Washington, DC, this Smithsonian Institution treasure trove of Native American art and artifacts is presented inside the **Alexander Hamilton US Custom House★★**, a Beaux-Arts landmark (1907, Cass Gilbert) overlooking Bowling Green, the Financial District's prettiest green space. Inside, the soaring oval **rotunda** is ringed with murals painted by Reginald Marsh in 1936–37. The museum's three roomy galleries branch off from this space, each containing an exhibit exploring some aspect of American Indian culture, history, or art. Recent shows included the astounding craftsmanship of the Pacific Coast tribes; and a survey of 77 works including a hand-painted set of Apache playing cards dating from 1880, a 1910 Nez Perce basketry hat, and a pair of Huron moccasins embroidered with moose hair.

New-York Historical Society★★

170 Central Park West. 212-873-3400. www.nyhistory.org. Open year-round Tue–Sat 10am–6pm (Fri until 8pm); Sun 11am–5:45pm. $10. B or C train to 81st St.

The Man Behind the Museum

Were it not for one New Yorker's passion for collecting, the Smithsonian might not have had a museum. Over the course of 45 years, George Gustav Heye (1874–1957), a wealthy investment banker, gathered almost a million objects from indigenous peoples throughout the Western Hemisphere. Heye cast his net wide and bought everything he could lay his hands on, starting with a deerskin shirt in 1897. Crass though it might have been, the strategy succeeded in filling first his personal museum *(at 155th St. & Broadway)*, then this one, and now much of the new one in Washington DC.

MUST SEE

An Urban Aviary

For a touch of spring in the dead of winter *(mid-February to mid-March)*, head to the New-York Historical Society, where in place of the Hudson River school paintings in Dexter Hall, you'll find a rotating selection of John James Audubon's famous *Birds of America* watercolors, accompanied by recorded calls and songs of depicted species. Items that belonged to Audubon, including ornithological models and personal keepsakes, round out the story of his "magnificent obsession" with winged creatures.

It may be New York's oldest museum, but curators at the historical society approach its rich trove of material with a keenly modern eye. The society was founded in 1804 to preserve the history of the US, and since then it has amassed a collection that embraces three centuries of Americana, with a special focus on New York material from the late 1700s to early 1900s. Thanks to a $10 million renovation and the opening in November 2000 of the Henry Luce Center, today the museum's holdings are presented in a more complete format than ever before.

The Historical Society serves as the world's most comprehensive collection of artifacts relating to the September 11, 2001, terrorist attacks. Blockbuster shows have addressed such topics as New York's role in the slave trade and the legacy of founding father Alexander Hamilton, a New Yorker.

Dexter Hall – *Second floor*. Thomas Cole's five-painting series *The Course of Empire* and other masterworks by Hudson River school artists are displayed salon-style along with smaller landscapes and portraiture by Rembrandt Peale and others.

Henry Luce III Center for the Study of American Culture – *Fourth floor*. Presented in what's called "working storage" format, nearly 40,000 objects are on view here. Holdings range from George Washington's camp bed at Valley Forge to the world's largest collection of Tiffany lamps, with thousands of odds and ends in between. For an entertaining commentary on dozens of items in this browser's delight, take a self-guided audio tour.

Whitney Museum of American Art★★

945 Madison Ave. at E. 75th St. 212-570-3600. www.whitney.org. Open year-round Wed–Thu & Sat–Sun 11am–6pm, Fri 1pm–9pm. Closed Mon, Tue & major holidays. $15 (pay what you wish Fri 6pm–9pm). 6 train to 77th St.

A diehard champion of emerging artists, the Whitney also has one of the world's best collections of 20C American art. The museum grew out of the personal art collection

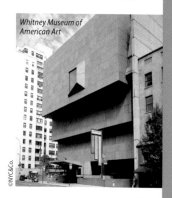
Whitney Museum of American Art

©NYC&Co.

of sculptor and art collector **Gertrude Vanderbilt Whitney** (1875–1942), the rebellious daughter of railroad titan Cornelius Vanderbilt. After starting the Whitney Studio Club in her Greenwich Village studio, she began to acquire works by living American artists, including painters Edward Hopper, Willem de Kooning, Ellsworth Kelly and Robert Motherwell, as well as sculptors Alexander Calder, Louise Nevelson and Isamu Noguchi. Her holdings outgrew two homes, moving to this, its third, in 1966. The stark granite structure by Marcel Breuer and Hamilton Smith is cantilevered over a sunken sculpture garden.

Permanent Collection – Now comprising 18,000 works, the Whitney's holdings are displayed in rotating exhibits on the fifth floor. Count on finding masterworks from the first half of the 20C (Marsden Hartley, Georgia O'Keeffe) along with postwar and contemporary artists (Jackson Pollock, Kiki Smith, Andy Warhol).

Temporary Exhibits – The museum's frequently changing exhibits explore daring, innovative and often controversial topics. In recent years film, video, installation art and mixed media have become popular forms.

International Center of Photography

[M2] *on the map on the inside front cover. 1133 Sixth Ave. at W. 43rd St. 212-857-0000. www.icp.org. Open year-round Tue–Sun 10am–6pm (Fri until 8pm). Closed Mon & major holidays. $12. B, D, F or V train to 42nd St.*

"Concerned photography" forms the heart of the collection here. The museum was founded in 1974 by Cornell Capa, whose brother Robert took dramatic photos of the fighting during the Spanish Civil War and World War II. Since then the museum's holdings have grown to encompass 100,000 prints, with a special strength in documentary reportage. There is plenty of room for beauty, scandal and whimsy as well. The ICP's vaults also include work by the fashion photographer David Seid-ner, whose portraits beautifully mimic the composition of the Old Masters, and Henri Cartier-Bresson, who took most of his pictures with a tiny Leica. The ICP devotes all of its gallery space to large temporary exhibitions, mounting about 20 per year. Some are drawn from the permanent collection; others come from other museums and partner facilities like the eminent George Eastman House in Rochester, New York.

Rest of the Best: Manhattan Museums

Rubin Museum of Art★★

150 W. 17th St. at Seventh Ave. 212-620-5000. www.rmanyc. org. Open year-round Mon & Thu 11am–5pm, Wed 11am–7pm, Fri 11am–10pm, weekends 11am– 6pm. Closed major holidays. $10. A, C or E trains to 14th St.

Buddhas abound at this stunning Chelsea museum, the first Western institution dedicated solely to the art of Bhutan, Tibet, Nepal and other parts of the Himalayas. The space has cool stone floors and warm, polished-wood accents, along with a corkscrew staircase. Some 900 paintings, sculpture, textiles and ritual objects spanning two millennia form permanent and temporary exhibits; the museum also hosts traveling shows. See the "What Is It?" exhibit on the second floor for an intriguing introduction to Himalayan art.

New Museum
235 Bowery, New York, NY 10002 www.newmuseum.org. 212-219-1222
This museum's name remains literal while it is still young, but only time will tell if it can remain 'new'. New Museum first appeared in the gritty Bowery district in Dec 2007, but has quickly become a local landmark. Emerging from a cluster of small buildings, the elegant white shoe-box architecture was dreamt up by Tokyo-based architects to be a new home in NYC for contemporary art and an 'incubator' for new ideas.

Asia Society and Museum★

725 Park Ave. at E. 70th St. 212-288-6400. www.asiasociety. org. Open year-round Tue–Sun 11am–6pm (Fri until 9pm Labor Day–July 4). Closed major holidays. $10. 6 train to 68th St/Hunter College.

Founded in 1956 by John D. Rockefeller III, New York's premier Asian cultural center radiates Eastern calm, with a sinuous white-steel staircase, curved shoji screens, and

Rubin Museum of Art

©2004 Peter Aaron/Esto/NYC&Co.

bamboo-floored galleries filled with ancient Hindu and Buddhist sculpture.

Chelsea Art Museum★

556 W. 22nd St. at Eleventh Ave. 212-255-0719. www.chelseaart museum.org. Open year-round Tue–Sat 11am–6pm (Thu until 8pm). $8. C or E train to 23rd St.

An exhibition of modern paintings from master painters of the Shanghai painting academy, and a group show exploring the concept of the bogeyman are just two of the recent shows mounted here on the western fringe of Chelsea's gallery district. The museum is also home of the Miotte Foundation, which is dedicated to archiving and conserving the work of French painter Jean Miotte (b.1926), an early proponent of Art Informel.

The Forbes Galleries★

62 Fifth Ave. at W. 12th St. 212-206-5548. www.forbes galleries.com. Open year-round Tue, Wed, Fri, and Sat 10am–4pm. Closed major holidays. 1, 4,5 or 9 train to 14th St.

This little museum was known for owning the largest collection of Fabergé Easter eggs in the world until February 2004, when the Forbes family sold them to a Russian oil magnate for more than $100 million. Many interesting objects remain, however, including 12,000 toy soldiers; more than 500 miniature boats; Abraham Lincoln's opera glasses; and the bill for Paul Revere's ride.

Museum of Arts & Design★

[M3] on the map on the inside front cover. 2 Columbus Circle. 212-956-3535. www.madmuseum. org. Open year-round daily 10am–6pm (Thu until 8pm). Closed major holidays. $9 (pay what you wish Thu 6pm–8pm). E or V train to 5th Ave.-53rd St.

Since its founding in 1956 as the American Craft Museum, this organization has showcased traditional and contemporary design. The museum celebrated its 2008 move to Columbus Circle with an exhibition drawn from its collection of works in metal, glass, wood, metal, ceramic and mixed media.

National Academy Museum★

1083 Fifth Ave. at E. 89th St. 212-369-4880. www.nationalacademy. org. Open year-round Wed & Thu noon–5pm, Fri–Sun 11am–6pm. Closed major holidays. $10. 4, 5 or 6 train to 86th St.

Though it may look rather modest from the outside, this 1902 town house contains 10,000 square feet of exhibit space. Here the museum displays rotating selections from its impressive, 5,000-piece collection of American art, which includes work by former National Academy of Art members Winslow Homer, John Singer Sargent and Jasper Johns.

Neue Galerie★

1048 Fifth Ave. at E. 86th St. 212-628-6200. www.neuegalerie. org. Open year-round Thu–Mon 11am–6pm (Fri until 9pm). Closed Tue–Thu & major holidays. $15. 4, 5 or 6 train to 86th St.

MUST SEE

Cafe Sabarsky

1048 Fifth Ave., lobby of Neue Galerie. Open Mon & Wed 9am–6pm; Thu–Sun 9am–9pm. 212-288-0665. Linzertorte, anyone? Named after Galerie cofounder Serge Sabarsky, this popular cafe is a culinary destination even when the galleries are closed, offering excellent tortes and strudels, smooth Viennese coffee, and Austro-Viennese staples like goulash and herring sandwiches. The setting was designed to re-create the heady atmosphere of early-20C Viennese coffeehouses, and it succeeds, especially when the piano player is in the house (*Wed–Thu 2pm–5pm, Fri 6pm–9pm*).

David Schlegel/Neue Galerie

Neue Galerie

This Museum Mile newcomer was founded by cosmetics mogul Ronald Lauder in 2001 to display early-20C Austrian and German art. Mrs. Cornelius Vanderbilt III's Beaux-Arts mansion provides a sumptuous backdrop for paintings by Gustav Klimt, Wassily Kandinsky and Paul Klee, as well as decorative arts by Bauhaus heavyweights Mies van der Rohe and Marcel Breuer.

Studio Museum in Harlem★

144 W. 125th St., between Seventh & Lenox Aves. 212-864-4500. www.studiomuseum.org. Open year-round Sun & Wed–Fri noon–6pm, Sat 10am–6pm. Closed Mon, Tue & major holidays. $7. 2 or 3 train to 125th St.

Established in 1968 to provide studio space for African-American artists, this museum has since grown into a major visual art and performance center. In addition to temporary shows, a rotating selection from the 1,600-piece collection is always on view.

Museum of Sex

233 Fifth Ave. at 27th St. 212-689-6337. www.museumof sex.com. Open year-round daily 11am–6:30pm (Sat until 8pm). Closed Thanksgiving Day & Dec 25. $14.50. 6 train to 28th St.

Birds do it, bees do it. So why not have a museum about it? Past exhibits have traced the evolution of pornographic movies, and the origins of the pin-up girl from Victorian times. Many items on display are plucked from the permanent collection, including erotic films, books, posters and toys.

Sports Museum of America

26 Broadway. 212-747-0900. www.sportsmuseum.com. Open daily year-round 9am–7pm. $24. 4 or 5 train to Bowling Green.

Put yourself in the skates of a pro hockey goalie or the cleats of an NFL referee via the interactive exhibits at this high-tech downtown newcomer. The collection includes some 600 sports artifacts, including the original Heisman trophy.

MUSEUMS

HISTORIC SITES

New York tends to look toward the future, not the past. But history is key to understanding this booming metropolis. The following sites offer glimpses of the Big Apple when it was just a tiny fruit.

City Hall★★

In City Hall Park, bounded by Broadway, Park Row, Lafayette & Chambers Sts. Visit by guided tour only (see sidebar). R or W train to City Hall.

New York's second official city hall, inaugurated in 1812, was designed by Joseph F. Mangin and John McComb Jr., who shared a prize of $350 for their efforts. Atop the graceful cupola is *Justice* with her scales; out front stands a statue of patriot Nathan Hale, who famously said, "I only regret that I have but one life to lose for my country" before being hanged by the British in

1776. Abraham Lincoln's body lay in state here in April 1865; 120,000 New Yorkers paid their respects. City Hall was half brownstone, not by design but by political penny-pinching, until 1956. Today it hosts welcoming ceremonies for visiting dignitaries and is the end point of ticker-tape parades.

Interior Highlights – The gallery is ringed by Corinthian columns, which support a coffered dome pierced by a small circular window. The Governor's Room holds a desk used by George Washington.

City Hall Park★★ – The publicly accessible corner of the park, cupped by Park Row and Broadway, sports benches, a spiffy fountain, and gas lamps.

Visiting City Hall

City Hall is only open to the public by the free, one-hour guided tours held Wednesday at noon, departing from Heritage Tourism Center at the south end of City Hall Park (Broadway at Barclay).

South Street Seaport★★

Bounded by Water and John Sts., the East River and Peck Slip. 212-748-8600. www.southstreet seaportmuseum.org. Free to wander; $10 to visit ships and museum (see sidebar). 2, 3, 4 5, J, M or Z train to Fulton St.

This waterfront historic district and shopping hub ranks as New York's third largest tourist attraction. Indeed, for some it might be too touristy – on warm days its pleasant cobblestone streets and wide-plank wharves are packed with sightseers, peddlers, and street performers.

But that's only half the picture. Spread throughout the district are half a dozen first-rate historical

sites maintained by the **South Street Seaport Museum**★★, including maritime art galleries, a fleet of 19C vessels, and an old-fashioned print shop. During the summer, open-air concerts draw throngs of visitors to the piers.

Schermerhorn Row Galleries★★ – *12 Fulton St. between Front & South Sts.* Built between 1811 and 1813 as countinghouses and warehouses, these handsome brick structures now hold the South Street Seaport Museum's formidable collection of maritime arts and artifacts, including paintings, delicate scrimshaw (whalebone carvings), and ivory, lacquer and silk souvenirs from the China trade.

Pier 17 Pavilion★ – You'll find more than 100 shops and restaurants inside this three-story glass and steel structure, which offers excellent views.

Street of Ships★ – The seaport boasts the largest fleet of historic vessels in the nation; several are in use for maintenance and hauling; others are permanently moored; you can board and explore the *Peking* and the *Ambrose* moored along Piers 15 and 16.

Bowne & Co. Stationers – *211 Water St. between Fulton & Beekman Sts. Open Wed–Sun 10am–5pm. Museum ticket not required.* At this charming 19C print shop, which

South Street Seaport

©Jeff Greenberg/NYC&Co.

still turns out wedding invitations and book plates, you can help make a Walt Whitman book on a treadle-operated press dating from 1901.

Harbor Cruises – Sail New York Harbor aboard the 1885 schooner *Pioneer*, the only iron-hulled American merchant sailing vessel still afloat. Sponsored by the South Street Seaport Museum, cruises depart from Pier 16 *(May–Sept; 2hrs round-trip; advance reservations recommended; 212-748-8786).*

HISTORIC SITES

75

World Trade Center Site

©iStockphoto.com/Archives

World Trade Center Site★★

Bounded by Church, Liberty, West & Barclay Sts. www.lower manhattan.info and www.renew nyc.com. E train to World Trade Center; N or R train to Cortlandt St.

The world's largest commercial complex stood here from 1970 until the morning of September 11, 2001, when two hijacked planes were flown into the Twin Towers, killing 2,979 people and bringing the 110-story structures – in which 50,000 people had worked – to the ground. It was the deadliest terrorist attack in US history. Rescue and recovery efforts began immediately, but there were few survivors of what *New Yorker* writer Hendrik Hertzberg called "the catastrophe that turned the foot of Manhattan into the mouth of hell." Eight buildings in all were destroyed. Workers carted off 1.5 million tons of steel and debris until the site was clear in May 2002, well ahead of schedule.

Rebuilding the site has proved far more difficult, thanks to the vast size of the project, the vast sums of money involved, and the number of parties with strong and often conflicting visions of its future.

Master Plan – Ultimately, the site will encompass an assortment of office buildings, memorials, parks and cultural venues, arranged according to a master plan created by Polish-born architect Daniel Libeskind and a revised design

Visiting the Site

Shortly after the debris was cleared in 2002, city officials opened a viewing platform on Church Street so that visitors could pay respects to the dead and watch the progress of rebuilding. The platform is now gone, but photo panels and a list of victims' names are on view near the top of the steps of the PATH station. The Tribute WTC Visitor Center at 120 Liberty Street *(open Mon, Wed–Sat 10am–6pm, Tue noon–6pm, Sun noon–5pm; 212-393-9160; www.tributewtc.org)* has visitor information and gallery displays *($10 donation)* and sponsors walking tours of the site. The Winter Garden provides a view of the World Trade Center site and an exhibit charting the future of downtown Manhattan.

Promenade★★

From Castle Clinton to the **Staten Island Ferry** Terminal, this walkway offers magnificent views of the bay, including the Statue of Liberty, Ellis Island and Governors Island.

released by the Lower Manhattan Development Corporation. The centerpiece of the design is a 1,776 ft high-rise dubbed the Freedom Tower, surrounded by a cluster of shorter, angular glass office buildings. The two "footprints" of the original World Trade Center towers will be preserved as reflecting pools.

African Burial Ground National Monument★

Visitor center at 290 Broadway. 212-637-2019. www.nps.gov/ afbg. Open Mon–Fri 9am–5pm (memorial open daily 9am–5pm). Closed major holidays. 4, 5 or 6 train to Brooklyn Bridge/City Hall.

Archaeologists happened upon this forgotten 18C site, called the "Negroes Burying Ground" on period maps, in 1991 during excavations for a new federal building. The remains of an estimated 20,000 people were interred here, a testament to the slave trade in colonial New York. Tours of the site and its memorial depart from the visitor center *(reservations recommended).*

Castle Clinton National Monument★

Battery Park. 212-344-7220. www.nps.gov/cacl. Open year-round daily 8:30am–5pm. Closed Dec 25. 4 or 5 train to Bowling Green; 1 train to South Ferry.

This old fort has had nine lives. Well, at least five. It was completed in 1811 on an artificial harbor island created to protect Manhattan from possible attack during the War of 1812. That attack never happened, so in 1823 the fort was deeded to New York City and leased out as a restaurant and concert hall called Castle Garden. French general Lafayette was feted here in 1824, and in 1850 "Swedish nightingale" Jenny Lind made her American debut on its stage, courtesy of circus ringleader P.T. Barnum. In 1855 the fort was returned to state hands and was opened as an immigrant landing depot. The harbor between the castle and the shoreline was filled in and turned into a park in 1870. After a 50-year stint as the home of the New York Aquarium (now at Coney Island), Castle Clinton, with its 8 ft thick walls and gun ports, was designated a national monument in 1950. It's now best known as the place where you buy tickets for the Statue of Liberty ferry, though the National Park Service maintains a visitor center here and conducts tours throughout the day.

Castle Cinton National Monument

©Peter Wrenn/MICHELIN

HISTORIC SITES

Stone Street Historic District

Just steps away from Fraunces Tavern, Stone Street is one of the Financial District's most charming thoroughfares. On warm days its cobblestone expanse is festooned with the umbrella tables of restaurants and pubs. On cool and rainy days these spots provide a cozy respite from the concrete jungle.

Try an espresso and a madeleine at the cheerful **Financier** patisserie *(no. 62; 212-344-5600; www.financierpastries.com)*. For pub grub and pints, try **Ulysses' Bar** *(no. 58; 212-482-0400; www.ulyssesbarnyc.com)*, serving lobster every Monday night and "cobblestone brunch" Sundays from 11am to 4pm.

Federal Hall National Memorial★

[K] *on the map on the inside front cover. 26 Wall St. 212-825-6888. www.nps.gov/feha. Open year-round Mon–Fri 9am–5pm. Closed weekends & major holidays. J, Z or 2, 3, 4 or 5 train to Wall St.*

Federal Hall marks the spot of two historic firsts. New York's first city hall was opened here in 1702. Then in 1789, Federal Hall hosted the swearing-in of George Washington as the nation's first president. Alas, that structure was demolished in 1812 and sold as salvage for $425, but its 1842 replacement is sufficiently grand (and Greek) to recall the democratic ideals of the Founding Fathers. A towering bronze likeness of Washington stands outside on a platform if you need reminding. The recently remodeled interior is distinguished by its splendid central rotunda rimmed with balconies. You'll find a city visitor center in the main lobby.

Fraunces Tavern

54 Pearl St. 212-425-1778. www.frauncestavernmuseum.org. Open year-round Mon–Sat noon–5pm. $4. Closed major holidays. N or R train to Whitehall St.

With its slate roof and cream-colored portico, this handsome brick house gives visitors a sense of New York City as it might have appeared during the American Revolution. In 1719, Etienne de Lancey, who later gave his family name to Delancey Street, built a home here. Samuel Fraunces bought it in 1762 and turned it into a tavern. For ten days in 1783, Fraunces Tavern served as George Washington's last residence as general of the Patriot army, and on Dec 4 of that year, in the tavern's Long Room, he bade farewell to his troops before returning to his Mount Vernon estate. The building

Fraunces Tavern
©Jeff Greenberg/NYC&Co.

you see is only partly original; much of it was reconstructed in the early 20C. Today the ground floor is used as a bar/restaurant, and the upper floors display early-American decorative arts in period rooms. Don't miss the collection of 45 paintings by John Ward Dunsmore depicting scenes from the Revolutionary War.

General Grant National Memorial

© Jeff Greenberg/NYC&Co.

General Grant National Memorial★

Riverside Dr. at W. 122nd St. 212-666-1640. www.nps.gov/gegr. Open year-round daily 9am–5pm. Closed Jan 1, Thanksgiving Day & Dec 25. 1 train to 116th St.

Who's buried in Grant's tomb? The question that stumped 1950s game-show contestants continues to perplex visitors to his final resting place, a towering Neoclassical monument on a quiet bluff overlooking the Hudson River. A West Point graduate, Ulysses S. Grant (1822–85) made his name as Commander of the Union Army during the Civil War, then served two terms in the White House. "Let us have peace," he wrote to the Republican Party in 1868 when he decided to run for president

under its auspices. These words are now engraved above the portico of this white-granite mausoleum, which contains the remains of Grant and his wife, Julia, as well as a small museum. But who's actually *buried* in Grant's tomb? No one – he and Julia lie in an above-ground crypt. Introductory talks *(on the hour)* help explain the history of the memorial and provide access to the crypt.

Gracie Mansion★

East End Ave. at 89th St. 212-639-9675. www.nyc.gov. Visit by one-hour guided tour only Wed 10am, 11am, 1pm & 2pm (reservations required). $7.

This Federal-style country manor (1799), today the official residence of the city's mayor, hosted dignitaries including Alexander Hamilton and John Quincy Adams. The current restoration features fine Federal- and Empire-style furnishings.

Morris-Jumel Mansion★

W. 160th St. & Edgecombe Ave. 212-923-8008. www.morrisjumel. org. Open year-round Wed–Sun 10am–4pm. Closed Mon, Tue & major holidays. $4. C train to 163rd St.

This Palladian-style hilltop mansion has stories to tell. Built for British colonel Roger Morris in 1765 as a summer retreat, the house today is Manhattan's oldest residence, containing a wealth of fine antiques and architectural details. Morris abandoned the house in 1775 because his Loyalist sentiments were no longer appreciated in the colonies. George Washington com-

HISTORIC SITES

79

Morris-Jumel Mansion

Morris-Jumel Mansion

A born-and-bred New Yorker, Theodore Roosevelt (1858–1919) was not your average city kid. As a sickly child, he was encouraged to exercise. The advice stuck, and the outdoors would become Roosevelt's lifelong passion. After going to college at Harvard, he worked as a rancher in the Dakota Territory, served as a colonel in the Rough Riders, hunted, collected specimens, and authored some 30 books. This in addition to being the 26th president of the United States (1901–09) and the winner of the Nobel Peace Prize in 1906. Roosevelt lived at this site from birth until the age of 14. Although the original home structure was demolished in 1916, this Victorian brownstone was constructed in its image; its five period rooms are decorated with original furnishings to appear as they did after his death.

mandeered the mansion during the Battle of Harlem Heights. taking advantage of its strategic views of the surrounding terrain. For a time the building served as an inn, and in 1810 it was acquired by French wine merchant Stephen Jumel, who preferred Napoleonic social circles to New York Society (the bed in the house was a gift from French Emperor Napoleon, who was a friend of the Jumels).

Theodore Roosevelt Birthplace National Historic Site★

28 E. 20th St. 212-260-1616. www.nps.gov/thrb. Open year-round Tue–Sat 9am–5pm. Period rooms may be visited by guided tour (40min) only; tours are held on the hour 10am–4pm, except noon. First-floor galleries may be viewed anytime. $3. Closed major holidays. 6 train to 23rd St.

Tweed Courthouse★

52 Chambers St. 212-639-9675. www.nyc.gov. Visit by 40min guided tour only, year-round Fri 2pm (reservations required).

A whopping $13 million was appropriated for construction of this courthouse between 1862 and 1870, and still the building wasn't finished *(for an idea of*

Gramercy Park Bites

Teddy Roosevelt's old neighborhood, Gramercy Park, is now well known for its gourmet vittles. For lunch or an afternoon snack, try **71 Irving Place Coffee and Tea Bar** *(71 Irving Pl. between E. 18th & 19th Sts.; 212-995-5252)*, a friendly, garden-level cafe that serves up homemade quiche, waffles, sandwiches and soups, as well as some of the city's best coffee. Or whisk away to India via the tea room at **Tamarind** *(41–43 E. 22nd St.; 212-674-7400)* where you can sample exotic teas, pastries and sandwiches and other light Indian fare.

MUST SEE

where the money went, see "Boss" Tweed, opposite). Restored in 2001, the Anglo-Italianate edifice boasts one of the city's finest 19C interiors, including a stunning 3-story octagonal rotunda.

Villard Houses (New York Palace Hotel)★

[J] *on the map on the inside front cover. 451–457 Madison Ave. at E. 50th St. E or V train to Fifth Ave./53rd St.*

In 1881 Henry Villard, a Bavarian immigrant who founded the *New York Evening Post* and the Northern Pacific Railroad, hired the esteemed architectural firm McKim, Mead and White to design a group of six town houses – one for himself and the other five for

sale. Inspired by a 15C Italian palazzo, the architects set six four-story structures around a U-shaped courtyard. Villard moved in with his family in 1883 but declared bankruptcy shortly afterward and had to sell the complex. It passed from private hands to the New York Archdiocese (St. Patrick's Cathedral is directly across the street) and then, in the 1970s, to Harry Helmsley, a developer who wanted to tear down the houses to build a hotel. The Landmarks Preservation Commission stopped him, so he built a 55-story skyscraper directly on top of the houses instead. The good news is that, as long as you don't look up, the houses appear much as they did when they were built, and some of the sumptuous interiors are preserved.

Villard Houses

New York Palace Hotel

HISTORIC SITES

Urban Center Books

457 Madison Ave. 212-935-3595.
www.urbancenterbooks.org.
This friendly little bookstore on the first floor of the Villard Houses has 9,000 titles on architecture, urbanism and design. The shop was founded by the nonprofit Municipal Art Society in 1980 in an effort to foster a more informed discussion of architecture and the design arts in New York City – a goal no doubt informed by the decision to balance a skyscraper on the Villard Houses' heads.

Interior – To get a sense of the grandeur of the original homes, enter the courtyard fronting Madison Avenue and step inside the central mansion, now the lobby of the posh New York Palace Hotel.

Urban Center – The Municipal Art Society, a feisty local preservation group since 1893, shares the north wing of the Villard Houses with several other nonprofit organizations. Here you'll find the Urban Center Bookstore *(left)* as well as free public galleries *(open Mon–Wed & Fri–Sat 10am–6pm, Sun 11am–5pm)* with rotating exhibits on architecture and design. You might also want to drop in to pick up a schedule of the Society's walking tours, which are widely considered among the most in-depth and engaging in the city.

Meatpacking District

Bounded by West 15th, Hudson and Gansevoort Sts. and the Hudson River.

In the 1850s New York was the nation's largest center of beef production with slaughterhouses, meatpacking plants and storage facilities lining its east and west sides. Meat processing operations shifted largely to the Midwest around the turn of the century, a move welcomed by New Yorkers, especially after Upton Sinclair's *The Jungle* (1906) illuminated the industry's dangerous and un-sanitary conditions. Though a few meat companies remain in busi-ness here, the area has blossomed today into an uber-hip shopping, dining and clubbing destination.

New York Stock Exchange

[L] *on the map on the inside front cover. 8–18 Broad St. at Wall St. www.nyse.com. 2, 3, 4 or 5 train to Wall St. Closed to visitors since Sept. 11, 2001.*

The New York Stock Exchange occupies a stunning eight-story Greek Revival building, home to the "Big Board" of 3,200 publicly traded companies with a global market value of $25 trillion. Its beginnings however, were a bit more humble: the exchange was formally established on May 17,

---

Trading Places

- On an average day, 1.46 billion shares, valued at $67 billion, are traded on the NYSE.
- NYSE is the world's largest stock exchange.
- The trading area of the NYSE is two-thirds the size of a football field.
- NYSE can process 4,000 orders, quotes and cancels per second.

1792, when 24 brokers met under a buttonwood (sycamore) tree outside the entrance at 20 Wall Street. Today, the classical facade hides one of the most technically sophisticated financial operations on the globe.

HISTORIC CHURCHES

Cathedral of St. John the Divine★★

Amsterdam Ave at W. 112th St. 212-316-7540. www.stjohndivine. org. Open Mon–Sat 7am–6pm, Sun 7am–7pm. 1 train to 110th St./ Cathedral Pkwy.

This massive stone edifice, the seat of the Episcopal Diocese of New York, is reputedly the largest Gothic cathedral in the world. Its construction, begun in 1892, was never completed. The design includes a **Great Rose Window** (with 10,000 pieces of glass) overlooking the 601-foot-long nave.

Saint Patrick's Cathedral★★

[N] *on the map on the inside front cover. Fifth Ave. between 50th & 51st Sts. 212-753-2261. www.saintpatrickscathedral.org. Open daily 6:30am–8:45pm. B, D, F or V train to 47th–50th Sts.*

Midtown skyscrapers dominate Saint Patrick's, the largest Roman Catholic church in the US. When construction began in 1853, the James Renwick-designed cathedral was considered "out in the country," but by the time it was completed in 1879 the neighborhood was a fashionable residential quarter. The centerpiece of the interior is a 57-foot-high bronze canopy, or baldachin.

©William Perry/Dreamstime.com

St. Patrick's Cathedral

St. Paul's Chapel★★

Broadway between Fulton & Vesey Sts. 212-233-4164. www.trinitywallstreet.org. Open Mon–Fri 10am–6pm, Sat 8am–3pm, Sun 7am–4pm. A or C train to Broadway-Nassau St.

Directly across the street from the World Trade Center site stands this picturesque chapel (1766), the oldest public building in continuous use in Manhattan. George Washington worshiped here regularly after his inauguration; today the chapel contains memorabilia from September 11, 2001.

Trinity Church★★

74 Trinity Pl., at Broadway & Wall St. 212-602-0800. www.trinitywall street.org. Open daily 7am–6pm Sat 8am–4pm, Sun 7am–4pm. Guided tours daily 2pm. 2, 3, 4 or 5 train to Wall Street.

This lovely Episcopal church, with its 280 ft spire, was the tallest building in New York when it was completed in 1846. The green, shady churchyard is dotted with old tombstones; the most famous marks the grave of former Treasury secretary Alexander Hamilton.

HISTORIC SITES

PARKS

Far from being a concrete jungle, New York City has plenty of green space – if you know where to look. From the tiny vest-pocket parks sprinkled throughout the Village to the 843-acre Central Park, they come in all shapes and sizes. Some offer bike rentals, hot dog vendors and paddleboats; others just provide a quiet place to read a book. Take your pick: there are 1,700 to choose from. Here are some of the best.

Central Park★★★

Bounded by 59th & 125th Sts. and Central Park West & Fifth Ave. www.centralparknyc.org.
N, R or W train to Fifth Ave.-59th St. A, B, C, D or 1 train to 59th St./ Columbus Circle.

Manhattan's playground is justifiably one of the most famous urban parks in the world and a great day out for **kids**. Not only is it massive – 2.5 miles long and half a mile across – but it is rich and varied, offering a multitude of views; tons of recreational activities; and plenty of room to stroll, skate, cycle or just explore. Amazingly, it is totally man-made. In 1844 newspaper editor William Cullen Bryant urged the city government to acquire a "wasteland, ugly and repulsive" north of 42nd Street (the city's northern border

at the time) for use as a park. The city complied, buying what was then a swamp inhabited by squatters who raised pigs and goats. Calvert Vaux and Frederick Law Olmsted's naturalistic design was selected, and in 1858 clearing began. Some 3,000 mostly Irish workers and 400 horses moved an estimated billion cubic feet of earth over a period of 19 years to make the blueprint green. In the northern part, rocky crags and dense thickets of trees were made to resemble the landscape of the Adirondack Mountains; in the south are more pastoral sections of rolling meadows, winding paths and delicate bridges.

Today stately rows of skyscrapers and apartment buildings encircle the park, but Olmsted's vision remains stunningly intact.

Central Park

©Jeff Greenberg/NYC&Co.

Tavern On The Green

West side of the park at 67th St. 212-873-3200. www.tavernonthegreen.com.
The famed tavern is a perfect Sunday brunch spot, with stained-glass windows and glittering crystal chandeliers. Weather permitting, head for the outdoor cafe and bar, which is a dazzling sea of white lights and glowing lanterns at night.

Best of Central Park

For the **Carousel, Central Park Wildlife Center** *and* **Swedish Cottage Marionette Theatre**, *see Musts for Kids.*

Belvedere Castle – *At 79th St.* Calvert Vaux built this fanciful structure in 1872. It is home to a charming nature observatory, which has hands-on exhibits about the city's flora and fauna.

Bethesda Terrace – *At 72nd St.* This lovely sandstone plaza resembles a Spanish courtyard with its arcaded bridge, sweeping stairs and central fountain. It adjoins the Mall, a wide allée lined with handsome elms and sculptures depicting famous writers.

Lake – *Between 71st & 78th Sts.* For a bit of old-fashioned fun, row a boat or hire a gondola to take you across this 22-acre expanse of water, or simply enjoy the view from the Loeb Boathouse, an acclaimed restaurant and cafe on the east side of the park between 74th and 75th streets.

Shakespeare Garden – The rustic four-acre garden on the rocky hillside between Belvedere Castle and the Swedish Cottage is scattered with plaques bearing quotations from the Bard.

Strawberry Fields – *West side at 72nd St.* Artist Yoko Ono contributed to the restoration of this 2.5-acre, teardrop-shaped garden honoring her husband, the late Beatle John Lennon, who was murdered nearby in 1980.

Bryant Park★★

W. 42nd St. at Sixth Ave. www.bryantpark.org. B, D, F or V train to 42nd St.- Bryant Park; 7 train to 5th Ave.

With its delicate green folding chairs, pebble walkways and London plane trees, this gracious formal park behind the New York Public Library is Midtown's only large green space. Designated public land since the late 17C, in 1853 and 1854 the site hosted New York's first world's fair. Thirty years later it was named for the poet and activist William Cullen Bryant. If you happen to notice

Activities, Events and Information

Central Park's main visitor center is located in the Dairy, a whimsical 1871 structure just west of the Children's Zoo at 65th Street. Here you'll find maps, guides, history books and souvenirs, as well as information about the day's special events and activities *(call 212-794-6564 for seasonal hours)*. The Central Park Conservancy's website *(212-310-6600; www.centralparknyc.org)* is also an excellent resource. In-line and ice skates *(in season)* may be rented at the Wollman Rink *(212-439-6900)*; rent boats and bicycles at Loeb Boathouse *(212-517-2233)*.

PARKS

Bryant Park

©Andrew F Kazmierski/iStockphoto.com

more than the usual number of laptop users here, it's because the whole park was outfitted with free wireless Internet in 2002. Other perks include **free outdoor movies** on Monday nights in summer, and concerts (*check the website for the schedule*).

Battery Park★

Bordered by Battery Pl. & State St. 4 or 5 train to Bowling Green; 1 train to South Ferry.

On the southwestern tip of Manhattan, the maze of stone and steel monoliths dominating the Financial District suddenly gives way to a 21-acre expanse of greenery whose twisting paths are lined with vendors, street performers and artists selling their wares. Running along the harbor, the park's **promenade★★** offers stellar views of the Statue of Liberty.

Things To See In Battery Park
Statue of Liberty★★★ – Ferries to the world-famous monument and to the **Ellis Island Immigration Museum★★** leave from Battery Park. *See Landmarks and Museums.*

Castle Clinton National Monument★ – Formerly West Battery, this round fort stood offshore until 1870, when the land in between it and the Financial District was filled in. It contains the Statue of Liberty ticket office as well as a National Park Service visitor center. *See Historic Sites.*

Sphere★★ – Near the north entrance of the park, at the intersection of Battery Place and State Street, is one of the most moving artifacts of September 11, 2001 – a 15-foot-diameter, 22-ton brass ball by Fritz Koenig that once glittered in the World Trade Center's vast plaza. Salvaged from the rubble, the sphere now resembles a battered suit of armor. It stands beside an eternal flame.

Sphere in Battery Park

Brigitta L. House/Michelin

Washington Arch★

Designed by Stanford White in 1891, this white marble Village landmark was built to memorialize George Washington's inauguration as the first US president.

The arch measures 30ft across and 77ft high; gracing the sides are sculptures of Washington, one a soldier, the other a civilian.

©iStockphoto.com/Blaney Photo

Union Square★

Bounded by E. 14th & E. 17th Sts. and Park Ave. & University Pl. 4, 5, 6, L, N, R, Q or W train to 14th St./Union Square.

Walks and benches beneath a thick canopy of trees make the park a pleasant place to stroll or rest. At the tiered plaza at the southern end, street performers strut their stuff and political activists stage vigils and protests, a tradition that goes back to the early 20C, when several radical organizations had offices in the area. Andy Warhol established his pop-cultural "Factory" in the ornate Decker Building (1893) at 33 Union Square West in the early 1960s; it has since been converted into condos and a wine store.

Washington Square★

At the south end of Fifth Ave., at the intersection with Waverly Pl. Any train to W. 4th St.-Washington Square Park.

This lively square at the heart of Greenwich Village teems with students, skateboarders, dog-walkers, chess players and other locals at all hours of the day and night. Originally a marshland and a favorite hunting ground of the early colonists, the site became a potter's field in the 18C (about 1,000 skeletons were unearthed during renovations in the 1960s). Following its transformation into a park in 1826, it spurred the growth of a fashionable residential enclave of redbrick town houses, including the well-preserved row on Washington Square North.

Henry James's novel, *Washington Square*, written in 1881, was set in a house that once stood at no. 18.

Union Square Greenmarket★

E. 17th to E. 14th Sts., between Park Ave. & University Pl. www.cenyc.org. To accommodate park construction, the market will relocate to the south end of the park until Fall 2009. From 8am to 6pm on Monday, Wednesday, Friday and Saturday, Upstate New York's farm bounty comes to this bustling market – a favorite of chefs citywide. Arrive early for the best selection of tubers and herbs, fresh poultry and eggs, fresh flower arrangements, and wonderful pastries and breads.

PARKS

WALKING TOURS

Time to lace up your boots and hit the streets. Whether you join an organized tour or go at your own pace, you'll find that New York's architecture, views and street life richly reward explorations on foot.

LOWER EAST SIDE

Map p. 29. Despite being one of New York's hippest 'hoods, the Lower East Side has, for the most part, a refreshing lack of attitude and an astounding amount of local pride. "Come one, come all" has been its message to visitors since the 1880s, when it became the quintessential American melting pot. Though today's immigrants tend to be young artists, musicians, designers and restaurateurs, history lives on in the district's one-of-a-kind tenement museum and many famous ethnic eateries.

Walking Tours

The Lower East Side Business Improvement District, which runs the Visitor Center *(261 Broome St.; www.lowereastsideny.com)*, sponsors a walking tour at 11am every Sunday *(Apr–Dec)*; meet at Katz's Deli *(Houston & Ludlow Sts.)*.
A **podcast walking tour**, available for download *(free)* from the website, directs you on a route starting from the Eldridge Street Synagogue and ending at the Essex Street Market, with vivid descriptions of the neighborhood's historical and cultural icons; stops include Canal Street, **Katz's Deli**, Russ & Daughters, and **Guss' Lower East Side Pickles**. The tenement museum and citywide walking tour companies, such as **Rent a New Yorker** *($10; 212-982-9445; www.rentanewyorker. com)* and **Big Onion Walking**

Tours *($15; 212-439-1090; www. bigonion.com)* conduct tours of this rich neighborhood as well.

Art tours

Every Last Sunday on the Lower East Side (or ELS on the LES), neighborhood artists open their studios and galleries to the public *(1pm–5pm)*. A free guided tour starts from the Lower East Side Visitor Information Center at 1pm. To visit galleries on your own, pick up an "art loop" map at the visitor center. For more information, go to www.lowereastsideny.com.

CENTRAL PARK

Manhattan's beloved backyard, this 843-acre haven of greenery, light and air draws more than 25 million people each year. Situated in the island's geographical center, Central Park measures 2.5mi long by .5mi wide, extending from 59th to 110th Streets, and Fifth Avenue to Central Park West. Framed by the silhouettes of surrounding buildings, the man-made park offers a quiet oasis in the heart of bustling Manhattan, and many opportunities for recreation.

Walking Tour

▶   *Enter Central Park South at Fifth Ave. & E. 60th St. from Grand Army Plaza. Walk north to the Wildlife Center.*

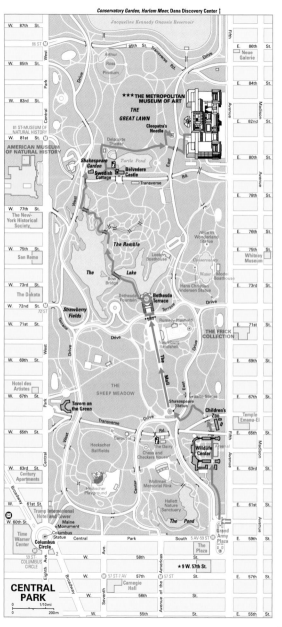

Conservatory Garden, Harlem Meer, Dana Discovery Center

Jacqueline Kennedy Onassis Reservoir

W. 87th St.

86 ST

W. 85th St.

85th St. Transverse Rd.

Fifth

E. 86th St.
Neue Galerie

West

Drive

West Drive

Park

W. 83rd St.

Central

81 ST-MUSEUM OF NATURAL HISTORY

W. 81st St.

Arthur Ross Pinetum

★★★ THE METROPOLITAN MUSEUM OF ART

THE GREAT LAWN

E. 84th St.

Madison

E. 82nd St.

Cleopatra's Needle

AMERICAN MUSEUM OF NATURAL HISTORY

Delacorte Theater

Shakespeare Garden
Swedish Cottage
Belvedere Castle

Turtle Pond

Transverse

East

E. 80th St.

Avenue

W. 77th St.

The New-York Historical Society

West

Drive

East Rd.

E. 78th St.

W. 75th St.
San Remo

W. 73rd St.
The Dakota

W. 72nd St.

72 ST

W. 71st St.

The Ramble

The   *Lake*

Bow Bridge

Loeb Boathouse

Bethesda Fountain

Bethesda Terrace

Alice in Wonderland Statue

Conservatory
Water
Model Boathouse

Hans Christian Andersen Statue

E. 76th St.

E. 75th St.
Whitney Museum

E. 73rd St.

Terrace

Strawberry Fields

Drive

Rumsey Playfield

Naumburg Bandshell

Drive

THE FRICK COLLECTION

E. 71st St.

West

Drive

The Mall

East

E. 69th St.

W. 69th St.

Hotel des Artistes

W. 67th St.

THE SHEEP MEADOW

Balto Statue

Shakespeare Statue

E. 67th St.

Temple Emanu-El

Park

Tavern on the Green

Transverse   Drive

Children's Zoo

Fifth

E. 65th St.

W. 65th St.

Heckscher Ballfields

Carousel   Rd.

The Dairy
Chess and Checkers House

Wildlife Center

Arsenal

Madison

Avenue

Central

W. 63rd St.
Century Apartments

Broadway

W. 61st St.

Trump International Hotel and Tower

W. 60th St.

Time Warner Center

Columbus Circle

59 ST COLUMBUS CIRCLE

Heckscher Playground

Wollman Memorial Rink

Hallett Nature Sanctuary

E. 63rd St.

Maine Monument

Columbus Statue

Central

W.

58th

Eighth Ave.

Park

South

The Pond

Grand Army Plaza

5 AV-59 ST

The Plaza

E. 61st St.

Avenue

E. 59th St.

St.

Americas

W. 57 ST-7 AV

CENTRAL PARK

0   1/10 mi

0   200 m

Broadway

Seventh

Carnegie Hall

56th

Avenue of the

W. 57 ST

★ 9 W. 57th St.

St.

E. 57th St.

St.

W.   55th   St.   E.   55th   St.

WALKING TOURS

89

Just before the Wildlife Center, look west to see Wollman Memorial Rink, a popular spot for ice-skating in winter. To the south a crescent-shaped **pond**, surrounded by luxuriant vegetation, borders the Hallett Nature Sanctuary on a rocky outcrop.

▶ *Enter the Wildlife Center.*

Central Park Wildlife Center

East side between 63rd & 66th Sts. Map available at entrance. Open Apr–Oct Mon–Fri 10am–5pm, weekends & holidays 10am–5:30pm. Rest of the year daily 10am–4:30pm. $8 (includes admission to children's zoo). 212-439-6500. www.wcs.org.

This 5.5-acre zoo houses more than 450 animals in a habitat that represents three climatic regions: the tropical zone, the temperate regions and the polar circle. Kids can feed the domesticated animals in the Children's Zoo *(feed available for purchase)*. Notice the Delacorte Clock over the entrance arch, with its moving bronze animal figures.

▶ *Exit the children's zoo at the north end and walk under 65th St. Bear left at the fork, then left again to take the wide*

steps to cross East Dr. Enter the southern end of the Mall at the statue of Shakespeare.

The Mall

This straight, wide path is lined with elms and sculptures of famous writers. At the north end, the Naumburg Bandshell is still used for performances. Summer evening events are staged at SummerStage at the Rumsey Playfield, east of the band shell. Lying west of the Mall, the Sheep Meadow attracts throngs of people to its green lawn, which also offers superb views of the city skyline.

To the far west of the Sheep Meadow stands the famed restaurant Tavern on the Green, housed in a former sheep barn (1870).

▶ *From the Mall, take the steps down to Bethesda Terrace.*

Bethesda Terrace

Considered the centerpiece of the park, this lovely sandstone plaza resembles a Spanish courtyard with its sweeping stairs and central fountain. Crowning the fountain is a statue by Emma Stebbins titled *Angel of the Waters* (1868).

▶ *From the fountain, take the pathway to the left.*

The Lake

A graceful iron bridge, Bow Bridge has been the subject of many a photograph. To the west lie the **Strawberry Fields** and the International Garden of Peace honoring musician John Lennon, one of the famous Beatles. It lies steps away from the Dakota apartment building, where Lennon lived and was murdered. To the east sits the Loeb

Lake, Central Park

©Jimi King/BigStockPhoto.com

Boathouse, a popular eating spot in summer. Between the lake and Fifth Avenue, Conservatory Water attracts mariners of all ages with model sailboats.

▶ *Enter the Ramble. To reduce your chances of getting lost, stay on paths on the west side of the Ramble, keeping the lake in view as much as possible.*

The Ramble

Interrupted by a meandering brook, this 38-acre wooded hill north of the lake is threaded with tree- and bush-lined paths that wind among large boulders.

▶ *You will cross two bridges before you reach West Dr. Then turn northward on West Dr.*

Swedish Cottage

This log structure, a model of a Swedish schoolhouse, was built in Central Park in 1877. It now serves as home to the **Marionette Theatre**, which presents puppet shows throughout the year *(see Musts for Kids for hours and prices)*. In the **Shakespeare Garden**, adjacent to the cottage, flowers, herbs, trees and shrubs mentioned in the works of the Bard can be seen. Small plaques display quotes from the playwright pertinent to a garden setting.

▶ *Go up the stairs to Belvedere Castle.*

Belvedere Castle

Complete with merlons and crenels, Belvedere Castle was designed by Vaux as an imitation medieval Scottish castle (1872). Its site atop Vista Rock permits views of the northern end of the park. Just north of Belvedere Castle lie Turtle Pond and the Delacorte Theater. Beyond, the **Great Lawn** occupies the site of the Receiving Reservoir, opened in 1842 to supply the city water system. Today it is best known as the setting for performances by the Metropolitan Opera and the New York Philharmonic.

▶ *From Belvedere Castle, walk north around Turtle Pond, then east toward the Metropolitan Museum of Art.*

Just before reaching the museum, note **Cleopatra's Needle**, a 77ft pink-granite obelisk (16C BC) from Heliopolis, given to the City of New York in 1880 by the Khedive Ismael Pasha. Translated hieroglyphs tell the story of Pharaoh Thutmose III.

FIFTH AVENUE★★★

A hundred years ago, the strip of Fifth Avenue from East 59th Street to East 96th Street was called the **Gold Coast** for its grandiose mansions overlooking Central Park. Today's **Museum Mile** embraces the northern third of that stretch—from East 82nd Street (the Metropolitan Museum of Art) extending up to East 105th Street (El Museo del Barrio). The following 2-mile walk embraces the Gold Coast and Museum Mile, making it a little more than two miles total.

▶ *Begin the tour at the intersection of 58th St. & Fifth Ave.*

WALKING TOURS

Grand Army Plaza★★

Fifth Ave. between E. 58th St. & E. 60th St.

Cut in half by Central Park South, this oval plaza marks the end of Midtown's Fifth Avenue luxury shopping district and the start of the Upper East Side's "Gold Coast." On the southern end splashes the 1915 **Pulitzer Fountain**, by Carrère and Hastings (the statue of the Roman goddess Pomona is by Karl Bitter). A huge gold-leaf bronze sculpture of Gen. William Tecumseh Sherman, by Augustus Saint-Gaudens (1903), stands on the north side. Nearby, **horse-drawn carriage**s often stand ready to take visitors for iconic rides around the south end of Central Park. Several significant buildings surround the plaza.

The Plaza Hotel★

Designed by Henry J. Hardenbergh in the French Renaissance style in 1907, the Plaza Hotel was a New York institution of status for nearly a century. Coming-out parties and charity balls drew the cream of New York society; overnight guests included the Duke and Duchess of Windsor and the Beatles.
The structure itself was one of the first buildings in New York to be named a landmark, but the designation applied only to the exterior facade. Developer El-Ad Properties bought the hotel in 2004 and began a $400 million renovation that reconfigured the bulk of its 800 guest rooms as condominiums. Today several of the majestic public rooms, including the Oak Room, the Grand Ballroom and Palm Court, have been restored to their original grandeur.

Paris Theatre

4 W. 58th St. at Fifth Ave.
212-688-3800.

Classic revivals and first-run foreign films (subtitled, not dubbed, of course) play at this charming cinema, one of the few left in Manhattan that hasn't been chopped up to house multiple screens. Its neon marquee is vintage 1960s, whileinterior walls are blue velvet.

General Motors Building

767 Fifth Ave. between E. 58th & E. 59th Sts.

Looming over the east side of the plaza, this 50-story tower (1968) is articulated by white marble piers, alternating with black glass. In the forecourt plaza rises the stunning 32ft glass-cube of the **Apple Store** (2006), open 24/7 for product try-outs and technical assistance. On the ground floor sits the beloved toy store FAO Schwarz, and the CBS television studio where "The Early Show" is broadcast each weekday morning: show up outside between 8am and 8:30am and you may get on camera *(212-975-4061; www.cbsnews.com)*.

Sherry-Netherland★

781 Fifth Ave. at E. 59th St.

The hotel/apartment building (1927) rises 38 stories from a brick base to a French Château-style tower. Above the 24th floor each apartment takes up a full floor. The small lobby has marble mosaic floors; custom-made chandeliers; and hand-painted, wood-paneled elevators. The sidewalk clock outside was installed when the building opened in 1927.

Hotel Pierre

2 E. 61st St. at Fifth Ave.

Opened in 1930, the luxury hotel was named after its owner, the celebrated chef Charles Pierre, who built it with a group of Wall Street backers. Most of the 700 rooms were leased annually by a wealthy clientele, either as primary residences or pieds-à-terre. Today the hotel, which is owned by the Taj hotel group, holds a mix of condominium owners, full-time renters and overnight guests. The Pierre's most famous moment was in 1972 when five men in tuxedoes tied up 16 hotel workers and looted the vault, which held an estimated $11 million in cash and jewels.

810 Fifth Avenue

This elegant limestone apartment house (1926) has only one unit on each of its 13 floors. Famous former residents include William Randolph Hearst, Nelson Rockefeller, and Richard Nixon, who lived with his family on the fifth floor between 1963 and 1968.

New India House

3 E. 64th St. at Fifth Ave.

This Beaux-Arts mansion was originally built (by Warren & Westmore, architects of Grand Central Terminal) as a private residence for Mrs. Caroline Astor's daughter Carrie. It's now the headquarters of the Consulate of India and the Indian delegation to the United Nations. Note especially the copper mansard roof with its ocular windows.

Temple Emanu-El★

1 E. 65 St. at Fifth Ave.
Open year-round Sun–Thu 10am-4:30pm. Services Fri 5:15pm, Sat 10:30am. 212-744-1400.
www.emanuelnyc.org.

Located on the site of Mrs. Astor's former mansion, this Byzantine Romanesque synagogue was completed in 1929. It is the leading Reform synagogue in New York and the largest in the world. The majestic main sanctuary, rising to 103ft, can hold 2,500 worshippers. The ceiling, the marble columns in low relief, and the great arch covered with mosaics are reminiscent of the basilicas of the Near East. The **sanctuary** harbors the Holy Ark, which contains the Torah scrolls.

The Frick Collection★★★

1 E. 70th St. at Fifth Ave.
See Museums.

7 East 72nd Street★

At Fifth Ave.

This building and its neighbor at 9 East 72nd Street were both designed as private residences. Flagg and Chambers designed no. 7, a five-story Renaissance Revival town house in 1899; Carrère and Hastings designed the larger mansion at no. 9 in 1896. The Lycée Français de New York occupied both structures from 1964 until 2001, when the mansions were sold as single-family residences. Asking prices were $15 million and $25 million, respectively.

WALKING TOURS

Harkness House

1 E. 75th St. at Fifth Ave.

An intricate wrought-iron fence protects this Italian-style palazzo (1900), built for Edward S. Harkness, son of a partner of John D. Rockefeller. Today the building houses the Commonwealth Fund, a philanthropic organization.

New York University Institute of Fine Arts

1 E. 78th St. at Fifth Ave.

This immense limestone town house (1912, Horace Trumbauer) was modeled after a Louis XV-style chateau in Bordeaux, France. In 1915 American Tobacco Co. founder James B. Duke and his family lived here. The family donated the house to New York University in 1957.

Ukrainian Institute of America

2 E. 79th St. at Fifth Ave.
Open year-round Tue–Sun noon–6pm. $5. 212-288-8660.
www.ukrainianinstitute.org.

Architect C.P.H. Gilbert was renowned among the rich for his opulent French Gothic designs, of

which this landmark 1898 castle is typical: it even has a (dry) moat. Financier Isaac D. Fletcher, its original owner, left the mansion, along with his art collection, to the Metropolitan Museum of Art in 1917. The Ukrainian Institute of America bought the building in 1955. Step inside to view the magnificent **woodwork** and **chandeliers**; exhibits by Ukrainian artists or on Ukrainian themes are mounted on three floors.

Goethe-Institut

1014 Fifth Ave. between E. 82nd & E. 83rd Sts. Gallery hours year-round Mon–Fri 10am–5pm, Sat noon–5pm. 212-439-8700. www.goethe.de/newyork.

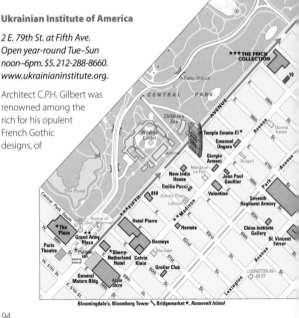

of the Goethe-Institut, one of 144 centers promoting German language and culture worldwide. Films, lectures, debates and museum-quality exhibits of German art are presented on an ongoing basis.

Neue Galerie★

1048 Fifth Ave. at E. 86th St.
See Museums.

Guggenheim Museum★★

1071 Fifth Ave.at E. 88th St.
See Museums.

The Republic of Germany purchased this five-story limestone town house (1907, Welch, Smith & Provot) in 1960. Today it's home to the New York branch

National Academy Museum★

1083 Fifth Ave. at E. 89th St.
See Museums.

Cooper-Hewitt, National Design Museum★★

2 E. 91st St. at Fifth Ave.
See Museums.

Jewish Museum★

1109 Fifth Ave. at 92nd St.
Open year-round Sat–Thu 11am–5:45pm (Thu until 8pm).
Guided tours (45min) available Mon–Thu; check website for times.
Closed major & Jewish holidays.
$12. 212-423-3200. www.thejewish museum.org.

Founded in 1904 as part of the Jewish Theological Seminary of America *(3080 Broadway)*, this museum houses a 28,000-piece collection of Judaica that offers insight into 4,000 years of Jewish history. The French Gothic-style mansion, built in 1909 for Felix M. Warburg, a prominent Jewish banker who emigrated to the US from Germany in 1894, was donated to the seminary by his wife, Frieda, in 1947. Since 1993, it has undergone several renovations. Large temporary shows are presented on the second floor. On the third and fourth floors is a permanent installation "Culture and Continuity: The Jewish Journey," in which 800 works from the permanent collection are arranged to examine Jewish identity from antiquity to the present. The media center *(3rd floor)* offers visitors access to the National Jewish Archive of Broadcasting.

Museum of the City of New York★★

1220 Fifth Ave. at 103rd St.
See Museums.

El Museo del Barrio

1230 Fifth Ave. at 104th St.
Currently closed for renovation; scheduled reopening fall 2009.
212-831-7272. www.elmuseo.org.

This museum and cultural center presents art from the Caribbean and Latin America.
El Museo was founded in a public-school classroom in 1969 by Puerto Rican artists and activists from *el barrio* ("the neighborhood") of East Harlem *(96th St. to 125th St., Fifth Ave. to the East River)*. Today the museum works with other institutions to create major traveling exhibitions of Latin American art. It also presents rotating selections from its permanent collection, which is especially strong in photography.

BROOKLYN HEIGHTS★★

2, 3 train to Clark St.

Heavily fortified during the Revolution, Brooklyn Heights was the site of General Washington's headquarters during the Battle of Long Island. In the mid-19C the neighborhood developed as a choice residential area, largely because of its closeness to Manhattan, and it remains an exclusive address, with brownstones and town houses representing almost every style of 19C American architecture lining its narrow, tree-shaded streets. The Heights' main commercial drag – home to most of its restaurants and shops – is **Montague Street**, though Atlantic Avenue has some good options, too.

Walking Tour

▶ *Distance: 2.8mi.
Begin at Monroe Pl.*

Leaving the subway station, walk toward Monroe Place. At the corner of Clark and Henry streets stands the Hotel St. George, once the largest hotel in New York City. The building has since been converted into co-ops, luxury apartments, and dormitories for nearby Pace University.

▶ *Turn onto Monroe Place.*

At **45 Monroe Place** stands the New York State Supreme Court's Appellate Division. The Classical Revival building dates from 1938 and has two huge Doric columns flanking the entrance.

▶ *Turn left at Pierrepont St.*

The handsome 1881 Queen Anne-style brick building at no. 128 houses the **Brooklyn Historical Society,** the borough's only history museum, comprised of a few small art and history exhibits drawn from the society's extensive permanent collection *(open Wed–Fri and Sun noon–5pm, Sat 10am–5pm; closed Jan 1, July 4, Thanksgiving and Dec 25; $6; 718-222-4111; www.brooklynhistory.org).*

▶ *Backtrack on Pierrepont St. and continue to the corner of Henry St.*

82 Pierrepont Street represents a splendid example of the Richardsonian Romanesque style, with its bulky massing and its rough, unfinished masonry surfaces, rounded arches and bas-relief carving. Built in 1890 as a private residence, it was later enlarged and converted into apartments. Turning onto Willow Street, note **nos. 155, 157** and **159**, three Federal-style houses sporting handsomely detailed entranceways. A skylight in the pavement in front of no. 157 allows daylight to filter down into a tunnel that connects no. 159 to **no. 151**, formerly a stable and now an apartment. Farther up the street, on the opposite side, **nos. 108-112** illustrate the picturesque Queen Anne style, with their great variety of building materials and blend of styles.

▶ *Continue on Willow St. and turn right onto Orange St.*

At the corner of Hicks and Orange Streets stands the 1914 parish house of the historically significant **Plymouth Church of the Pilgrims** down the block *(visit by guided tour only, Mon–Fri 10am–4pm & Sun noon–2pm; stop in at 75 Hicks Street and ask for assistance, or call ahead; 718-624-4743 ; www.plymouthchurch. org).* The first Congregational Church in Brooklyn, this simple brick meetinghouse dating from 1846 served for 40 years as the pulpit for abolitionist Henry Ward Beecher and a stop on the Underground Railroad. President Lincoln worshiped here in 1860; tour guides will point out his pew. The church is also well known for its large stained-glass windows by Tiffany.

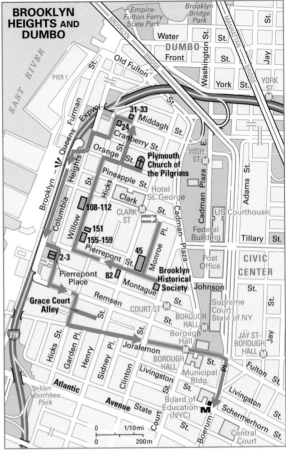

BROOKLYN HEIGHTS AND DUMBO

Backtrack to Hicks St. and continue two blocks north; turn left onto Middagh St.

Several Federal-style clapboard houses, built in the 1820s, line the street. Among the best preserved are the double frame house at **nos. 31-33** and the charming dwelling at **no. 24**. To get to the vibrant shopping and dining district fondly known as DUMBO (*see opposite*), remain on Middagh and turn right on Columbia Heights. Otherwise, continue to the Esplanade as described below.

Take Willow St. to Cranberry St. and continue toward the East River to the Brooklyn Heights Esplanade.

Overlooking the harbor, the esplanade offers excellent **views★★** of the Financial District; the view is especially impressive in the early evening when the lights glimmer across the river. Behind the terrace lies a series of houses with lovely private gardens.

▶ *Walk along the esplanade; turn left onto Pierrepont St. and right onto Pierrepont Pl.*

Note the elegant brownstone mansions at **nos. 2** and **3 Pierrepont Place**.

▶ *Continue on Pierrepont Pl., which be-comes Montague Terrace; turn left onto Remsen St. and right onto Hicks St.*

Off to the left is **Grace Court Alley**, a picturesque mews that was the stable alley for the fine homes on Remsen Street.

▶ *Continue along Hicks St. and turn left onto Joralemon St.*

The intersection of Hicks and Joralemon streets was the location of the country home of Philip Livingston, a signer of the Declaration of Independence. It is reported that on August 29, 1776, General Washington met at Livingston's home with his chiefs of staff to plan the evacuation of his army.

▶ *Continue east on Joralemon St. to Court St.*

The Civic Center area presents a jarring contrast to the residential section, with its monumental public buildings such as Borough Hall, the former Brooklyn City Hall and the massive Richardsonian Romanesque central post office.

▶ *Continue on Joralemon St. to Boerum Pl. and turn right.*

New York Transit Museum★

[M] *on map, opposite. Boerum Pl and Schermerhorn St. See Must See: Best of the Boroughs.*

DUMBO

One of the most vibrant new neighborhoods in Brooklyn, DUMBO (the acronym for Down Under the Manhattan Bridge Overpass) stretches roughly from Fulton Street to the East River. Formerly a waterfront industrial area, its moody cobblestone streets are lined with imposing warehouse buildings, many of them reborn as loft apartments and galleries.

A number of top-notch restaurants and gourmet stores have opened here in the last few years as well. The best time to visit is Saturday afternoon, when most of the galleries and shops are open. Another lively option if your timing is right is the **First Thursday Gallery Walk**, featuring open studios and gallery receptions as well as live music on the first Thursday of the month *(5:30–8:30pm; www.dumbonyc.com)*. For a meal break, try **Bubby's** *(1 Main St.; 718-222-0666; www.bubbys.com)* a TriBeCa import that serves up homey staples like pie and chicken. Sweet tooth? Head for **Jacques Torres Chocolate** *(66 Water St.; 212-414-2462; www.jacquestorres.com)* for its housemade truffles, cookies and European-style hot chocolate. If you need to take a load off, Brooklyn Bridge Park is a great place to rest or picnic, especially if you've just walked over the legendary span.

BEST OF THE BOROUGHS

Manhattan may be the heart of New York City, but a lot of life goes on in the four "outer" boroughs: the Bronx, Queens, Brooklyn and Staten Island, all of which were incorporated into the city in 1898. Here you'll find not only the vast majority of New Yorkers, but some of New York's best-loved – and least crowded – attractions.

THE BRONX

Home of the New York Yankees (aka "the Bronx Bombers"), the Bronx is New York's only borough located on the mainland. It was named after Jonas Bronck, a Swedish emigré who arrived here in June 1639. Today about half the borough's residents are Hispanic and 25 percent of its area is parkland. The 4,5, and 6 trains run to the Bronx from Manhattan's East Side; from the West Side, take the 1, B or D trains. To get to the zoo or the Botanical Garden, see below.

Bronx Zoo★★★

Fordham Rd. at Bronx River Pkwy. 718-367-1010. www.wcs.org. Open Apr–Oct Mon–Fri 10am–5pm, weekends & holidays 10am–5:30pm; rest of the year open daily 10am–4:30pm. $15. 2 or 5 train to E. Tremont Ave./W. Farm Sq. or take the BXM11 express bus ($5 each way; exact change or MetroCard required) from Madison Ave. (stops between 27th and 99th Sts) to the zoo's Gate B.

The country's largest urban zoo is set in a gorgeous 265-acre woodland park. From elegant ibex to goofy gibbons, the animals here enjoy homes that mirror their natural habitats. Founded in 1899, today the zoo showcases more than 4,000 animals and is an important breeding center for endangered species.

Best of the Bronx Zoo

Skyfari★★ – Travel about the treetops from the zoo center to Wild Asia on this high-flying gondola. It's a quick and beautiful way to get across the park.

Tiger Mountain★★ – The zoo's spectacular tiger exhibit puts you just a whisker away from the largest member of the cat family.

Wild Asia★★ – The Bengali Express Monorail passes through 38 acres of free-roaming tigers, guar cattle, red pandas and rhinoceroses.

Congo Gorilla Forest★★ – This 6.5-acre African rain forest counts more than 300 animals, including one of the largest breeding groups of lowland gorillas.

Children's Zoo★ – Kids can feed farmyard animals and see others in natural environments.

MUST SEE

New York Botanical Garden★★

200th St. and Kazimiroff Blvd. 718-817-8700. www.nybg.org. Open Tue–Sun 10am–6pm. Closed Mon, Thanksgiving Day & Dec 25. $20 includes all gardens, tours and tram. B, D or 4 train to Bedford Park Blvd., then the Bx 26 bus east to Moshulu Gate entrance.

Green thumbs shouldn't miss this horticultural landmark, located directly north of the Bronx Zoo. Founded in 1891, it is one of the largest and oldest gardens in the country. Numerous walking trails wind through its 250 acres past such favorites as the Rose Garden, the Rock Garden, the Native Plant Garden and the Daylily Collection. The site also features 50 acres of original forest. Peak season is late spring/early summer, though you'll see plenty of plants in bloom throughout the year.

Enid A. Haupt Conservatory★★ – Opened in 1902, this glorious Victorian structure showcases global plant communities from rain forests to deserts.

New York Botanical Gardens

©NYC&Co.

Everett Children's Adventure Garden★ – Hands-on exhibits allow kids and families to explore how plants live and function.

Wave Hill★

W. 249th St. & Independence Ave. 718-549-3200. www.wavehill.org. Open mid-Apr–mid-Oct Tue–Sun 9am–5:30pm; rest of the year Tue–Sun 9am–4:30pm. Closed Mon (except holiday Mon) Jan 1, Thanksgiving & Dec 25. $6 (free Sat 9am–noon and all day Jan–Apr, Jul–Aug, Nov–Dec). You can take the 1 subway train then transfer to a shuttle, or the Metro-North Hudson Line commuter train from Grand Central Terminal to Riverdale and transfer to a shuttle (see website).

From its spectacular perch above the Hudson River, Wave Hill – a gardener's paradise – seems worlds away from the city. This enchanting 28-acre estate was built as a country home in the 1840s and has had some illustrious occupants, including Theodore Roosevelt's family and Mark Twain. Today 18 acres of its grounds have been landscaped into seven separate gardens, containing more than 3,000 species. Not to be missed: the herb garden, the alpine garden, the dry garden, the wild garden, the pergola and the conservatory.

🪆 Yankee Stadium

See Musts for Fun.

Touring Tip

For another way to get to the garden, take the Metro-North Harlem line from Grand Central Station to the Botanical Garden stop, directly outside the garden gate. The trip takes only 20 minutes!

BROOKLYN

New York's most populous borough occupies the western tip of Long Island. Founded by the Dutch in 1636, the area was named Breuckelen ("broken land") after a small town near Utrecht. The population exploded after the Brooklyn Bridge opened in 1883. Today Brooklyn is a mix of separate neighborhoods, from staid Brooklyn Heights to honky-tonk Coney Island to verdant Park Slope, the last a popular haven for young well-to-do families. New to Brooklyn? Get your bearings at Brooklyn Borough Hall *(209 Joralemon St. at Court St.; open Mon–Fri 10am–6pm; 718-802-3846; www.visitbrooklyn.org)*, where you'll find neighborhood maps, hotel and restaurant listings (there are new ones cropping up every day), calendars of events, transportation information and more.

Brooklyn Bridge★★★

See Landmarks.

Brooklyn Botanic Garden★★

900 Washington Ave. 718-623-7200. www.bbg.org. Open mid-Mar– Oct Tue–Fri 8am–6pm, weekends & holidays 10am–6pm. Rest of the year Tue–Fri 8am–4:30pm, weekends 10am–4:30pm. Closed Mon & major holidays.$8 (free Sat 10am–noon, all day Tue & weekdays mid-Nov–Feb). 2 or 3 train to Eastern Pkwy.; B, Q or S train to Prospect Park.

Bordering the east edge of Prospect Park, this refreshing oasis covers 52 acres and includes one of the country's finest assemblages of roses. Its outdoor gardens include a Shakespeare garden and a Japanese garden. The **Steinhardt Conservatory★** houses the country's largest bonsai collection.

Walking Tours
For an insider's view of Brooklyn, the **Brooklyn Historical Society** *(128 Pierrepont St.; 718-222-4111; www.brooklynhistory.org)* does tours of the area and keeps the borough's only history museum.

©Jeff Greenberg/NYC&Co.

Brooklyn Heights

Brooklyn Heights★★

If you decide to walk over the Brooklyn Bridge, consider taking a stroll around this lovely neighborhood at the other end *(See Walking Tours)*. It's a wealthy enclave of narrow, tree-lined streets bordered with historic brownstones. Willow and Pierrepont streets are particularly picturesque. Montague Street is the commercial strip, with cafes and high-end boutiques. And don't miss the **esplanade**, which runs along the East River from Montague to Orange Street and affords magnificent views of the Financial District across the river.

©NYC&Co.

Brooklyn Museum of Art

Brooklyn Museum of Art★★

200 Eastern Pkwy. 718-638-5000. www.brooklynmuseum.org. Open year-round Wed–Fri 10am–5pm, weekends 11am–6pm. Closed Mon, Tue, Jan 1, Thanksgiving Day & Dec 25. $8. 2 or 3 train to Eastern Pkwy/Brooklyn Museum.

Best known for its Egyptian collection and its superb cache of American paintings, the Brooklyn Museum is among the largest art museums in the US.
It illustrates art history from ancient times to the present, with selections from its 1.5-million-piece collection. The monumental Beaux-Arts structure, designed by McKim, Mead and White, was opened in 1897, and has been repeatedly modified. In 2003 viewing space for the Egyptian collection doubled, the Beaux-Arts Court displaying European painting was totally refurbished, and the museum opened a public study center for its collection of American art.

First Floor – African art★★, arts of the Americas and a sculpture garden.

Second Floor – Asian and Islamic art; Chinese jades and Persian art.

Prospect Park★

Main entrance at Grand Army Plaza (intersection of Flatbush Ave. & Prospect Park West). Events hot line: 718-965-8999. www.prospectpark.org.
After a visit to the museum, check out Brooklyn's most cherished park, a 585-acre wonderland of meadows and gardens designed in 1896 by Olmsted and Vaux, creators of Central Park. A road traces its periphery, and paths cut through its interior, which has plenty of ball parks and recreation facilities, as well as a carousel, a band shell, a pond and a small zoo. For lunch, exit the west side of the park and go two blocks to **Seventh Avenue**, a family-friendly strip of restaurants, cafes and boutiques.

BEST OF THE BOROUGHS

Third Floor – The stunning **Egyptian art collection★★★**, 700 years of European paintings, and ancient Middle Eastern art.

Fourth Floor – 19C and 20C decorative arts, including a Wedgewood gallery.

Fifth Floor – "American Identities: A New Look" presents works by Copley, Sargent, Cassatt, O'Keeffe and Frank Lloyd Wright alongside Native American and Spanish colonial art.

You'll also find the **Elizabeth A. Sackler Center for Feminist Art★**, highlighting 40 years of women's contributions to the art world.

New York Transit Museum★

Boerum Pl. & Schermerhorn Sts., Brooklyn Heights. 718-694-1600. www.mta.info/mta/museum. Open year-round Tue–Fri 10am–4pm, weekends noon–5pm. $5. 2, 3, 4 or 5 train to Borough Hall.

Public transportation buffs will find everything they wanted to know about how New Yorkers get around in this former subway station, with historic subway cars, exhibits on how the tunnels were excavated, old turnstiles and more.

Brooklyn Academy of Music★

See Performing Arts.

New York Aquarium★★

W. 8th St. & Surf Ave., Coney Island. 718-265-3474. www.nyaquarium. com. Open Jun–Aug Mon–Fri 10am–6pm (weekends 7pm); rest of the year closing times vary from 4:30pm to 5:30pm. $13 ($9 ages 3–12). F or Q train to W. 8th St./New York Aquarium.

The weather outside might be frightful, but for the creatures at this indoor-outdoor facility, the water is always delightful. The first New York Aquarium — reputedly the first aquarium in the US — opened in 1896 in what is now Castle Clinton National Monument *(see Historic Sites)*. The present facility has been a Coney Island institution since 1957. In large outdoor pools, whales, seals, sea lions, dolphins and Pacific walrus go through their paces *(check at entrance for feeding schedule)*. Indoor aquariums display more than 8,000 specimens and 300 species from around the world.

Alien Stingers★★ – This exhibit showcases sea jellies, corals and anemones.

Conservation Hall – Rays glide through a floor-to-ceiling tank.

Sea Cliffs★ – The 300-foot-long North Pacific coastline habitat contains penguins, mullets, sea horses, walruses, and octopuses and other creatures, which can be viewed above and below the water.

Coney Island

See Musts for Kids.

New York Aquarium

©Wildlife Conservation Society

QUEENS

With an area of 120 square miles and a population topping two million, New York's biggest borough draws thousands of immigrants each year to its relatively affordable housing and its tight-knit ethnic communities – but for years it wasn't much of a draw for tourists. That is slowly changing as film studios and art museums make use of abandoned factories in the Long Island City and Astoria neighborhoods. Inland, sports thrive at **Shea Stadium** (home of the New York Mets baseball team), the **USTA National Tennis Center** (where the US Open is played each September) and **Aqueduct Racetrack** (which hosts thoroughbred horse racing). Of course, many visitors come here whether they want to or not: LaGuardia and Kennedy airports are both in Queens.

The Noguchi Museum★★

9-01 33rd Rd., at Vernon Blvd., Long Island City. 718-204-7088. www.noguchi.org. Open Wed–Fri 10am–5pm, weekends 11am–6pm. Closed Mon, Tue, Jan 1, Thanksgiving Day & Dec 26. N or W train to Broadway.

The world-renowned sculptor Isamu Noguchi (1904–88) had lived and worked in a converted factory space next to this building from 1961 until 1981, when he built the present facility as a studio and museum. Noguchi, who was born in Los Angeles but raised in Japan, sculpted a range of dynamic works in New York, from the stainless-steel *News* (1938–40) for the entrance of the Associated Press building at 50 Rockefeller Center to *The Red Cube* (1967) in the plaza in front of the Marine Midland Bank *(140 Broadway at Liberty St.)* in the Financial District. Today this tranquil indoor-out-

The Noguchi Museum

Noguchi Museum New York/©2004 Elizabeth Felicella

door museum in the heart of Queens displays 250 of Noguchi's sculptures in stone, wood, clay and metal, as well as working models for many of his large-scale public projects. Try to visit on a pleasant day, so you can linger in the peaceful garden.

Museum for African Art★

36-01 43rd Ave. at 36th St., Long Island City. 718-784-7700. www.africanart.org. Currently under construction; call or check website for location and hours of traveling shows. Office and museum store open Mon–Fri 10am–5pm.

The only independent museum in the country dedicated to African art and culture has mounted dozens of major shows exploring Africa's artistic traditions and

cultural heritage. Work is progressing on the museum's new home on Fifth Avenue in Manhattan *(projected completion late 2009).* In the meantime, the museum mounts exhibitions in various locations throughout the city; check the website for information.

Museum of the Moving Image★

35th Ave. at 36th St., Astoria (during construction enter on 37th St. near 35th St.). 718-784-0077. www. movingimage.us. Open Tue–Fri 10am–4pm (Fri until 6:30pm); hours may vary during construction. $7.50. R or V train to Steinway St.

This eye-popping place uses its trove of film-related paraphernalia to describe the art, craft and business of making moving images, defined as anything from a flip book to Pac-Man. The museum

Museum for African Art

Museum for African Art

MUST SEE

was founded in 1988 in a portion of the former Kaufman Astoria Studios, which were built by Paramount Pictures in the 1920s and used by Paul Robeson, the Marx brothers and Rudolph Valentino. The studios, abandoned in 1971 and revived in the 1990s, now bustle with film and television shoots. The museum is currently undergoing a major expansion and renovation *(projected completion 2010)*; some galleries remain open, and the museum sponsors screenings, panel discussions and premiers at other theaters around the city *(check website for schedules and information)*.

P.S. 1 Contemporary Art Center★

22-25 Jackson Ave. at 46th Ave. 718-784-2084. www.ps1.org. Open year-round Thu–Mon noon–6pm. Closed Jan 1, Thanksgiving Day, Dec 25. $5 suggested donation (free with MoMA ticket within 30 days of purchase). 7 train to Courthouse Square.

An affiliate of MoMA since 1999, P.S. 1 has been one of the city's most exciting venues for up-and-coming contemporary art since 1976, when it took over this 1893 school building (the "P.S." stands

for "public school"). The five-story center nurtures new talent with a range of educational programs and a broad vision of what constitutes art nowadays. You'll usually find at least one site-specific installation here as well as something from MoMA, which uses the mammoth space to display large-scale works. The rest is up in the air – that's the fun of it.

Louis Armstrong House Museum★

34-56 107th St., Corona. 717-478-8274. www.satchmo.net. Visit by 40min guided tour only, Tue–Fri 10am–5pm, weekends noon–5pm. $8. 7 train to 103rd St./Corona Plaza; walk north on 104th St., turn right on 37th Ave. and left on 107th St.

This modest, 2-story brick house was home to American jazz icon Louis "Satchmo" Armstrong from 1943 until his death in 1971. The house and personal effects, which appear mostly as they did during Armstrong's lifetime, reveal the beloved jazzman's unpretentious, fun-loving nature. A special bonus: snippets of recordings Armstrong made about his home life, riffing on everything from music to brussels sprouts.

Astoria

The friendly neighborhood of Astoria is well known throughout New York City for its Greek food. Dripping with honey and butter, the baklava at **Omonia Cafe** *(32-20 Broadway; 718-274-6650)* is some of the freshest around. A local institution, **Uncle George's** *(33-19 Boadway; 718-626-0593)* is a family-friendly Greek diner where you can get a huge meal–the rotisserie chicken with lemon potatoes is a specialty– with wine for well under $20. **S'Agapo Taverna** *(34-21 34th Ave.; 718-626-0303)*, just a block from the Museum of the Moving Image, is a lovely place for a dinner of whole grilled fish or just a glass of retsina and the *pikilia orektiton*, a sampling of dips with fresh-baked pita.

STATEN ISLAND

Sometimes referred to as "the forgotten borough," Staten Island is primarily a bedroom community, sharing more in common with New Jersey than with New York. Still, the 🚢 **Staten Island Ferry** is a thrilling – and free – ride, and while you're over there, you might as well take a look around.

Staten Island Ferry★

212-639-9675.
www.siferry.com.
Departs year-round daily from Whitehall Terminal at the southern tip of Manhattan about every 30min (hourly midnight–6am).
1 train to South Ferry; R or W train to Whitehall St.

Who said there were no free rides in life? The Staten Island Ferry, which shuttles commuters back and forth between Manhattan and "the forgotten borough," is a free 🚢 **tour** – and it offers some of the best views of Manhattan and the Statue of Liberty that you're likely to find at any price. On the five-mile voyage, which takes 25 minutes each way, the boat skirts the Statue of Liberty. On the return trip, you can zoom in on the lower New York skyline.

Alice Austen House Museum★

2 Hylan Blvd. 718-816-4506. www. aliceausten.org. Open Mar–Dec Thu–Sun noon–5pm. Closed Jan, Feb & major holidays. $2 suggested donation. From the ferry terminal, take S51 bus to Hylan Blvd (15min).

Pioneer photographer Alice Austen (1866–1952) captured turn-of-the-century life in New York City, snapping elite society gatherings and immigrant scenes alike. Restored according to her own photographs, this Victorian cottage displays changing exhibits, including prints from her glass-plate negatives.

Staten Island Ferry

©Jeff Greenberg/NYC&Co.

Alice AustenHouse Museum	BY A	Museum of Tibetan Art	BZ B
Conference House	AZ	Moravian Cemetery	BY
Greenbelt Environmental		Snug Harbor Cultural Center	BY
Education Dept.	BY C	Staten Island Ferry	BY
Historic Richmond Town	BZ	Staten Island Museum	BY
Jacques Marchais		Zoo	BY

BRIDGES	
Bayonne Bridge	BY
Goethals Bridge	AY
Outerbridge Crossing	11 AZ
Verrazano-Narrows Bridge	12 BY

Historic Richmond Town★

441 Clarke Ave. 718-351-1611. www.historicrichmondtown.org. Open Jul–Aug Wed–Fri 11am–5pm, weekends1pm–5pm. Rest of the year Wed–Sun 1pm–5pm. Closed Mon, Tue & major holidays. $5. From the ferry terminal, take S74 bus to Richmond Rd./ St. Patrick's Pl (30min).

Summertime is "living-history season" at this 25-acre village, with costumed interpreters demonstrating crafts (tinsmithing, print-making) and telling stories about life in the former county seat. Don't miss the late-17C Voorlezer

House, thought to be the oldest elementary school in the US.

Jacques Marchais Museum of Tibetan Art★

338 Lighthouse Ave. 718-987-3500. www.tibetanmuseum.org. Open year-round Wed–Sun 1pm–5pm. Closed major holidays. $5. From the ferry, take S74 bus to Lighthouse Ave (30min).

This museum has a rare collection of art and artifacts from Tibet, Nepal, China, Mongolia and India. Topping Lighthouse Hill amid terraced gardens and lily ponds, the museum buildings resemble a small Buddhist mountain temple.

EXCURSIONS FROM NEW YORK CITY

You'll be surprised how quickly the city melts away as you head north along the Hudson River or east out to Long Island. Drive north along US-9 and you'll discover a rich landscape of highlands and history. If you're craving the feel of sand between your toes, jump on the Long Island Parkway to reach some of the finest beaches and best-protected harbors on the Atlantic Coast.

HUDSON RIVER VALLEY★★★

Take I-87 North to I-287 West to US-9 North and continue north, following Rte. 9d along the east bank of the river. After seeing sites in Hyde Park, backtrack south and cross the river at Poughkeepsie, returning along the west bank on Rte. 9W . See map p. 157. Tourist information 845-291-2136; www.travelhudsonvalley.org. Historic homes may be visited by guided tour only.

A remarkable concentration of historic homes in the Hudson River Valley reflects the early-17C Dutch settlement pattern, which carved feudal estates out of the land flanking the river. When the English took over in 1664, they turned these estates into lordly manors. In the 1800s the region's wild beauty inspired artists of the Hudson River school – including Frederic Edwin Church,

Thomas Cole and Albert Bierstadt – to paint sweeping landscapes. Today, along with historic mansions, you'll find small towns (Cold Spring, Rhinebeck) nestling near the riverbanks, chock-a-block with antiques stores, boutiques and bistros.

Boscobel Restoration★★

Rte. 9D, 4mi north of junction with Rte. 403, Garrison. 845-265-3638. www.boscobel.org. Open Apr–Oct Wed–Mon 10am–5pm. Nov–Dec Wed–Mon 10am–4pm. Closed Jan–Mar, Tue, Thanksgiving Day & Dec 25. $15.

Fans of the Federal style love this elegant manor, built in the early 1800s but moved in pieces to this site overlooking the Hudson in the 1950s. The restored interior features graceful arches, fireplaces embellished with classical motifs, carved woodwork and Duncan Phyfe furnishings.

The Castle on the Hudson

400 Benedict Ave., Tarrytown. 914-631-1980 or 800-616-4487. www.castleonthehudson.com. 31 rooms. Over $300. Resembling a medieval castle with its towers and arched windows, this 1910 mansion-turned-inn tops a hill overlooking the Hudson, 25 miles north of New York City. Inside, period tapestries soften the stone walls, and hand-carved four-poster beds and custom-made chandeliers decorate the guest rooms. Save time for a meal at **Equus**, where you'll dine on memorable French cuisine.

MUST SEE

Home of FDR National Historic Site★★

Rte. 9, Hyde Park. 845-229-9115. www.nps.gov/hofr. Open year-round daily 9am–5pm. Closed Jan 1, Thanksgiving Day & Dec 25. $14 (free children under 15).

You'll feel as if you know the Roosevelt family personally after a visit to this 300-acre estate, which is bursting with historic memorabilia. Franklin Delano Roosevelt's father bought the site in 1867, and FDR was born here in 1882. In the rose garden, a simple white-marble monument marks the final resting place of FDR and his wife, Eleanor.

Vanderbillt Mansion National Historic Site★★

Rte. 9, Hyde Park. 845-229-9115. www.nps.gov/vama. Open year-round daily 9am–5pm. Closed Jan 1, Thanksgiving Day & Dec 25. $8.

This sumptuous Beaux-Arts estate, designed in 1898 for Frederick W. Vanderbilt, recalls a bygone era of wealth and opulence. The art and furnishings in the house range from Renaissance to rococo, typifying the lavish lifestyle of American "nobility" in the early 20C.

Culinary Institute of America

1946 Campus Dr., Hyde Park. 845-471-6608. www.ciachef.edu.
Here, 2,400 chefs-in-training hone their skills in five restaurants (you may be sampling the work of the next star in the culinary firmament). Reservations required.

Kykuit★★

Rte 9 North, Sleepy Hollow. 914-631-9491. www.hudson valley.org. Open mid-May–early Nov Wed–Mon 9am–4pm (weekends until 5pm). Closed mid-Nov–late Apr. Tours $15–$38.

Dutch for "lookout," Kykuit (pronounced "KYE-cut") is the most picturesque of the Hudson Valley estates. The house was built between 1906 and 1913 by John D. Rockefeller Jr. for his father, the patriarch of Standard Oil. In all, Kykuit has housed four generations of Rockefellers. Inside you'll find antique Chinese porcelains, tapestries and a fine collection of modern art amassed by Nelson D. Rockefeller. The lovely terraced **gardens★** contain sculptures by such artists as Picasso, Louise Nevelson and Isamu Noguchi.

Kykuit Estate

EXCURSIONS

rary sculptures with individually tailored settings that present each work to best effect. The pastoral landscape of meadows, hillsides, forests and terraced lawns features works by Alexander Calder, Mark diSuvero, Henry Moore, Louise Nevelson, Isamu Noguchi and many others. Most of the works were installed on-site.

West Point★★

On the west bank of the Hudson off US-9 West; take the exit for West Point/Highland Falls. 845-938-2638. www.usma.edu. Visitor center open daily 9am–4:45pm. Grounds may be visited by 1hr or 2hr guided tour only; call 845-446-4724 or go to www.westpointtours.com for schedule. $11–$13.

The prestigious U.S. Military Academy was established here in 1802, on the site of Fortress West Point, a 1778 series of fortifications overlooking the Hudson at one of its most narrow points. In 1780 Benedict Arnold, the fort's commander, schemed to hand West Point over to the British (the plan was thwarted). In the academy's first year, 10 students graduated; today there are more than 4,200 cadets here.

Try to plan your visit to coincide with one of the academy's spectacular **parades**, known for their precision of movement *(Sept–Nov & late Apr–May)*. Be sure to visit the **museum★★**, where you'll find out everything you ever wanted to know about the history of the military.

Storm King Art Center★

On the west bank of the Hudson off Rte. 9; exit Rte. 107 and turn left; turn right on Rte. 32 and follow signs. 845-534-3115. www.stormking.org. Open Apr–mid-Nov Wed–Sun 11am–5:30pm (early–mid-Nov closing 5pm). Closed rest of the year. $10.

This unique outdoor museum combines large-scale contempo-

LONG ISLAND★★

From end to end, Long Island is a study in extremes. On the western tip you have ultra-urban Brooklyn and Queens; on the eastern tip, 118 miles away, lie the dramatic bluffs of Montauk. In between are vast tracts of suburban development. But that's not all. Long Island boasts many sandy beaches and seafaring towns. Although the North Shore is rockier and more dramatic than the South Shore (which is protected by several long barrier islands), both are equally worth exploring.

Long Island has three major highways: The Long Island Expwy. (I-495, aka "the LIE"), the Northern State Pkwy. and the Southern State Pkwy. The Queens–Midtown Tunnel, accessible at E. 42nd St., leads directly onto the Long Island Expwy. For tourist information, contact Long Island Convention and Visitors Bureau; 631-951-3900; www.licvb.com.

The Long Island Museum★★

Rte. 25A at Main St., Stony Brook. 631-751-0066. www.longisland museum.org. Open year-round Wed–Sat 10am–5pm, Sun noon–5pm. Closed Mon, Tue & major holidays. $9 ($4 ages 6–17).

This kid-friendly complex incorporates museums of art, history and carriages, as well as a blacksmith shop, a schoolhouse and a barn. Plan on spending most of your time in the carriage museum, ogling the 250 horse-drawn carriages that range from Gypsy wagons to children's vehicles (pulled by goats or dogs).

Old Bethpage Village Restoration★★

1303 Round Swamp Rd., Old Bethpage. 516-572-8400. www.nassaucountyny.gov. Open Mar–Dec Wed–Fri 10am–4pm, weekends 10am–5pm. $10.

Take a stroll through this pre-Civil War village and watch the weaver make cloth, the farmwife prepare a meal, and farmers work their fields. More than 55 historic buildings have been moved here from their original locations and staffed with costumed interpreters, creating a museum that's especially fun for families.

Beach on Fire Island, Lond Island

©John Archer/iStockphoto.com

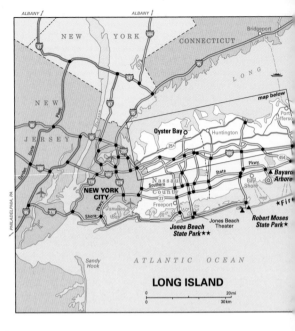

LONG ISLAND

0   20mi
0   30km

The Hamptons★★

South Shore, about 100mi east of New York City. www.thehamptons.com.

Home to the glitterati, Long Island's most renowned vacation spot forms a loose-knit chain of towns running 35 miles along the South Shore, from Westhampton Beach to Amagansett.
Try tony **Southampton★** for superb estates and pricey shops, and the port of **Sag Harbor★** *(northeast of Southampton via Rtes. 27 & 79; www.sagharborchamber.*

com) for charm. Westhampton Beach is a lively resort where New Yorkers – especially writers, musicians and artists–like to spend their weekends.

East Hampton has long attracted writers and artists (Childe Hassam, Jackson Pollock and Stuart Davis all lived here).

The laid-back town of **Montauk**, at the island's easternmost tip, offers beachfront hotels, seafood restaurants and bars along with dramatic cliffs and sea views. A 15-mile-long public beach runs from Moriches Inlet to Shinnecock Inlet.

The Lobster Roll

1980 Montauk Hwy., Amagansett. 631-267-3740. Closed Nov–mid-Apr.
Sand dunes may surround this highway shanty, but don't let the beachy atmosphere fool you. The famous lobster rolls draw celebrity locals like Barbra Streisand, Kathleen Turner and Alec Baldwin.

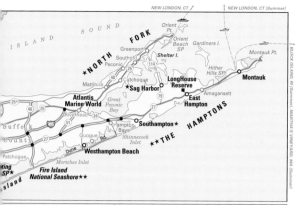

Planting Fields★★

*Planting Fields Rd., Oyster Bay.
516-922-8600.
www.plantingfields.com.
Grounds open year-round daily
9am–5pm. Closed Dec 25. $6/car
(except Nov–Apr weekdays).*

Flower power rules at financier
William Robertson Coe's former estate, 409 acres of which have been
preserved as an arboretum, with
greenhouses, rolling lawns, formal
gardens, hiking paths and more.
The exquisite Tudor mansion may
be visited by guided tour *(Apr–Sept
noon–3:30pm; $6.50; 516-922-9210).*

Cold Spring Harbor Whaling Museum

Cold Spring Harbor Whaling Museum

Cold Spring Harbor Whaling Museum★

301 Main St., Cold Spring Harbor. 631-367-3418. www.cshwhaling museum.org. Open year-round Tue–Sun 11am–5pm, daily in summer. $5 ($4 ages 5–18).

More fun for kids, this museum brings back the town's 1850s heyday as a whaling port. Exhibits include a fully equipped 19C whaleboat, harpoons, navigational instruments, an orca skull and scrimshaw (whalebone carvings), the whaler's folk art.

Sagamore Hill National Historic Site★

Cove Neck Rd., Oyster Bay. 516-922-4788. www.nps.gov/sahi. Mansion open by guided tour only, late May–Labor Day daily 9am– 5pm; rest of the year Wed–Sun 10am–4pm. Closed major holidays. $5.

Though this site includes a museum and a visitor center, the 1885 Queen Anne mansion, Teddy Roosevelt's former residence, is the main attraction here. Many of its 23 rooms appear as they did during Roosevelt's presidency (1901–09), with more than 90 percent of the family's original furnishings.

Raynham Hall Museum

20 W. Main St., Oyster Bay. 516-922-6808. www.raynham hallmuseum.org. Open Jul–Labor Day Tue–Sun noon–5pm; rest of the year Tue–Sun 1–5pm. Closed major holidays. $4.

This old colonial farmhouse was the home of Samuel Townsend, whose son Robert was George Washington's chief intelligence agent in New York City during the American Revolution. For a time the house served as a British headquarters, despite the fact that the Townsends' sympathies lay with the Patriots. Inside you'll see period furniture and memorabilia dating from the 1770s through the 1870s.

Vanderbilt Museum★

180 Little Neck Rd., Centerport. 631-854-5555. www.vanderbilt museum.org. Open year-round Tue–Sun noon–5pm. Closed Jan 1, Thanksgiving Day & Dec 25. $7.

William K. Vanderbilt II – "Willie K" – was a lifelong traveler, expert yachtsman and racecar driver. The 24-room, Spanish Revival-style mansion houses natural history collections in the Habitat Wing. There's also a marine museum with ship models, and a planetarium.

Beaches of Long Island

Had enough of history? Then hit the beach! On the North Shore, **Sunken Meadow State Park**★ *(631-269-4333; www.nysparks.com)* has a large, fine-sand beach as well as recreational activities like hiking and golf. On the South Shore you can spread your towel at **Jones Beach State Park**★★ *(516-785-1600; www.nysparks.com)*, a barrier island boasting 6.5 miles of beaches along ocean and bay; car-free **Fire Island**★, which encompasses the 1,400-acre **Fire Island National Seashore**★ *(631-289-4810; www.nps.gov/fiis)* and an idyllic beachfront state park; or the **Hamptons**★★.

MUST SEE

Old Westbury Gardens★

71 Old Westbury Rd., Old Westbury. 516-333-0048. www.oldwestbury gardens.org. Open mid-Apr–Oct Wed–Mon 10am–5pm (last entry 4pm). $10.

The formal English gardens, with their grand allées, statues and lakes, form the centerpiece of this historic 160-acre estate, former home of John S. Phipps and his family. The Charles II-style mansion is beautifully preserved; don't miss the fine period furnishings, decorative objects and paintings by Thomas Gainsborough and John Singer Sargent.

Sands Point Preserve★

127 Middleneck Rd., Port Washington. 516-571-7901. www.sandspointpreserve org. Estate open year-round daily 10am–5pm. Guided tours of Falaise ($6) May–Oct noon, 1pm, 2pm & 3pm.

This former Gold Coast estate, bought as undeveloped land in 1900 by Howard Gould (son of railroad magnate Jay Gould), reflects the opulent lifestyles of New York's wealthy "robber baron" families during the Gilded Age. Gould built the massive, Tudor-style Hempstead House *(not open to the public)* before selling the property to Daniel Guggenheim in 1917. Falaise, Guggenheim's Normandy-style manor house, perches on a bluff above Long Island Sound, and contains a wonderful collection of 16C and 17C French and Spanish antiques. Don't miss the spectacular views of Long Island Sound from the loggia at the rear of the house.

North Fork★
www.northfork.org.

Roughly 25 miles east of Stony Brook, the Long Island Expressway ends and the island splits in two, like the tines of a fork. For decades the South Fork, home to the Hamptons and white-sand beaches, has gotten the lion's share of the tourist trade, but in recent years the more-rural North Fork is taking on new life, thanks to a boomlet of charming bed-and-breakfast inns and award-winning wineries. Strung out along 24 miles of Route 25, the North Fork's quaint towns boast a number of new wine bars and exciting new restaurants, all amid rolling farmland, vineyards and orchards. For an introduction to the area's viticultural scene, stop in at the **Tasting Room** in Peconic for tastings of wines from ten boutique North Fork wineries *(2885 Peconic Ln.; 631-765-6404; www. tastingroomli.com).*

Bayard Cutting Arboretum State Park★

Rte. 27A, Oakdale. 631-581-1002. www.nysparks.com. Open Apr–Oct Tue–Sun 10am–6:30pm (last entry at 5pm); rest of the year 10am–5:30pm (last entry at 4pm). $6/vehicle.

Created in 1887 by William Cutting according to plans by legendary landscape architect Frederick Law Olmsted, thie arboretum covers 690 acres of woodlands and planted areas. Many of the specimens in the pinetum date back to the original plantings of fir, spruce, pine and other evergreens. Rhododendrons and azaleas *(in bloom May–June)* border the walks and drives; wildflowers add blazes of color throughout the park.

FOR FUN

Don't get stressed if you can't see everything on your trip to New York. That's just what a New Yorker would do. Instead, try to relax and have fun, mixing up museum visits with simple pleasures. Here are some places to start.

It's All In the Approach

Staten Island Ferry★

Year-round daily 24hrs/day roughly every 30min (hourly midnight–6am). 212-639-9675 (311 within New York). www.si ferry.com. R or W train to Whitehall St.; 1 train to South Ferry.

For a quick (25 minutes each way) **tour** with dazzling views of the Statue of Liberty and New York Harbor, hop onto the free Staten Island Ferry – the best sightseeing deal in town *(see Boroughs)*.

Brooklyn Bridge★★★

For the classic approach to Manhattan, take a stroll across the Brooklyn Bridge and back via the pedestrian walkway on the north side *(entrance near the Brooklyn Bridge/City Hall subway station)*. The walk takes about a half an hour each way. The best part? Drinking in the incomparable views of Manhattan's skyline at your own pace.

Roosevelt Island Tram

Departs every 15min from Second Ave. & E. 59th St. year-round Sun–Thu 6am–2am, Fri–Sat 6am–3:30am. 212-832-4555. www.rioc.com.

Try the 4-minute tram ride across the East River to pleasant Roosevelt Island for awe-inspiring bird's-eye views in each direction.

🏙 Seasonal New York

As the proverb goes, for everything there is a season, and that is certainly true in New York. Even if fall and spring offer the best chance of nice weather, summer and winter have lots of fun traditions as well. Here are a few.

Winter
Under the watchful gaze of *Prometheus* lies a winter wonderland – **Rockefeller Center's sunken skating rink** *(212-332-7654)*. It's cozy – okay, tiny – but taking a turn on the ice in such a splendid setting is unforgettable. If you need more room to execute your Hamill Camel, head uptown to Central Park's tree-framed **Wollman Rink**, near Columbus Circle *(212-439-6900; www.wollman skatingrink.com)*. Skate rentals are available at both rinks.

Ice skating at the Rockefeller Center

Brigitta L. House/Michelin

Another holiday tradition: Check out the **window displays at Macy's** *(34th St. & Sixth Ave.)* and **Saks Fifth Avenue** *(Fifth Ave. & 49th St.)*. If you're at Saks, be sure to mosey across the street to see the nine-story **Christmas tree** ablaze with tiny lights in Rockefeller Plaza. For a break from the holiday chill, nab tickets for **Christmas Spectacular** at Radio City Music Hall, featuring the high-kicking **Rockettes** *(see Performing Arts)*, or the New York City Ballet's annual production of **George Balanchine's Nutcracker** *(212-870-5570)*.

Summer

July and August can be hot and sticky, and many New Yorkers flee the city, missing out on a great civic tradition: **free performances**, offered by some of the Big Apple's most renowned theatrical troupes and music groups. The **Metropolitan Opera**, the **New York Philharmonic** and the **Public Theater** all offer freebies in New York's parks. **SummerStage** in Central Park hosts some terrific performers as well. *For more information, see Calendar of Events or check local listings.* Another warm-weather tradition: a float on the Lake in Central Park. **Rowboats** are available for rent

from the Loeb Boathouse, or you can hire a **gondola** (complete with gondolier) for a more leisurely experience *(212-517-2233; www.thecentralparkboathouse.com)*.

Times Square★★

Seventh Ave. & Broadway between W. 42nd & W. 46th Sts. Any train to Times Sq.-42nd St.

Packed with people day and night (night is a relative term, as it never goes dark here), Times Square is the blazing heart of New York; a sensory burst of gigantic neon advertisements and electronic tickers, Jumbotrons, traffic, crowds and vendors. The newly renovated (some say sanitized) district stretches along Broadway and Seventh Avenue between 42nd and 46th streets and overflows into the side streets, which host dozens of Broadway theaters *(see Performing Arts)*. Times Square is especially festive at night, when after-theater audiences pour out into the streets to enjoy its bright lights and carnivalesque atmosphere. Don't expect to find any "old" New York here – with its corporate logos and international crowds, the area is now more than ever the crossroads of the world. Among the most audacious newcomers:

119

- **The ESPN Zone**
  (1472 Broadway at W. 42nd St.)
  is not only a sports store but a massive arcade and sports bar with more than 200 TV screens.
- **Toys R Us**
  (1514 Broadway at W. 44th St.)
  is a toy store and a small amusement park, complete with an indoor Ferris wheel and an animatronic dinosaur.
- **Virgin Megastore**
  (1540 Broadway at W. 45th St.)
  claims to be the world's largest music/entertainment emporium, with 70,000 square feet of space.

Circle Line Cruises

Pier 83 (W. 42nd St. at West Side Hwy.). 212-563-3200. www.circleline42.com.

Anchors aweigh! Taking a narrated boat ride is one of the best ways to learn about the city – Manhattan is an island, after all. And these guides know their stuff, peppering their running historical commentary with the latest in New York gossip (for instance, which celebrity paid how many millions for their apartment?).

The full island tour takes three hours, and on a sunny day the time breezes by. But there are shorter tours, too. Look online or check at the ticket counter for options, schedules and prices – and keep in mind that a Circle Line cruise is included with a CityPass discount ticket booklet *(see p. 17)*.

Carriage Rides in Central Park

©Jeff Greenberg/NYC&Co.

🐴 Carriage Rides in Central Park

Carriages line up on Central Park South (59th St.) between Fifth & Sixth Aves. and at Tavern on the Green. Central Park Carriages; 212-736-0680; $35–$100, depending on time of day & length of ride. N, R or W train to Fifth Ave.

Horse-drawn carriages have been a fixture in Central Park since the Victorian era. This old-fashioned mode of transport remains one of the most romantic and popular ways to see the southern tip of Central Park, even (or especially!) during the winter months, when drivers will give you a blanket to snuggle up in.

To arrange a carriage ride elsewhere in the city, try the number above or:

- **Manhattan Carriage Co.** – *212-664-1149*
- **Chateau Stables** – *212-246-0520.*

MUST DO

Grand Central on the Half Shell

Grand Central Terminal, lower level. 212-490-6650. www.oysterbarny.com. S, 4, 5, 6 or 7 train to Grand Central-42nd St.

Sure, its vaulted ceiling is magnificent (the tiles were designed by 19C artisan Rafael Gustavino), but the **Grand Central Oyster Bar** doesn't coast on atmosphere. New Yorkers come here for some of the best fresh seafood in the city. Settle in at the counter and order oysters Rockefeller and clam chowder – it's a tradition – or have a full meal in the restaurant. The steady flow of diners makes for great people-watching.

Lights, Camera, Action!

You've seen them on TV – people just like you sitting in the studio audiences of your favorite programs, hooting and hollering, groaning or laughing on cue. If that's what you're after, try to get tickets to a taping. Though most tickets are spoken for months or even years in advance, you may be able to get stand-by tickets if you're willing to call at a specific time or wait in line.

Here's how to get information about some of the shows:

- **Good Morning America** – *212-580-5176, www.abcnews.com.*
- **Late Night with Conan O'Brien** – *212-664-3056, www.nbc.com.*
- **The Late Show with David Letterman** – *212-247-6497, www.cbs.com.*
- **Live with Regis and Kelly** – *www.bventertainment.go.com.*

- **Saturday Night Live** – *212-664-3056, www.nbc.com.*
  If all else fails, you can jostle for a spot on camera outside the street-level **Today Show** studio (*Rockefeller Plaza at 49th St.; Mon–Fri 7am–10am; www.nbc.com*), or take a **guided tour of NBC studios** (*see Landmarks/ GE Building*).

Madame Tussauds

234 W. 42nd St. between Seventh & Eighth Aves. 800-246-8872. www.nycwax.com. Open Mon–Fri 10am–8pm, weekends 10am–10pm. $35. Any train to Times Square.

If a picture's worth a thousand words, then how many is a wax model worth? Judge for yourself at this popular "museum," named after a woman who made death masks from the guillotined heads of prominent victims of the French Revolution. In this branch of the famous London museum you will find more than 200 popular and historical personalities come eerily to life in galleries that show them off, warts and all (when they say realistic, they mean it!). Behind the Scenes tours detail the art and craft of making wax figures; there's also a 4D movie in the in-house theater.

See a Game at Yankee Stadium

161st St. & River Ave., the Bronx. Tour and ticket information at www.yankees.com. B, D or 4 train to 161st St.-Yankee Stadium.

After playing 85 seasons in their beloved Yankee Stadium, in 2009 the **New York Yankees** take up residence in a gleaming new home located just north of the

FOR FUN

121

orginal facility. Though the new Yankee Stadium boasts upgraded amenities, it's still "the House That Ruth Built": the dimensions of the new field match those of the old one, including the short right-field porch that was designed to maximize Ruth's left-handed swing. A game here is the modern-day equivalent of watching a gladiatorial contest in the Roman Coliseum. As the pin-striped Bronx Bombers take the field with military precision, the crowd explodes with hoots and hollers and, if the game is a good one, continues in the same vein for hours – fueled by a steady diet of beer, hot dogs and Cracker Jacks. If you're not around for the Apr–Oct season or if games are sold out (they often are), take a stadium tour. This way you'll get to check out various areas of the stadium plus Monument Park, where bronze plaques commemorate Yankee legends Lou Gehrig, Joe DiMaggio, Mickey Mantle and others.

Serendipity 3

225 E. 60th St. between Second & Third Aves. 212-838-3531. www.serendipity3.com. Open Sun–Thu 11:30am–midnight (Fri until 1am; Sat until 2am). N, R, W, 4, 5 or 6 train to Lexington Ave.-59th St.

Visitors rarely come upon this kid-friendly general store/soda fountain/restaurant serendipitously anymore. On the contrary: they flock to it, especially on weekends, when it provides the perfect pre- or post-Bloomingdale's boost. The place was founded in 1954 as New York's first "coffeehouse boutique"; Andy Warhol declared

it his favorite sweet shop and is said to have paid his bill here with drawings. Today frozen hot chocolate – served in parfait glasses, topped with fluffy whipped cream and sucked through a straw – is the specialty of the house. This patented delicacy, along with upscale diner fare, is served under an array of Tiffany lamps, amid a fascinating arrangement of historic bric-a-brac.

Biking In the City

For more information about biking in the city, visit www.bikenewyork. org or www.nycbikemaps.com

Though navigating Manhattan streets on a bike is unlikely to reduce your stress level, it's still possible to have some two-wheeled fun in New York. The city's parks department maintains a 32-mile bike circuit that takes cyclists from the Battery up the West Side, past the George Washington Bridge almost to the northern tip of Manhattan, then down the Harlem and East rivers and back to the Battery. A few spots along the north and east sections require a little street maneuvering; the smoothest paths and best views are up and down the West Side. Several bike shops can outfit you with a set of wheels, a helmet and a map.

A few to try:

- **Gotham Bikes** – *112 W. Broadway at Duane St. 212-732-2453. www.gothambikes.com*
- **City Bicycles** – *315 W. 38th St. 212-563-3373. www.citybicycles.net*
- **Bike and Roll** – *557 12th Ave. at 43rd St. 212-260-0400. www.bikeandroll.com*

Street Festivals

Whether a blockbuster event drawing throngs of revelers or a modest block party sponsored by a local neighborhood association, you'll likely find a parade, street fair, church festival or fun run going on somewhere in New York regardless of when you visit. You don't have to be a local to head on out and enjoy cultural traditions, sample the food, take in the street performers, do a little shopping...who knows?

If you like being around crowds, there's Chinatown's world-famous **Lunar New Year** parade in late January, the **Macy's Thanksgiving Day Parade** and the granddaddy of them all, the **New Year's Eve** celebration in Times Square. Fifth Avenue's **Museum Mile Festival** in late spring draws thousands to its live performances, outdoor art activities and free museum admissions. September brings the popular **Feast of San Gennaro** celebrations to **Mulberry Street** in Little Italy, a perfect time to sample Italian specialties (sign up for the cannoli-eating contest if you dare). *For more information, see Calendar of Events.*

Sports Museum of America

26 Broadway, at Beaver St. (entrance on Beaver St.). 212-747-0900. www.sportsmuseum.com. Open year-round daily 9am–7pm (last ticket 5:30pm). $24. 4 or 5 train to Bowling Green, or 1, R or W train to Rector St.

Ever imagined what a hockey game looks like from a goalie's point of view? Or pictured yourself as a pro football referee, making the tough call? Interactive multimedia exhibits put visitors in the middle of the action at this high-tech new museum in downtown Manhattan.

Chelsea Piers★

Pier 62, West Side Hwy. at W. 23rd St. 213-336-6666. www.chelseapiers.com

For a change from sightseeing, head to this enormous waterside sports complex, reclaimed in the mid-1990s from a couple of long-neglected piers. There's something here for every recreational taste;

the piers offer an ice-skating rink, bowling alley, pool, batting cages, toddler gym, rock-climbing wall, even a driving range and beach volleyball!

The High Line

212-206-9922. www.thehighline.org. Entrances at Gansevoort, 14th, 23rd and 30th Sts.

Paralleling the Hudson River between Gansevoort Street and 34th Street, a disused 1930s elevated railroad bed looms over the bustling thoroughfares. Climb on up and you'll find one of Manhattan's most unique public spaces: a pleasant, airy corridor of gardens, benches, water features and paths bending gently among the surrounding buildings with views of the river and the cityscape. It's a great place for a stroll. Plans call for the park eventually to extend all the way from the Meatpacking District to Penn Station.

FOR FUN

FOR KIDS

Don't be fooled by its cosmopolitan air – New York City loves to kid around: A city of parents, it teems with fun activities for families. Here's a roundup of some of our favorites.

American Museum of Natural History★★★

Central Park West between 77th & 81st Sts. 212-769-5100. www.amnh.org. Open year-round daily 10am–5:45pm. $15 adults, $8.50 children. Closed Thanksgiving Day & Dec 25. B or C train to 81st St. or 1 train to 79th St.

There's plenty of awesome stuff here to keep kids mesmerized for hours. Dinosaurs are a good place to start. Check out the huge barosaurus skeleton in the entrance rotunda, then ogle hundreds of specimens in six dazzling **fossil halls★★** on the fourth floor – the museum has the largest collection of vertebrate fossils in the world. Then proceed to the adjoining **Rose Center for Earth and Space★★**. Exhibits on the blue planet and its place in the universe are high-tech marvels, as are the space shows, which take place every half-hour in the

Hayden Sphere: tip back in your comfy chair and let Robert Redford be your guide *(advance tickets: 212-769-5200).*
For more kid-friendly activities at the museum, go to www.amnh.org/kids.

Bronx Zoo★★★

Bronx River Pkwy. at Fordham Rd. 718-367-1010. www.wcs.org. Open Apr–Oct Mon–Fri, 10am–5pm; weekends & hos 10am–5:30pm; rest of the year daily 10am–4:30pm. $15 adults, $11 children (ages 3-12).2 or 5 train to West Farms Sq./E. Tremont Ave.; an express bus ($5 each way; exact change or MetroCard required) makes stops along Madison Ave. to the zoo's Gate B.

The country's largest urban zoo is set in a woodland park that's so pretty you might forget that just around the corner you could meet a giraffe or an ostrich. From elegant ibex to goofy gibbons,

Siberian Tiger at Bronx Zoo

©Vladimir Korostyshevskiy/Dreamstime.com

MUST DO

the animals here enjoy homes that mirror their natural habitats as much as possible, thanks to the Wildlife Conservation Society, which runs the place.

The Tiger Mountain★★ exhibit lets you see eye to eye with these Siberian cats. A **Children's Zoo**★ *($3)* houses more than 500 animals and lets kids climb a rope spider web, try on a turtle's shell and feed goats, chickens and other barnyard critters.

Central Park★★★ for Kids

Bounded by 59th St & 110th St., Central Park West & Fifth Ave. 212-310-6600. www.centralpark nyc.org. N, R or W train to Fifth Ave.- 59th St.; A, B, C, D or 1 train to 59th St./Columbus Circle.

Besides offering plenty of space for sports and strolls, Central Park has attractions that appeal to kids of all ages. For more information on visiting the park, including details on boat and bicycle rental and ice skating, see the *Parks* chapter; for the day's calendar of events, drop by the visitor center in the Dairy, just south of the carousel *(call for seasonal hours; 212-794-6564).*

Carousel – *Midpark at 65th St. 212-879-0244. www.centralpark carousel.com. Open Apr–Nov daily 10am–6pm. Rest of the year daily (weather permitting), 10am–dusk.* This 1908 carousel incorporates 58 hand-carved, hand-painted horses – some life size! Taking it for a whirl is a New York tradition.

Central Park Wildlife Center – *East side between 63rd and 66th Sts. 212-439-6500. Open Apr–Oct Mon–Fri 10am–5pm; weekends 10am–5:30pm. Rest of the year daily*

10am–4:30pm. $8 adults, $3 children 3–12. Animals in this 5.5-acre zoo have space to roam in natural settings. Among the biggest (literally) crowd pleasers are the frisky sea lions, which are fed at 11:30am, 2pm and 4pm. Kids can pet and feed goats, sheep and a Vietnamese pot-bellied pig at the **Tisch Children's Zoo**, which is especially popular with the stroller set.

Belvedere Castle – *Midpark at 79th St. 212-772-0210. Open year-round Tue–Sun 10am–5pm. Closed major holidays.* The Henry Luce Nature Observatory features kid-friendly hands-on exhibits about the city's flora and fauna.

Swedish Cottage Marionette Theatre – *W. 79th St. and West Dr. 212-988-9093. Shows weekends 1pm; weekday showtimes vary. $6 adults, $5 children. Reservations required.* Original puppet shows are staged daily at this charming 1877 Swedish schoolhouse, many drawn from fairy tales and using puppets handmade by a dedicated band of puppeteers.

Empire State Building ★★★

Fifth Ave. & 34th St. 212-736-3100. www.esbnyc.com. Open year-round daily 8am–2am (last elevator up at 1:15am). $19 adults, $17 ages 12-17, $13 ages 6-11. Any train to 34th St-Herald Square. See Landmarks.

Kids love a trip to the top of this 102-story Art Deco landmark, where they can get dizzying views of New York City and its neighboring states. High-speed elevators zip up to the 86th floor, which has both a glass-enclosed area and spacious outdoor promenades.

FOR KIDS

Viewing Lower Manhattan from Empire State Building

©Bildagentur/Tips Images

High-powered binoculars let you zoom in on your favorite sites.

Statue of Liberty★★★

Liberty Island. 212-363-3200. www.nps.gov/stli. Closed Dec 25. For visitor information, see Landmarks.

A trip to New York wouldn't be complete without getting up close and personal with Lady Liberty, the towering symbol of democracy in New York harbor. Though the winding corkscrew staircase to the crown has been closed, you can still go inside the statue to see the original torch and a full-size replica of Lady Liberty's face (be sure to reserve a Monument Pass in advance!), plus historical exhibits and videos. Take the elevator to the 10th-floor observation platform, which boasts awesome views.

Lower East Side Tenement Museum★★

108 Orchard St. at Broome St. 212-982-8420. www.tenement.org. Open daily 11am–5pm. Visitor center and gift shop open Mon and Wed–Fri 11am–6pm (Thu until 8:15pm); weekends 10:45am–6pm. Closed major holidays. Tenements may be visited by 1hr guided tour only; call or check website for tour schedule and advance tickets. $17 adults, $13 students. F train to Delancey St.

Kids ages five and older – especially ones from the country or the suburbs – will never forget a visit to one of the cramped tenement apartments at 97 Orchard Street, especially if Victoria Confino is their guide. This early 20C teenager, played by a sassy young actress, will show you her apartment and relate in witty detail how work was parceled out, how marriages were arranged and how much monthly rent her family paid for the tiny space – $15, including coal.

New York Aquarium★★

W. 8th St. & Surf Ave., Brooklyn. 718-265-3474. www.nyaquarium. com. Open Jun–Aug daily10am– 6pm (weekend closing at 7pm). Rest of the year closing times vary. $13 adults, $9 children (ages 2-12). F or Q train to W. 8th St.

Just off the Coney Island boardwalk, this world-renowned aquarium – it's run by the Wildlife

---

Family Fun in the Big Apple

For more tips on what to do with kids – from suggested itineraries to parents' testimonials – go to New York City's official tourist website (*www.nycvisit.com*), and type "kids" into any search box.

Conservation Society – shows off 8,000 slippery critters in naturalistic indoor and outdoor habitats. Kids can explore the world of jellies in the **Alien Stingers**★★ exhibit and view octopi, walrus, sea lions, seahorses and penguins in the underwater viewing galleries of **Sea Cliffs**★.

Sea turtle at the New York Aquarium
©Sandy Matzen/BigStockPhoto.com

South Street Seaport Museum★★

12 Fulton Street, near Piers 15–17. For visit information, see Museums.

Apart from the shops and restaurants, younger visitors can have a terrific time at the museum's weekend family programs. On Saturdays kids can make arts, crafts and music, carve scrimshaw, learn knot-tying, or take a boat tour.

Museum of the City of New York★★

1220 Fifth Ave. at E. 103rd St. 212-534-1672. www.mcny.org. For visit information, see Museums.

The third-floor **Toy Gallery** in New York's history museum features an astonishing array of playthings, from plush teddy bears to intricate mechanical banks. Don't miss the exquisite dollhouses, including a 1769 Ann Anthony Pavilion, and a 1920s brownstone complete with artwork by Marcel Duchamp.

Forbes Galleries★

62 Fifth Ave at W. 12th St. 212-206-5548. www.forbesgalleries.com. For visit information, see Museums.

The wealthy Forbes family gathered an amazing trove of delightful objects now on display. Wander at will among the 12,000 toy soldiers arranged in battle scenes, or the 500 miniature boats ranging from Noah's ark to ocean liners. There are also versions of the popular board game Monopoly.

Just for Kids: Art Museums

Art museums have come a long way from the dry, brainy, kid-unfriendly experiences of yesteryear. These days children (and their parents) can take their pick of innovative programs, including workshops, podcasts and gallery explorations especially designed to engage and entertain kids and keep them coming back for more. Check out the Metropolitan Museum of Art's **Hello, Met!** program *(www.metmuseum.org)* or MoMA's **A Closer Look For Kids** *(www.moma.org)*. The Brooklyn Museum's Saturday **Arty Facts** program is designed just for kids ages 4–7 *(ww.brooklynmuseum.org)*. Check museum websites for schedules and extra online activities.

FOR KIDS

Cyclone Rollercoaster, Coney Island

©Terraxplorer/iStockphoto.com/

Sony Wonder Technology Lab★

[C] *on the map on inside front cover. In the Sony Plaza Building, 550 Madison Ave. at E. 56th St. 212-833-8100. www.sonywondertechlab.com. Open year-round Tue–Sat 10am–5pm. Closed Sun, Mon & major holidays. For advance reservations (highly recommended), check the website. E or V train to Fifth Ave./53rd St.*

Interactive exhibits at this futuristic play space in Sony Plaza will dazzle even the most tech-savvy kid. Take your card (issued at the entrance) and swipe it through the slot at each exhibit to watch, paint, create, and play. You can learn how movies are made and make a trailer of your own; create a computer racing game in the GameBuilder section; choose an instrument and join up with a (virtual) musical artist to be part of a performing group; and make a sand painting by projecting your own shadow on an interactive wall, among other things. A HD theater screens High-Def movies Parents take note: If this is one of

your child's must-sees, reserve at least a week ahead.

Coney Island

Brooklyn. www.coneyislandusa. com. Open daily in summer, weekends in fall and spring. D, F, N or Q train to Stillwell Ave.

New York's beachfront amusement park is a little seedy but still tons of fun. Take a stomach-dropping ride on the **Cyclone**, a 1927 wood-framed roller coaster, ride the gigantic Ferris wheel or catch a circus sideshow. A stroll along the wood-plank boardwalk that skirts the beach is a Coney Island tradition, as is a paper boat of fried clam strips; a drippy ice-cream cone, or a Coney Island hot dog from **Nathan's Famous** *(1310 Surf Ave. at Stillwell Ave.).*

Children's Museum of Manhattan

212 W. 83rd St. (between Broadway & Amsterdam Ave.). 212-721-1234. www.cmom.org. Open Tue–Sun 10am–5pm. Closed Mon & major holidays. $10 (adults & children). 1 train to 79th St.

MUST DO

Kids can spend many happy hours at Manhattan's only museum geared just for children. Five floors of hands-on exhibits explore the environment, forensic science, healthy living, world cultures and much more. Sections like "Little West Side" and "Playworks" cater to babies and preschoolers; a series of long-term temporary exhibits bring art and science to kids ages 6 and up.

Shopping Just for Kids

"When can we leave?"...something you won't be hearing from the little ones at these stores:

- **FAO Schwarz** – *Fifth Ave. at 58th St. 212-644-9400. www.fao.com.*
- **Toys R Us** – *Broadway at 44th St. 212-644-9400. www1.toysrus.com.*
- **American Girl Place** – *Fifth Ave. at 49th St. 877-247-5223. www.americangirl.com.*
- **Alexander Doll Co.** – *615 W. 31st St. 212-283-5900. www.madamealexander.com.*

Intrepid Sea, Air & Space Museum

Pier 86 (W. 46th St. at Twelfth Ave.). 212-245-0072. www.intrepid museum.org. Open Apr–Sept Mon–Fri 1am–5pm, weekends & holidays 10am–6pm; Oct–Mar Tue–Sun 10am–5pm. $19.50, ages 6–17 $14.50.

Berthed at a parklike pier in the Hudson River, the 1943 aircraft carrier USS *Intrepid* measures 898 feet and weighs in at 42,000 tons. During its 31 years of active service the massive vessel was a veritable city, providing its 3,500-member crew with everything from a haircut to an ice-cream sundae. Renovated in 2008, the *Intrepid* is the focal point of a state-of-the art museum complex with interactive displays. Its restored aircraft collection features the British Airways Concorde that crossed the Atlantic Ocean in 2 hours and 53 minutes. You can even explore the USS *Growler*, a guided-missile submarine.

USS Intrepid, Sea, Air & Space Museum

©Dantang/iStockphoto.com

PERFORMING ARTS

You can hardly think of New York City without thinking of Broadway shows, Off-Broadway shows, and Off-Off Broadway shows. As the undisputed arts capital of the US, New York offers entertainment for nearly every taste and budget. Here's a list of some of the most popular options in the city, but it's by no means comprehensive.

For daily schedules and critics' picks, see Practical Information, Media.

Broadway★★

The Broadway Line: 888-276-2392. www.livebroadway.com.

They say the neon lights are bright on Broadway – and rightly so. "The Great White Way" is synonymous with the country's best and most popular theater productions. Of course, this street isn't the only one lined with theaters; it merely forms the spine of the **Theater District★**, which extends roughly between 40th and 53rd streets from Sixth to Eighth avenues. Crowd-pleasing musicals abound, with some of the best hoofers burning up the boards and bringing down the house in shows like *The Lion King, Chicago, Hairspray* and *The Producers*. Serious drama balances the musical productions; recent revivals have included *A Man for All Seasons* and *Equus*.

Billboards on Broadway
Brigitta L. House/Michelin

Movie stars and pop-music legends will often open shows that run for years with rotating casts – some better than the originals.

TKTS

Waiting until the last minute doesn't always mean paying top dollar when it comes to theater tickets. If you're flexible with what you want to see, you can save 25 to 50 percent on tickets at TKTS. You can buy tickets for same-day evening performances and matinees at the **Times Square booth** *(Broadway & W. 47th St.; tickets for 2pm matinees go on sale at 10am; tickets for 8pm shows go on sale at 3pm)* or at the **South Street Seaport booth** *(corner of John & Front Sts.; tickets for evening shows go on sale at 11am; matinee tickets available a day in advance)*. Digital signs at both locations indicate which shows have tickets; availability changes hourly. For the best selection, arrive early, though sometimes tickets are released just before the 8pm curtain *(cash & traveler's checks only at Times Square location)*. For more information, check online at www.tdf.org/tkts.

Sometimes the play's not the only thing: several Broadway theater buildings are stars in their own right: *See Off-Broadway on following pages.*

Lyceum Theater

149–157 W. 45th St. between Broadway & Ave. of the Americas.

This 1903 structure boasts a grand Beaux-Arts facade and undulating marquee. It is the oldest New York theater still used for legitimate productions, and was the first to be landmarked.

Lunt-Fontanne Theater

205 W. 46th St. between Broadway & Eighth Ave.

The palazzo-style building was designed in 1910 by Carrère and Hastings. *The Sound of Music* premiered here.

Barrymore Theater

243-251 W. 47th St. between Broadway & Eighth Ave.

The marquee of this 1928 theater is held up by stunningly ornate ironwork. *A Streetcar Named Desire* had its Broadway debut here in 1947.

Lincoln Center★★

Columbus Ave. between W. 62nd & W. 65th Sts. 212-546-2656. www.lincolncenter.org.

Devoted to drama, music and dance, Lincoln Center for the Performing Arts is a 16-acre complex comprising five major theater and concert buildings, a library, a band shell and two outdoor plazas. Visually, the space is stunning, with sleek rectangular buildings of glass and Italian travertine marble arranged around a central foun-

Metropolitan Opera House

©Charles Weidig/BigStockPhoto.com

PERFORMING ARTS

The Rockettes

...5-6-7-8. The world's finest precision dance team began as the Missouri Rockettes in St. Louis in 1925, and they've been the star attraction at Radio City Music Hall since opening night – December 27, 1932. Today the annual Radio City Christmas Spectacular, with its cast of 140 leggy dancers, is a dazzling New York holiday tradition *(early Nov– late Dec; 2–5 performances daily)*.

The Famous Rockettes

Radio City Entertainment

tain. The centerpiece is the **Metropolitan Opera House**, with its 10-story colonnade. Although guided tours are available daily, the best way to appreciate Lincoln Center is to attend a performance. The regular season lasts from September through May; the summer season is filled with festivals and special events, including Lincoln Center Out of Doors, Midsummer Night Swing, Mostly Mozart, and the Lincoln Center Festival.

Backstage Tours – *Most weekdays 3:30pm; Sun 10:30am. Advance reservations recommended.* 212-769-7020. www.operaed.org. If you've always wanted to know what goes on behind the scenes, book a 90min in-depth tour of the Metropolitan Opera House. You'll be led from the shops where artisans create the sets, costumes and wigs; through the rehearsal space and dressing rooms; and finally to the vast stage and auditorium.

Resident Companies

Chamber Music Society of Lincoln Center – *212-875-5788. www.chambermusicsociety.org.* The nation's premier chamber music ensemble performs in 1,100-seat Alice Tully Hall, newly refurbished and reopened in spring 2009.

Jazz at Lincoln Center – *212-875-5350 (tours), 212-721-6500 (tickets). www.jalc.org.* Under the direction of Wynton Marsalis, the Lincoln Center Jazz Orchestra performs at the Time Warner Center at Columbus Circle *(Broadway & W. 60th St.).* Three spaces here are dedicated to jazz: the 1,100-seat Frederick P. Rose Hall, the 400-seat Allen Room, and the 140-seat Dizzy's Club Coca-Cola.

Metropolitan Opera – *212-362-6000. www.metopera.org.* The world-renowned company presides in the 3,788-seat Metropolitan Opera House. *For Backstage Tours, see above.*

New York City Ballet – *212-870-5570. www.nycballet.com.* The troupe performs in the 2,792-seat David Koch Theater, (formerly the New York State Theater), designed by Philip Johnson.

New York City Opera – *212-870-5570. www.nycopera.com.* With its emphasis on affordable productions and nonstandard repertoire, the New York City Opera also performs in the David Koch Theater.

New York Philharmonic – *212-875-5656. www.newyorkphilharmonic.org.* New York's resident symphony performs in 2,742-seat Avery Fisher Hall.

Radio City Music Hall★★

[P] *on the map on the inside front cover. 1260 Sixth Ave. at W. 50th St. 212-247-4777. www.radiocity.com.*

A treasured New York landmark, this Art Deco performance palace is a spectacular place to see a show – particularly the resident **Rockettes**, whose kick-line spectaculars are as mesmerizing as the place itself. Radio City opened its doors in 1932 and began by presenting the best vaudeville acts and silent pictures of its day. The 5,882-seat theater has been the site of some fantastic live performances (everyone from Frank Sinatra to Björk has graced its stage) as well as the annual Tony Awards for live theater.

Its famed proscenium arch rises six stories, and the state-of-the-art stage allows musicians in the orchestra and organists at the two electric Wurlitzers to be whisked away behind the walls or below the floor during performances – without missing a note!

©Ronen Perry/Wikimedia Commons

Radio City Music Hall

Brooklyn Academy of Music★

30 Lafayette Ave., Brooklyn. 718-636-4100. www.bam.org.

Widely regarded as New York's premier venue for avant-garde performance, Brooklyn Academy of Music (BAM) hosts live music, dance and theater in two historic buildings, plus experimental and first-run films in its Rose Cinemas. The elegant 1,100-seat opera house has hosted everyone from Enrico Caruso to Laurie Anderson. The 900-seat Harvey Theater is home to the Brooklyn Philharmonic Orchestra and is a favorite venue for cutting-edge theater troupes from around the world. BAM's annual **Next Wave Festival** *(Oct–Dec)* is one of the liveliest performing-arts festivals in the city.

Carnegie Hall

156 W. 57th St. at Seventh Ave. 212-247-7800. www.carnegiehall.org.

With its fine acoustics, majestic Carnegie Hall is one of the world's most prestigious concert venues. Named after steel magnate Andrew Carnegie, the Italian Renaissance structure opened in 1891 with Tchaikovsky's American conducting debut. Since then its stage has hosted luminaries from Gustav Mahler to Bob Dylan. Carnegie Hall has three performance spaces – the main 2,804-seat auditorium; the 268-seat **Weill Recital Hall**, which resembles a Belle Epoque salon; and the high-tech **Zankel Hall**, with 599 seats – and a museum.

BOX OFFICE

PERFORMING ARTS

BOX OFFICE

Apollo Theater

253 W. 125th St. 212-531-5305. www.apollotheater.org.

This world-famous Harlem theater has been a hotbed of African-American music and entertainment since 1934.

Every Wednesday night is **Amateur Night** – "where stars are born and legends are made." Who knows? You might see the debut of the next Ella Fitzgerald, James Brown, Michael Jackson or Lauryn Hill – all of whom launched their careers here. Tickets *($18–$40)* can be purchased at the box office *(open Mon, Tue, Thu & Fri 10am–6pm, Wed 10am–8:30pm, Sat noon–6pm)* or through Ticketmaster *(212-307-4100; www.ticketmaster.com)*.

City Center

131 W. 55th St between Sixth & Seventh Aves. 212-581-7907. www.nycitycenter.org.

After being threatened with demolition in the 1940s, this 1923 Shriner's temple reopened as a concert hall with ticket prices topping out at $2. Since 1994, the popular **Encores!** series has brought recognition to rarely heard works of American musical theater. The center also produces a popular **Fall for Dance** festival every autumn, featuring performances by dance companies from around the world. City Center hosts six resident performing companies, including the **Alvin Ailey American Dance Theater** *(www.alvinailey. org)* and the **American Ballet Theatre** *(www.abt.org). See Dance and Performance.*

Shahar Azran/Apollo Theater

MUST DO

©Jeff Greenberg/NYC&Co.

Times Square Crossover by night

Off-Broadway Theater

www.offbroadwayonline.com.

There are 150 spaces across the city that qualify as Off-Broadway theaters. While many of them lie outside the Theater District, the designation indicates more than their location. Off-Broadway tickets cost less than those to Broadway shows. Theaters are also smaller (100–499 seats), and performances more intimate. Some shows, like Stomp and Blue Man Group, remain on Off-Broadway for years (as did *The Fantasticks*, the longest-running musical in New York history). Others (*The 25th Annual Putnam County Spelling Bee*, *Rent, Proof, A Chorus Line*) start Off-Broadway and move to Broadway once they become bona fide hits. The following venues are all are based downtown:

Public Theater

425 Lafayette St. 212-260-2400. www.publictheater.org

Established in 1967 by Jospeh Papp, the Public mounts Shakespeare, new plays and musicals in its Lexington Avenue home, the former Astor library. The intimate Joe's Pub stage hosts new works and solo performers.

Atlantic Theater Company

336 W. 20th St. (Linda Gross Theater) and 330 W. 16th St. (Atlantic Stage 2). 212-645-1242. www.atlantictheater.org

Founded in 1985 by David Mamet and William H. Macy, the Atlantic has mounted works by Mamet, Woody Allen and Tom Donaghy among others. The organization has two stages and runs a respected acting school.

Stagedoor Annies

Can't leave New York without the autograph of your favorite theater star? Grab your program and an indelible pen and jostle with the crowds lining up in Shubert Alley, the pedestrian lane that runs from W. 44th to W. 45th Streets between Broadway and Eighth Ave. It's theater tradition.

New York Theater Workshop

79 E. 4th St. 212-460-5475.
www.nytw.org

Musicals, experimental drama and readings all fill the bill at this 195-seat space. The theater has featured works by Tony Kushner, Athol Fugard and Claudia Shear.

Playwrights Horizons

416 W. 42nd St. 212-279-4200.
www.playwrightshorizons.org.

This "writer's theater" presents work by both veteran and emerging playwrights on its two stages. There are also upwards of 20 readings each season.

Off-Off Broadway Theater

If Off-Broadway doesn't get you far enough away from the Great White Way, consider going Off-Off. This designation goes to venues with fewer than 100 seats. For the most part, these are productions done on a shoestring by playwrights whose work lies far outside the mainstream, or by actors and directors who want to "make theater" from scratch. These shows have short runs, and you can get tickets, usually for under $20 apiece, directly from the theaters. Consult the *Village Voice* for complete listings. A few venues to look for:

The Flea

41 White St. between Broadway & Church St., TriBeCa. 212-226-2407.
www.theflea.org.

Avant-garde work, such as that of wordsmith Mac Wellman, is presented in a space run by Jim Simpson, the husband of Sigourney Weaver.

HERE

145 Ave. of the Americas at Broome St., SoHo. 212-352-3101.
www.here.org.

This pleasant multi-use venue has three small stages, as well as an art gallery and a cafe. The theaters are often rented out by long-standing Off-Off Broadway companies, as well as actors trying solo material.

PS 122

150 First Ave. at E. 9th St., East Village. 212-477-5288.
www.ps122.org.

A former public school, this East Village mainstay puts on a range of offbeat performances, many mixing theater with music, dance or film.

Center Stage NY

48 W. 21st St., Chelsea.
212-929-2228.
www.centerstageny.com.

This 70-seat space is home to several theater organizations including Phillip Seymour Hoffman's Labyrinth Group.

Classical Music and Opera

Bargemusic

Fulton Ferry Landing, just south of the Brooklyn Bridge. Brooklyn. 718-624-2083 or 718-624-4061.
www.bargemusic.org.

Though few might have guessed that a coffee barge could be a proper setting for chamber music,

Opera Omnia

www.operaomnia.org. New York has something for everyone–even, it seems, for die-hard fans of baroque opera. Venues vary for this young company's productions of early operatic works; its inaugural production of Monteverdi's *Coronation of Poppea* drew rave reviews.

native New Yorker Olga Bloom thought it would, and made it so. That was 20 years ago, and since then Bargemusic has been going strong, holding about 100 world-class recitals a year. It's a totally unique musical evening.

To make it an all-Brooklyn night, have dinner at the nearby River Cafe *(1 Water St., 718-522-5200; www.rivercafe.com).*

Carnegie Hall

156 W. 57th St. at Seventh Ave., Central Midtown.

One of the world's most prestigious concert venues, the 1891 hall has three classical music stages.

Lincoln Center

Broadway between W. 57th & W. 62nd Sts., Upper West Side.

New York's premier cultural center has 12 constituent companies, including the Metropolitan Opera, The New York City Opera, the New York Philharmonic, and the New York City Ballet.

Symphony Space

2537 Broadway at W. 95th St., Upper West Side. 212-864-1414. www.symphonyspace.org.

The varied programming here includes the annual 12-hour Wall to Wall, a celebration of works by a specific composer as performed by a variety of musicians.

Miller Theater

2960 Broadway at W. 116th St., Upper West Side. 212-854-7799. www.millertheater.com

With tickets priced for a student budget, Columbia University's Miller Theater presents world-class musical performances ranging from Bach concertos to experi-

Lincoln Center

©S. Berger/NYC&Co.

The Center gets a Facelift

In March 2006 Lincoln Center broke ground on an extended series of renovations aimed at making the complex and its resident organizations more open and accessible to the public. Plans call for an innovative new Visitor Center designed by Tod Williams Billie Tsien Architects to occupy the former Harmony Atrium *(Broadway and Columbus Ave at 62nd St)*. Guided tours will depart from here, and the facility will house a full-service cafe, a visitor information desk, and a centralized box office where you'll be able to buy discounted same-day tickets to all performances by Lincoln Center and its resident organizations. The Visitor Center is projected to open in fall 2009.

mental work by living composers like Steve Reich and John Zorn.

DiCapo Opera Theater

184 E. 76th St. 212-288-9438. www.dicapo.com.

The troupe puts on a full slate of traditional, contemporary and family-friendly productions in its renovated 204-seat space on the lower level of the Church of St. Jean Baptiste.

Music Schools

To hear free classical music, try attending a student recital at the **Juilliard School** *(60 Lincoln Center Plaza; 212-769-7406; www.juilliard.edu)* or the **Manhattan School of Music** *(120 Claremont Ave. at W. 122nd St; 917-493-4428; www.msmnyc.edu)*. Both institutions rank among the country's best conservatories.

Dance and Performance

Brooklyn Academy of Music

30 Lafayette Ave. between Ashland Pl. & St. Felix St., Brooklyn. 718-636-4100. www.bam.org.

Boasting two major performance spaces and a cinema, BAM has become Brooklyn's version

of Lincoln Center. But while opera and classical music both have their place here, it's the annual **Next Wave Festival** (fall and winter) that garners the headlines, presenting a roster of established and emerging avant-garde dancers and performers.

City Center Theater

131 W. 55th St. between Ave. of the Americas & Seventh Aves., Central Midtown. 212-581-1212. www.citycenter.org.

This ornate auditorium has been hosting first-rate dance for decades. **The American Ballet Theater** performs here in the fall, the **Alvin Ailey American Dance Theater** in the winter, Paul Taylor's in the spring. Twyla Tharp and Merce Cunningham frequently drop in for shorter runs. The Off-Broadway Manhattan Theatre Club puts on plays at two smaller stages here.

Joyce Theater

175 Eighth Ave. at W. 19th St., Chelsea. 212-242-0800. www.joyce.org.

Modern dancers from such heavy-hitters as the **Martha Graham Dance Company** and the **Ballet**

Hispanico take the stage at this 472-seat Art Deco theater. A second, smaller space, **Joyce SoHo** *(155 Mercer St. between Houston & Prince Sts.; 212-431-9233)*, nurtures emerging talent.

Dance Theater Workshop

219 W. 19th St. at Seventh Ave., Chelsea. 212-924-0077. www.dancetheaterworkshop.org.

The 184-seat theater has contemporary dance and performance art shows, hosting 45 different artists or companies each season.

Baryshnikov Arts Center

450 W. 37th St., Midtown. 646-731-3200. www.whiteoak danceproject.com.

Dance and performance pieces by visiting companies are staged in the center's new 299-seat Jerome Robbins Theater. There's also an active artist-in-residence program and classical music concert series.

Modern Dance

New York is the undisputed capital of modern dance in the US, nurturing world-renowned companies since the form emerged in the early 20C. Not all the organizations headquartered here perform regularly in the city though, so check the websites to see if a New York performance is on the calendar during your visit.

- **Alvin Ailey American Dance Theater** – *212-405-9000. www.alvinailey.org.* December–January season at New York City Center.
- **Martha Graham Dance Company** – *212-521-3611.*

www.marthagraham.org. Performances at the Joyce Theater.
- **Merce Cunningham Dance Company** – *212-255-8240. www.merce.org.*
- **Paul Taylor Dance Company** – *212-431-5562. www.ptdc.org.* Feb–Mar season at New York City Center.

Movies and Filmmaking

Museum of the Moving Image★

35th Ave. at 36th St., Queens. 718-784-0077. www.moving image.us. For visit information, see Boroughs/Queens.

The excellent on-site film program here is well-known to local buffs. During its ongoing renovation, the museum is sponsoring screenings and premieres at other theaters throughout the city.

Brooklyn Academy of Music

30 Lafayette Ave. between Ashland Pl. & St. Felix Sts., Brooklyn. 718-636-4100. www.bam.org.

BAM's Rose Cinemas host a regular slate of new releases, and its popular **cinématek** program presents classics, festivals and thought-provoking retrospectives.

Film Society of Lincoln Center

70 Lincoln Center Plaza. 212-875-5600. www.filmlinc.com

Host of the renowned New York Film Festival *(see Calendar of Events)*, the Lincoln Center organization presents new films and major retrospectives year-round in the Walter Reade Theater.

PERFORMING ARTS

NIGHTLIFE

Jump on the subway at three or four in the morning and you'll find the rumor is true: New York really is the city that never sleeps. Gotham comes alive each night in its pubs and clubs, many offering music and live entertainment. Here's a selection of some of the most atmospheric venues. Check local listings for what's on tap when you're in town.

Listings

To see what's on while you're here, pick up a copy of the latest *Time Out New York* or *New Yorker* (both are available at newsstands) or grab a free *L Magazine* or *Village Voice* from a corner newspaper box or visitor information center.

Cabaret

Café Carlyle

35 E. 76th St. at Madison Ave., Upper East Side. 212-744-1600. www.thecarlyle.com.

A timeless institution, the Carlyle was singer Bobby Short's home base for decades prior to his death in 2005. The mural-bedecked space now hosts world-famous musicians from saxophonist Woody Allen to gravelly voiced alto Elaine Stritch.

Don't Tell Mama

343 W. 46th St. between Eighth & Ninth Aves., Theater District. 212-757-0788. www.donttellmamanyc.com.

This Restaurant Row institution offers a rowdy good time as Broadway hopefuls (including the waiters) and intrepid audience members take their turns belting out show tunes in the piano bar; two cabaret theaters have more traditional shows (covers $10–15).

Joe's Pub

425 Lafayette St. at Astor Pl. 212-539-8778. www.joespub.com.

Singer-songwriters the world over clamor to perform at this intimate downtown supper club, part of the Public Theater complex. Arrive early or make a dinner reservation to snag a good seat.

Oak Room

59 W. 44th St. at Sixth Ave., Midtown. 212-840-6800. www.algonquinhotel.com.

Ensconced in the **Algonquin Hotel**, which lent its name (and its bar) to the acid-witted writers who became known as the Algonquin Roundtable, the cozy Oak Room serves up first-rate cabaret. Recent performers have included Andrea Marcovicci and John Pizzarelli.

Metropolitan Room

34 W. 22nd St between Fifth and Sixth Aves., Chelsea. 212-206-0440. http://metropolitanroom.com.

An unassuming storefront facade leads to a comfy cabaret space with excellent acts. Fairly new on the scene, the Metropolitan has booked headliners including Maureen McGovern, Marilyn Maye and Andrea McArdle.

MUST DO

Cocktail Lounges

Bemelmans Bar

35 E. 76th St. at Madison Ave., Upper East Side. 212-744-1600. www.thecarlyle.com.

The sister venue of Cafe Carlyle *(above)* recently got a makeover that deepened its Rat Pack-era allure. Cocoon-like banquettes make listening to jazz here a decadent experience.

Campbell Apartment

15 Vanderbilt Ave., between E. 42nd & E. 43rd Sts., Midtown. 212-953-0409.

You can't help but be amazed when you enter this ornate vaulted space, which executive John W. Campbell turned into a sumptuous office in the 1930s. Today it's a one-of-a-kind bar that feels like a speakeasy – though it's just steps from bustling Grand Central Terminal. A hidden gem.

Lobby Lounge

8 W. 60th St. at Broadway, Upper West Side. 212-805-8800.

Not your ordinary hotel bar, the Lobby Lounge – perched on the 35th floor of the Mandarin Oriental Hotel in the Time Warner Center – has vertiginous views of Central Park South and the city beyond. Perfect for a nightcap or an afternoon tea.

Pravda

281 Lafayette St, between Houston and Prince Sts., SoHo. 212-226-4696.

This subterranean hotspot is the perfect place to retreat for a pre- or post-dinner cocktail downtown. Red banquettes and flickering candles set a cozy mood. The only things Russian about the place are the Cyrillic posters on the walls and the 70 varieties of vodka.

Rainbow Grill

30 Rockefeller Plaza, Midtown. 212-632-5100. www.rainbowroom.com.

Few bars are more romantic than this one, an Art Deco lounge with panoramic views of Manhattan from the 65th floor. Come for a cocktail and stay for a Northern Italian dinner (jackets requested; no T-shirts, jeans or sneakers). On selected Fridays and Saturdays, the adjoining Rainbow Room hosts a live big band for a night of dinner and dancing.

Rise

2 West St. at Battery Pl., Battery Park City. 917-790-2626.

Drink in panoramic vistas of the harbor and Statue of Liberty from this 14th-floor perch inside the swank Ritz-Carlton hotel, whose open-air terrace is a real treat on warm summer nights.

World Bar

845 United Nations Plaza (First Ave.) between E. 47th & E. 48th Sts., East Midtown. 212-935-9361.

This retro-chic cocktail lounge in Trump World Tower is popular with neighborhood diplomats. If you're feeling flush, try the World Cocktail, complete with edible gold.

Comedy Clubs

Comix

353 W. 14th St., between Eighth and Ninth Aves., Meatpacking District. 212-524-2500. www.comixny.com.

Opened in fall 2006, this is one of the bigger comedy ventures in town, with tiered seating around a stage large enough for sketch troupes but not too big for a single comic. Try to catch British expat and *Daily Show* regular John Oliver.

Gotham Comedy Club

208 W. 23rd St., between Seventh & Eighth Aves., Chelsea. 212-367-9000. www.gotham comedyclub.com.

One of New York's leading stand-up clubs, Gotham's roomy space hosts everyone from unknowns to celebrities – as long as they're funny. You be the judge. Jerry Seinfeld has been known to drop in here to test-drive his new material, and even the hosts make the most of their moments at the mike.

Upright Citizens Brigade Theater

307 W. 26th St. between Eighth and Ninth Aves., Chelsea. 212-366-9176. www.ucbtheatre.com.

Saturday Night Live-style sketch comedy and improv – sometimes even with SNL stars – are trotted out nightly here at bargain prices. Brigade alumni include writers for SNL, The Daily Show, 30 Rock and other TV shows.

Dance Clubs

APT

419 W. 13th St. between Ninth & Tenth Aves., Meatpacking District. 212-414-4245. www.aptwebsite.com.

Dress to impress if you want to get into this bi-level DJ lounge, a fixture on the underground music scene; the doormen can be highly selective about who gets in.

Cielo

18 Little W. 12th St. between Ninth Ave. & Washington St., Meatpacking District. 212-645-5700.

The sunken dance floor, world-famous DJs and throbbing sound system have drawn legions of clubgoers to this relatively small space in the Meatpacking District.

Club Shelter

Club Shelter

150 Varick St. between Spring and Vandam St, SoHo. 646-862-6117. www.clubshelter.com.

It may not be in the most happening 'hood, but this Saturday-night (and on into Sunday morning) house party has offered some of the best, sweatiest beats in the city for fifteen years, a virtual eternity in the notoriously fickle club world.

Lotus

409 W. 14th St., between Ninth and Tenth Aves. 212-243-4420. www.lotusnewyork.com.

The quintessential Meatpacking District club, this three-tiered glamour palace boasts a fancy restaurant, multiple lounges and a disco.

Sapphire

249 Eldridge St. between Houston & Stanton Sts., Lower East Side. 212-777-5153.

Sapphire has been spinning funk, hip-hop and house seven nights a week for more than a decade.

Happy "hour" lasts from 7pm to 10pm, and the cover is waived on Fridays and Saturdays before 11pm because, you guessed it, things don't really get going till well after midnight.

S.O.B.'s (Sounds of Brazil)

204 Varick St. at Houston St. 212-243-4940. www.sobs.com.

New York's premier world-music venue has tropical decor, a cabana-like bar, and a menu with tasty Brazilian and Portuguese specialties. When the music starts pumping, the crowd hits the dance floor.

Jazz Clubs

B.B. King Blues Club & Grill

237 W. 42nd St. between Seventh & Eighth Aves., Times Square. 212-997-4144. www.bbkingblues.com.

The massive Times Square club has hosted blues greats like Ray Charles, George Clinton and Peter Frampton. The Harlem Gospel Choir accompanies a buffet brunch every Sunday.

NIGHTLIFE

Blue Note Jazz Club

131 W. 3rd St., between Sixth Ave. & MacDougal St. 212-475-8592. www.bluenote.net.

Incredible acoustics, an intimate setting and a stellar lineup (often two top artists in one evening) make this one of the city's best jazz clubs. Continental cuisine is served late.

Iridium Jazz Club

1650 Broadway at W. 51st St. 212-582-2121. www.iridiumjazzclub.com.

This relative newcomer to New York's jazz scene has won fans with its impressive roster of artists (Les Paul, Arturo Sandoval, Eddie Daniels) and its 600-bottle wine list.

Jazz Gallery

290 Hudson St., between Dominick and Spring Sts., SoHo. 212-242-1063, www.jazzgallery.org.

This terrific little second-floor club is one of the city's great jazz secrets, with none of the commercialism of the larger venues and lots of hardcore regulars. Seats are folding chairs and benches. There's no bar, but you can get a glass of wine in a plastic cup. Trumpeter Roy Hargrove got his start here and sometimes comes back with his big band, a real treat.

Jazz Standard

116 E. 27th St., between Lexington & Park Aves. 212-576-2232. www.jazzstandard.net.

There's no minimum food or drink order here, because the owners are certain you'll want baby back ribs and pan-fried catfish from Blue Smoke restaurant upstairs. Superlative bookings and crystalline sound make this a great choice.

Lenox Lounge

288 Lenox Ave., between 124th & 125th Sts., Harlem. 212-427-0253. www.lenoxlounge.com.

When film producers search for an authentic Harlem club of the 1920s, they look no farther than the Lounge. Live jazz and blues are played six nights a week in the Zebra Room. Southern fried chicken, barbecued ribs, and crab cakes are served up daily.

Blue Note Jazz Club

©JTB/Photoshot

MUST DO

Smoke

2751 Broadway between W. 105th & W. 106th Sts., Upper West Side. 212-864-6662. www.smokejazz.com.

One of New York's most popular small clubs offers Monday-night jam sessions, Hammond B3 organ grooves and some of the city's hottest jazz stars (often with no cover charge) in a neighborhood with otherwise slim entertainment pickings.

 Village Vanguard

178 Seventh Ave. at W. 11th St., Greenwich Village. 212-255-4037. www.villagevanguard.com.

Photographs of Bill Evans and other jazz greats line the walls, and top-billing jazz musicians take the stage at New York's oldest jazz club, in Greenwich Village. Musicians often drop in after their gigs at other clubs for late-night jam sessions.

Rock and Pop

Beacon Theatre

2124 Broadway at W. 74th St., Upper West Side. 212-465-6500. www.beacontheater.com.

Come see touring singer-songwriters like Bob Dylan, Lenny Kravitz and Lucinda Williams at this wondrous 1929 venue, a stunning assemblage of rococo curlicues and red velvet that somehow manages to be vast and intimate at the same time.

Bowery Ballroom

6 Delancey St. between Bowery & Chrystie Sts., Lower East Side. 212-533-2111. www.bowery ballroom.com.

This onetime vaudeville club and shoe store has become a top venue for touring indie-rock bands since opening in 1998. Its main space has a wraparound balcony.

Fillmore NY at Irving Plaza

17 Irving Pl. at E. 15th St. 212-777-6800. www.irvingplaza.com.

Big indie bands like Built to Spill and the New York Dolls, as well as legends like Tom Jones and Deborah Harry, have played at this newly renovated club, now run by Live Nation; stand close to the stage for the best acoustics.

Madison Square Garden

Seventh Ave. between W. 31st & 33rd Sts., Garment District. 212-465-6741. www.thegarden.com.

The vast space that hosts the New York Knicks and the Westminster Dog Show also welcomes Elton John and Duran Duran when they come to town. Also onsite is a new, smaller space, the WaMu

NIGHTLIFE

Highline Ballroom

©Highline Ballroom

Theater, where the last row is less than 200 feet from the stage.

Radio City Music Hall

1260 Sixth Ave. at 50th St., Central Midtown. www.radiocity.com.

The **Rockettes** aren't the only ones to grace the stage of this 6,000-seat Art Deco landmark, part of the Rockefeller Center complex. So do big-name crooners, including Björk, Carly Simon, Alanis Morissette and Tony Bennett. It's worth it to get tickets just to see the magical interior.

Indie Rock and Avant-Garde

Arlene's Grocery

95 Stanton St. between Ludlow & Orchard Sts., Lower East Side. 212-358-1633. www.arlenes grocery.net.

Named for the Lower East Side bodega it once replaced, the tiny club hosts up to seven bands a night. Go Monday night for punk and heavy-metal karaoke. The bar opens at 1pm, music starts around 7pm, doors close at 4am.

Highline Ballroom

431 W. 16th St., between Ninth and Tenth Aves., Chelsea. 212-414-5994. www.highlineballroom.com.

Eclectic programming and ear-tingling acoustics define this new industrial-chic venue, opened in 2007 by the owner of the B.B. King Blues Club. Opening night featured Lou Reed; since then the stage has been graced by performance artist Diamanda Galas, indie rockers the Squirrel Nut Zippers, singer-songwriter Suzanne Vega and others. Upscale bar food includes mini Kobe beef burgers, and 25 cents of every ticket sale go to the restoration of nearby Highline Park.

Mercury Lounge

217 E. Houston St. between Ludlow & Essex Sts., Lower East Side. 212-260-4700. www.mercury loungenyc.com.

A long, dimly lit bar greets visitors to this indie- and roots-rock club. Behind the velvet curtain is an intimate (250-capacity) space with exposed brick walls, a raised stage and a formidable sound system.

Knitting Factory

74 Leonard St., between Broadway & Church St., Tribeca. 212-219-3132. www.knittingfactory.com.

Legendary home of the musical avant-garde, the club hosts live jazz and rock upstairs, more experimental music below – and 18 varieties of beer on tap.

Pianos

158 Ludlow St. between Rivington & Stanton Sts., Lower East Side. 212-505-3733. www.pianosnyc.com.

You'd think that a former piano factory would give patrons plenty of room to spread out. Not so at this bi-level supper club, a magnet for urban hipsters. There are often three bands a night – and a DJ. Happy hour lasts from 5pm to 7pm, and dinner is served till 1am.

The Living Room

154 Ludlow St. betweein Rivington & Stanton Sts., Lower East Side. 212-533-7235. www.livingroomny.com.

An intimate venue for the mellower crowd, the Living Room books

up-and-coming small groups and singer-songwriter.s

Blender Theater at Gramercy

158 Ludlow St. between Rivington & Stanton Sts., Lower East Side. www.irvingplaza.com

This smallish venue used to be a movie theater; head for the old stadium seats at the back if you need a break from the floor. The acoustics are great no matter where you plant.

Le Poisson Rouge

158 Bleecker St. between Sullivan and Thompson Sts., Greenwich Village. 212-796-0741. www.lepoissonrouge.com

With a mix of musical offerings and a crowd of regulars that can only be described as eclectic, this Greewich Village venue packs them in. Tables are set about the multilevel space around a central stage, where you might see anything from Lou Reed to They Might Be Giants, depending on the night.

©Gregphoto.com

Le Poisson Rouge

NIGHTLIFE

SHOPPING

Fashion victims unite! No matter if you have champagne tastes and a beer budget, there's something to suit everyone in New York City. Consider taking a guided shopping tour, a popular way to hit the hotspots and get the inside scoop on bargains *(Shop Gotham; 212-209-3370; www.shopgotham.com)*.

Fifth Avenue★★★

Upscale boutiques and department stores line world-famous Fifth Avenue between 34th and 59th streets. Even if you don't set foot inside a single one, their elaborate window displays turn a simple stroll into a dazzling adventure.

Fifth Avenue Roll Call

- **Bergdorf Goodman** – *Between 57th & 58th Sts.* 212-753-7300. *www.bergdorfgoodman.com.* Understated elegance has been the key to the store's lasting ap-

peal among "ladies who lunch" and the men who love them.

- **Cartier** – *At 52nd St.* 212-753-0111. *www.cartier.com.* French jewelry, sold at this Renaissance-style palazzo since 1917.

- **FAO Schwarz** – *At 58th St.* 212-644-9400. *www.fao.com.* Kids of all ages adore this world-famous toy store, founded by German immigrant Frederick August Otto Schwarz in 1862.

- **Rockefeller Center** – *47th–51st Sts.* 212-632-3975. *www.rockefellercenter.com.* Buy

Fifth Avenue Shopping

CENTRAL PARK

Grand Army Plaza

Crate & Barrel

Central · Park South

E. 59th St.

Plaza Hotel

General Motors · Baccarat

FAO Schwartz

W. 58th St. · Bergdorf Goodman ▲ · Bergdorf Goodman ● Ermenegildo Zegna · Chanel

Louis Vuitton ●

W. 57th St. · Tiffany & Co. · Burberry

Bulgari ● · Tourneau

Prada ● · Niketown

Harry Winston ● · Trump Tower

W. 56th St. · Henri Bendel ● · Hugo Boss · Escada

Fifth Ave. Presbyterian

W. 55th St. · St. Regis-Sheraton

Takashimaya ▲

W. 54th St. · Gucci

THE MUSEUM OF MODERN ART · Bruno Magli ● · Thomas Pink

53rd St. · St. Thomas · Fogal ● · Cellini

CBS Building · Hickey Freeman ● · Salvatore Ferragamo

W. 52nd St. · Cartier ●

· Versace ●

H&M ● · Jimmy Choo ●

W. 51st St. · St. Patrick's Cathedral

Radio City Music Hall · ROCKEFELLER CENTER

GE Building · Saks Fifth Avenue · Waldorf-Astoria

W. 50th St.

Channel Gardens

Lacoste ● · American Girl Place

W. 48th St.

AVENUE · FIFTH · Madison · Park · Lexington

● Retail Store ▲ Department Store

Fifth Avenue

anything from Japanese books to Italian leather in shops lining the plazas and concourses.

- **Saks Fifth Avenue** – *At 50th St. 212-753-4000. www.saks.com.* Upper floors at Saks' flagship feature exclusive upscale boutiques with plenty of clerks on call.

  🔹**Tiffany & Co.** – *At 57th St. 212-755-8000. www.tiffany.com.* For silver, pearls and diamonds, Tiffany is the *crème de la crème*.

- **Henri Bendel** – *At 56th St. 212-247-1100. www.henribendel. com.* Upscale womenswear and accessories take center stage at Bendel, reputedly the first US store to feature Coco Chanel.

- **Lord & Taylor** – *At 38th St. 212-391-3344. www.lordandtaylor. com.* Look for high-end brands for men and women at this landmark store, flagship of the oldest upscale department-store chain in the US.

- **Takashimaya** – *at 54th St. 212-350-0100. www.takashi-maya-ny.com.* East meets West in the sleek department store's tranquil interiors and carefully "curated" merchandise.

Times Square★★

42nd–46th Sts. & Broadway.

New York's commercial heart is ablaze day and night with stores and vendors vying for visitors' attention. Kids will love **Toys R Us** *(1514 Broadway; 800-869-7787; www.toysrus.com)*, where they can greet Barbie in a life-size house.

Madison Avenue★★

Though it has stiff competition from Fifth Avenue, Madison Avenue between 59th and 78th streets remains the most luxurious 🔹**shopping** strip in the city.

- Native son **Calvin Klein** anchors the southern end with a palace for clothing and home furnishings *(no. 654; 212-292-9000; www.calvinklein.com)*.

- **Barneys** has nine exuberant storys of chic brands *(no. 660; 212-826-8900; www.barneys.com)*

- Impeccable French accessories designer **Hermès** has a shop at 691 Madison Ave. *(212-751-3181; www.hermes.com)*.

- **Emilio Pucci** flogs wildly patterned togs at 24 E. 64th St. *(212-752-4777; www.emiliopucci.com)*.

Madison Avenue Stores			
Store	Address	Telephone	Website
Baccarat	625 Madison Ave.	212-826-4100	www.baccarat.com
Barneys	660 Madison Ave.	212-826-8900	www.barneys.com
Betsey Johnson	1060 Madison Ave.	212-734-1257	www.betseyjohnson.com
Calvin Klein	654 Madison Ave.	212-292-9000	www.calvinklein.com
Daum	694 Madison Ave.	212-355-2060	www.daum.fr
DKNY	655 Madison Ave.	212-223-3569	www.dkny.com
Emanuel Ungaro	792 Madison Ave.	212-249-4090	www.emanuelungaro.com
Giorgio Armani	760 Madison Ave.	212-988-9191	www.giorgioarmani.com
Polo Ralph Lauren	867 Madison Ave.	212-606-2100	www.polo.com
Prada	841 Madison Ave.	212-327-4200	www.prada.com
Steuben	667 Madison Ave.	212-752-1441	www.steuben.com
Swarovski	625 Madison Ave.	212-308-1710	www.swarovski.com
Valentino	747 Madison Ave.	212-772-6969	www.valentino.com

- **Emanuel Ungaro** has a pink staircase to match his signature floral print dresses *(no. 792; 212-249-4090; www.emanuelungaro.com).*
- Men gravitate toward **Giorgio Armani** for European-style suits and torso-hugging T-shirts *(no. 760; 212-988-9191; www.giorgioarmani.com).*
- Bronx-born **Ralph Lauren** (née Ralph Lifschitz) displays his timeless fashions in the opulent 1895 Gertrude Rhinelander Waldo House *(no. 867; 212-606-2100; www.polo.com).*
- Farther north you'll find the super-luxe French shoe store **Christian Louboutin** *(no. 965; 212-396-1884).*
- The Japanese designer **Issey Miyake** showcases wearable art at no. 802 *(212-439-7822; www.isseymiyake.com).*

Bridgemarket★

E. 59th St. & First Ave.

An immense, cathedral-like hall under the roadway to the Queensboro Bridge has been restored to its original grandeur, thanks to the efforts of British designer Terence Conran, who in the early 1990s signed on to develop a shop and restaurant on the site. Credit for the glorious results goes largely to the father-and-son team Rafael and Rafael Guastavino, Italian artisans who covered the vaulted ceilings with thousands of clay tiles in the early 1900s. Today the **Conran Shop** houseware and design emporium is a favorite among savvy shoppers *(407 E. 59th St.; 866-755-9079; www.conranusa.com).*

Madison's Sparkling Lineup

Baccarat *(no. 625; 212-826-4100; www.baccarat.com)* traces its lineage back to 1764. Its 4,500-square-foot US flagship has two floors of sparkling wares.

Daum *(no. 694; 212-355-2060; www.daum.fr)* has been around for 120 years and showcases designs specially created by avant-garde artists, including Salvador Dalí.

Lalique *(no. 712; 212-355-6550; www.cristallalique.com)* offers crystal as well as luxury goods including silk scarves, perfume and porcelain.

Steuben *(no. 667; 212-752-1441; www.steuben.com)* moved to this location in 2000, selling its trademark animal figurines as well as bowls and vases.

Swarovski *(no. 625; 212-308-1710; www.swarovski.com)*, a family-owned company based in Austria, is the world's leading manufacturer of full-cut crystal.

Diamond and Jewelry Way

W. 47th St. between Fifth & Sixth Aves. www.diamonddistrict.org.

This 750 ft long block is home to nearly 90 per cent of the diamond wholesale trade in the US. Listen closely, and even on the sidewalk you may hear cut, carat, color and clarity – the four "C"s – discussed in a bewildering variety of languages. Feel free to browse the heavily monitored showrooms.

Time Warner Center★

Broadway at Columbus Circle.

Cupping the west side of Columbus Circle with its vast semicircular facade, this huge complex (2004) contains 40 shops arranged around a four-story atrium. The most popular (among locals) is the gargantuan Whole Foods supermarket in the basement. Other stores include J. Crew clothing store, Godiva Chocolatier, Borders Books and Music, Hugo Boss, Sephora, TUMI luggage, Dean & DeLuca, Eileen Fisher, and Davidoff jewelers.

Don't miss the Time Warner Center's stellar lineup of celebrity chef-run restaurants, which includes Per Se (Thomas Keller), Masa (Masa Takayama), Porter House New York (Michael Lomonaco) and Landmarc (Marc Murphy).

Shopping Neighborhoods

Crystal District

The five-block stretch of Madison Avenue *(from 58th to 63rd Sts.)* is home to the world's richest concentration of crystal decorative objects and jewelry. The big names in this fragile world include Baccarat, Daum, Lalique, Steuben and Swarovski *(see below)*.

Nolita

Mulberry, Mott, & Elizabeth Sts. between Broome & Houston Sts. For shopaholics, the acronym for "North of Little Italy" has become synonymous with fashion daring and originality. In recent years, young designers fleeing the high rents of SoHo have turned Little Italy pizzerias and shoe-repair businesses into trendy boutiques. Cool, streamlined **Bio** features designer women's clothing, shoes, and handbags by emerging design talents *(29 Prince St., 212-334-3006; www.bio-nyc.com)*.

Sample Sales

One of the best ways to get designer clothes at rock-bottom prices in New York is to attend a sample sale or a trunk sale. This is when designers unload everything that didn't make it into mass production. Elbows can be sharp, but the savings are fantastic.

Check *New York Magazine* or *Time Out New York* for this week's sales.

57th Street

Considered one of the most exclusive shopping streets in the world, 57th between Park and Fifth avenues is home to art galleries, the Manhattan Art and Antiques Center and chic designer boutiques, including **Chanel** *(15 E. 57th St.; 212-355-5050 www.chanel. com)* and **Louis Vuitton** *(1 E. 57th St.; 212-758-8877 www.vuitton.com).*

Lower Manhattan

Known primarily as the financial center of the city, this area offers a varied shopping experience, including famed discount department stores **Syms** *(42 Trinity Pl.; 212-797-1199; www.syms.com)* and **Century 21** *(22 Cortlandt St.; 212-227-9092; www.c21stores.com).* Festive South Street Seaport incorporates more than 50 boutiques and restaurants, as well as the Pier 17 shopping center.

Lower East Side & East Village

These neighborhoods are chock-full of shops specializing in vintage apparel and clothes by up-and-coming designers. Orchard Street in the Lower East Side is the heart of the discount area. Note that many shops may close early on Friday and all day Saturday for the Jewish Sabbath. The greatest concentration of shops in the East Village is along 7th, 8th and 9th streets between First and Second avenues; try **Tokio 7** for designer hand-me-downs *(64 E. 7th St., 212-353-8443).*

SoHo & TriBeCa

Broadway between Houston and Canal is lined with trendy chain stores like H&M, Uniqlo, Forever 21 and Banana Republic.

Move west into the heart of SoHo, though, and you'll find more upscale offerings, like **A.P.C.**, an airy, minimalist loft space filled with a well-edited selection of top-quality basics for men and women *(131 Mercer St., 212-966-9685; www.apc.fr).* More tranquil, TriBeCa is home to upscale interior design stores like **Urban Archaeology** *(143 Franklin St., 212-431-4646; www.urbanarchaeology.com).*

girlprops.c

Inexpensive.....we never s

Shop in SoHo

Brigitta L. House/Michelin

Macy's

Greenwich Village

The city's bohemian enclave is known for its quaint boutiques, specialty shops, jazz clubs and coffeehouses. Bleecker Street is lined with old-world bakeries and Italian grocery stores. NYU students with eclectic tastes flock to the Village's music stores, including **Other Music** *(15 E. 4th St.; 212-477-8150; www.othermusic.com).*

Chelsea & the Garment District

Chelsea boasts exclusive art galleries along its west edge between Ninth and Tenth avenues. On its east edge, between Fifth and Sixth avenues, you'll find a number of large chain clothing stores, including J. Crew, Anthropolgie, Zara and H&M. In between are a number of interior design outfits. Just north of Chelsea sits **B&H**, the city's best camera store, with a vast selection of gadgets and gear and knowledgable salespeople to help you choose *(420 Ninth Ave. between 33rd & 34th Sts. 212-444-6600; www.bhphotovideo.com).*

Upper East Side

A bastion of high-end shopping, the area encompasses upscale fashion boutiques, and is home to world-famous **Bloomingdale's** department store *(below).*

Department Stores

- **Macy's★** – *151 W. 34th St., between Broadway & Seventh Ave. 212-695-4400. www.macys.com.* The world's largest department store holds 2.1 million square feet of space. The store's so big that it even has a visitor center *(34th St. balcony)* with information about where to find what. Foreign visitors can pick up an 11-percent discount card here.

- **Bloomingdale's** – *E. 59th St. & Lexington Ave. 212-705-2000. www.bloomingdales.com.* "Bloomie's," as it's affectionately called, has been an Upper East Side shopping mecca for decades. Here, high fashion applies to all the merchandise, from bonbons to shower curtains.

- **Century 21** – *22 Cortlandt St., between Broadway & Church Sts. 212-227-9092. www.c21stores. com.* You won't find gracious

SHOPPING

Photo credit: ©Natalia Bratslavsky/BigStockPhoto.com

service or orderly displays here. But if it's name-brand bargains you're after, you've come to the right place.

- **Saks Fifth Avenue** – *Fifth Ave. at 50th St. 212-753-4000. www.saks.com. See p 149.*
- **Lord & Taylor** – *Fifth Ave. at 38th St. 212-391-3344. www. lordandtaylor.com. See p 149.*

Auction Houses

Whether you're in the market for a priceless van Gogh or not, these establishments offering fine art, furnishings, books and decorative arts are well worth a visit. Advance viewings of items to be auctioned are usually held 3-5 days prior to the event. Visitors are welcome to participate in or watch the auction; advance reservations may be required for some events..

- **Christie's** – *20 Rockefeller Plaza. 212-636-2000. www.christies.com.*

- **Sotheby's** – *1334 York Ave. 212-606-7000. www.sothebys.com.*
- **William Doyle Galleries** – *175 E. 87th St. 212-427-2730. www.doylenewyork.com.*

Flea Markets

For one-of-a-kind collectibles at bargain prices, head to one (or more) of the city's flea markets. One group runs three of the most popular markets *(for more information: 212-243-5343; www. hellskitchenfleamarket.com)*:

Hell's Kitchen Flea Market – *W. 39th St., between Ninth & Tenth Aves.; open year-round weekends dawn–dusk.* 170 vendors selling all manner of vintage and retro goods.

- **Antiques Garage** – *112 W. 25th St.; open year-round weekends 9am–5pm.* Two floors of art, books, photographs, furniture and decorative arts.
- **25th Street Market** – *between Fifth and Sixth Aves.; open year-round weekends dawn–dusk.* Some 125 vendors of various and sundry items.

Food and Wine

- New York is a paradise for foodies. **Union Square Greenmarket★** *(see p 87)* is the most popular of New York's farmers' markets but there are

---

Museum Shops

Looking for an unusual gift? Visit the city's many museum shops, where items for sale are fashioned after pieces from the permanent collections and special exhibits–jewelry, sculptures, scarves, stationery, prints, posters and art books. Some also have sections for kids with toys, books and craft kits. A few to try:
American Folk Art Museum – *45 W. 53rd St.; www.folkartmuseum.org*
Metropolitan Museum of Art – *Fifth Ave. at E. 82nd; www.metmuseum.org*
American Museum of Natural History – *W. 79th St.; www.amnh.org*
Museum of Modern Art – *11 W. 53rd St.; www.moma.org*

dozens sprinkled throughout the five boroughs *(212-788-7476; www.cenyc.org)*.

🛒 **Zabar's** – *2245 Broadway at W. 80th St. 212-787-2000. www.zabars.com.* Zabar's stretches a city block and sells unusual foods from around the globe, including more than 600 varieties of imported cheeses.

- **Chelsea Market** – *75 Ninth Ave. between 15th and 16th Sts. www.chelseamarket.com.* Housed in an 1898 Nabisco factory, the market slots cafes and bakeries in among shops selling flowers, meat, cheeses, wines and other gourmet essentials.

- **Dean & Deluca** – *560 Broadway at Prince St. 212-226-6800. www.deandeluca.com.* The huge SoHo flagship store stocks a huge selection of cheeses, breads, pastries, and unique pantry ingredients.

- **Acker, Merrall & Condit** – *160 W. 72nd St. 212-787-1700. www.ackerwines.com.* The venerable wine merchant boasts a huge selection, including many fine and rare vintages.

- **Sherry-Lehman** – *505 Park Ave. 212-838-7500. www.sherry-lehman.com.* The friendly staff guide buyers through a vast but expertly selected inventory of wines & spirits. The annual catalogue is famous.

Home and Kitchen

- **ABC Carpet & Home** – *888 Broadway; 212-473-3000; www.abchome.com.* Six vast yet serene floors hold furniture, accessories, and everything you need for an elegant home.

- **Property** – *14 Wooster St.; 917-237-0123; propertyfurniture.com.* A sleek selection of contemporary furniture and accessories by European designers.

- **Moss** – *150 Greene St.; 212-204-7100; www.mossonline.com.* The shop feels like an art gallery, with scores of eye-catching (and wallet-busting) designs set against a crisp white interior.

- **Bower Kitchen Supply** – *75 Ninth Ave.; 212-376-4982; www.bowerykitchens.com.* The user-friendly restaurant supply house is chock-full of pots, pans, utensils, cutlery and servingware, all at reasonable prices.

©Courtesy of Moss

Moss

SPAS

A trip to New York can sometimes feel as hectic as staying at home, but it doesn't have to be that way. Whether you're fighting jet lag or your feet are aching after days of pounding pavements, a visit to one of these spas can be just what the doctor ordered.

Acqua Beauty Bar

7 E. 14th St. 212-620-4329.
Think you're already on vacation? Think again. Aqua Beauty Bar offers a range of "journeys" for the face, body and nails. Treatments range from high-tech facials (Medi-Lift, microdermabrasion) to an Indonesian Ritual of Beauty, complete with ground rice body scrubs and herbal masques. There's even an airbrushed Fantasy Tan for people who want a sun-kissed look.

Treatment Room, Acqua Beauty Bar

©Acqua Beauty Bar

Ajune

1294 Third Ave., between E. 74th & 75th Sts. 212-628-0044. www.ajune.com.

Aestheticians at this Uptown oasis offer personalized treatments for the muscle-sore and wrinkle-weary. Low-tech solutions include the facial *du jour*, which draws on the curative powers of fresh fruits and essential oils; and the ginger massage, which uses moisture and heat to work out all that tension

For those wanting eternal youth – or at least, the appearance of it – there are botox and collagen injections.

Bliss Spa

568 Broadway at Prince St., 2nd floor; 12 W. 57th St. between Fifth and Sixth Aves., 3rd floor; 541 Lexington Ave. at E. 49th St. 212-219-8970. www.blissworld.com.

Since opening its first tiny outpost in SoHo in 1996, Bliss has become one of New York's hottest spots for beautification and relaxation. The most popular facial is the Herbie, which combines a basic cleansing and exfoliation facial with a full-body rub-down and herbal wrap. The ultimate skin and massage treatment is the Ginger Rub. You'll be slathered in crushed ginger and essential oils, then wrapped in foil and left to steep on a bed of hot water. Afterward, melt into a 100-minute massage. *Ahhh....*

Eden Day Spa

388 Broadway, between Walker & White Sts. 212-226-0515. www.edenspany.com.

Relaxation is the name of the game at this TriBeCa staple, where treatments are refreshingly straightfoward. If you're really feeling indulgent, try the Day Dream: five hours of loving attention to your muscles, nails, skin and face.

MUST DO

Elizabeth Arden Red Door Salon & Spa

691 Fifth Ave. at 54th St. 212-546-0200. www.reddoorspas.com.

The extensive menu of services at Elizabeth Arden's Fifth Avenue flagship spa has something for every appetite. If it's a cut you need, the stylists here are top notch. Botox treatment? A plastic surgeon is on hand to administer one. However, the most popular choices remain the most basic ones: manicures and pedicures, facials, makeovers and aromatherapy massages.

Graceful Services

1097 Second Ave: at 57th St, 2nd floor. 212-593-9904. www.gracefulservices.com. Graceful Spa: 205 W. 14th St. at Seventh Ave., 2nd floor. 212-675-5145. www.gracefulspa.com.

For a body-tingling, mind-expanding massage at a great price, these sister spas can't be beat. Calling on ancient Chinese wisdom, therapists work to get your life energy, or "qi," moving with three different types of massage: Chinese, Swedish and shiatsu. The original Upper East Side location is more spartan than the newer, more luxurious

©Graceful Services
Massage at Graceful Services

Chelsea outpost, but both offer a full range of services.
Graceful Services other branch is located at 1097 2nd Ave (between 57th–58th St.); 212-593-9904. www.gracefulservices.com.

John Allan's Club

46 E. 46th St., 212-922-0361; 95 Trinity Pl., 212-406-3000. www.johnallans.com.

The people at this admirably efficient outfit know how to deliver maximum pampering in a minimum amount of time. The "Full Service" treatment, administered simultaneously by at least two clinicians, includes a shoe shine, a shampoo, a hair cut, a scalp massage, a hot-towel facial, a manicure and a beverage, and clocks in at only 35 to 45 minutes. It's perfect for busy Wall Street execs, Madison Avenue ad men – and scruffy travelers.

La Prairie Spa

Ritz-Carlton Hotel, 50 Central Park South. 212-521-6135. www.ritzcarlton.com.

Can't slow down enough for a full treatment – consider one of La Prairie's Manhattan Minutes spa packages. Jet Lag Therapy includes aromatherapy massage, foot reflexology, and a facial. After-Shopping Paradise blends foot massage with a pedicure. For the one-hour Changing Room special, both you and your clothes get a good steaming, while you're treated to a manicure, a facial and a makeover. Really pressed? The Stress Release Facial makes it all go away in just 30 minutes.

SPAS

SPORTS AND RECREATION

If New York's world-class monuments, museums and restaurants are stiffening your muscles and expanding your waistline, it's time to slot some exercise into the itinerary. After all, everyone needs to play once in awhile. *For New York's professional sports teams, see Practical Information.*

Central Park

Bounded by 59th St., Fifth Ave. 110th St. and Central Park West. www.centralpark.com.

The sylvan setting of New York's playground is a glorious place for a workout, with recreational facilities widely scattered among the park's rolling meadows and tourist attractions.

- **Central Park Tennis Center** – *West Drive between W. 94th and W. 96th St; open daily (weather permitting) Apr–Nov 6:30am–dusk; permit required; for permit information 212-360-8135.* 30 outdoor clay courts and 4 asphalt courts.
- **Lasker Pool** – *mid-park between 108th & 109th Sts.; open Jun daily 11am–3pm, Jul 1–Labor Day 11am–3pm and 4–7pm; 212-534-7639.*

- **Wollman Ice Skating Rink** – *east park at 63rd St.; open Nov–Mar Mon–Tue 10am–2:30pm, Wed–Thu 10am–10pm, Fri-Sat 10am–11pm, Sun 10am–9pm; 212-439-6900.*
- **Lasker Ice Skating Rink** – *mid-park between 106th and 108th Sts.; open Nov–Mar Mon–Thu 10am–3:45pm, Fri 10am–10pm, Sat 1–10pm, Sun 12:30–4:30pm. 212-534-7639.*
- **Running trails** – *trail and distance maps available at www.centralpark.com.* All park drives are closed to vehicular traffic from 10am–3pm on weekdays and all day on weekends, a great time to run in the park.
- **Basketball courts** – *Mid-park at 85th St. north of the Great Lawn; and mid-park at 97th St.*

Playing basebal in Central Park

©Wetback/iStockphoto.com

Chelsea Piers

West Side Hwy. at 23rd St. 212-336-6666. www.cheseapiers.com.

New York City's gargantuan public recreational complex occupies four former ocean liner piers on the Hudson River. Here you'll find not only standard workout facilities (weight rooms, aerobics studios, a swimming pool, basketball courts) but also a few things you wouldn't expect to see on a river pier, such as a beach volleyball court, batting cages, a driving range and a bowling alley.

- **Sports Center** – *open Mon–Fri 5:30am–11pm, Fri 5:30am–10pm; weekends 8am–9pm; day pass $50; 212-336-6000.* The center houses a quarter-mile indoor running track, a weight deck, a rock-climbing wall, basketball courts, a swimming pool, aerobics studios and spa services.
- **Golf Club** – *open daily 6:30am–midnight; $25/90 balls during peak hours, $25/147 balls during off-peak hours. 212-336-6400.* The heated outdoor driving range boasts 52 stalls on four tiers.
- **Sky Rink** – *open daily year-round; hours and fees vary; call for information; 212-336-6100.* Freestyle ice skating sessions are held on two rinks.

Biking and Jogging

In addition to Central Park, runners and cyclists make use of the Hudson River Greenway, which stretches from Battery Park to Washington Heights. The **New York Road Runners Club** *(9 E. 89th St. between Fifth and Madison Aves.; 212-860-4455; www.nyrr.org)* offers bathrooms,

Where To Get a Workout

Many private fitness centers are available to guests of major hotels; check with the concierge.

YMCA memberships are valid worldwide; for a list of New York facilities, call 212-630-9600 or www.ymca.net.

You can also try:

Crunch Fitness – 14 locations in New York; www.crunch.com; $16 day.

New York Health & Racquet Club – 10 locations in Manhattan; www.nyhrc.com; $20/day.

New York Sports Clubs – 40 locations in Manhattan; www.mysportsclubs.com; $25/day.

changing areas and lockers at their Upper East Side offices, plus information and support for runners. Cyclists can contact the **New York Cycling Club** *(212-828-5711; www.nycc.org)* to find out about routes, group rides and more. For information on renting a bike in New York, see Biking in the City p. 122.

Ice Skating

Taking a twirl on the ice amid the skyscrapers is an unforgettable experience in wintertime New York. In addition to the rinks in Central Park, try the following:

- **The Rink at Rockefeller Plaza** – *Open Oct–Apr Sun–Thu 8:30am–10pm, Fri–Sat 8:30am–midnight. Rates vary; skate rental $8. 212-332-7654*
- **The Pond at Bryant Park** – *Fifth Ave. between 40th & 42nd Sts. Open daily late Oct–late Jan Sun–Thu 8am–10pm, Fri–Sat 8am–midnight. Skate rental $12. 866-221-5157; www.thepondat bryantpark.com*

RESTAURANTS

The venues listed below were selected for their ambience, location and/or value for money. Rates indicate the average cost of a dinner appetizer, an entrée and a dessert for one person (not including tax, gratuity or beverages). Most restaurants accept major credit cards. Call for information regarding reservations, dress code and opening hours. For a list of restaurants by theme, see p. 169. A complete listing of restaurants mentioned in this guide appears in the Index.

Luxury	**$$$$**	over $75	Moderate	**$$**	$25–$50
Expensive	**$$$**	$50–$75	Inexpensive	**$**	under $25

Chanterelle dining area

©FChanterelle

LUXURY

Chanterelle

$$$$ **French**
2 Harrison St. at Hudson St.,
TriBeCa. 212-966-6960.
www.chanterellenyc.com.

This New York classic serves contemporary French cuisine in a gorgeous Art Nouveau-style dining room. While the menu changes monthly, the signature grilled seafood sausage remains a staple.

Sushi Yasuda

$$$$ **Japanese**
204 E. 43rd St. between Second &
Third Aves., East Midtown. 212-
972-1001. www.sushiyasuda.com.

Chef Naomichi Yasuda elevates sushi to new heights at his name-sake restaurant. His insistence on the freshest ingredients means that the menu changes daily. Look for Japanese eel and toro (fatty tuna), all served in the bamboo-sheathed dining room.

EXPENSIVE

Café Boulud

$$$ **French**
20 E. 76th St. between Fifth &
Madison Aves., Upper East Side.
212-772-2600.
www.danielnyc.com.

Famed French chef Daniel Boulud offers four different tasting menus here: La Tradition, with old-fashioned dishes; La Saison, with

©Café Boulud

Café Boulud

seasonal fare; Le Potager, with market-fresh produce; and Le Voyage, inspired by world cuisines.

'Cesca

$$$ Italian
164 W. 75th St. at Amsterdam Ave., Upper West Side. 212-787-6300. www.cescanyc.com.

Southern Italian fare headlines the menu at this Upper West Side spot, including dishes like tuna with white beans, serignola olives with preserved lemon, and swordfish with caponata. If that doesn't tickle your fancy, try one of the daily specials.

©Firebird Restaurant

Firebird Restaurant

Firebird

$$$ Russian
365 W. 46th St. between Eighth & Ninth Aves., Midtown. Closed Mon. 212-586-0244. www.firebirdrestaurant.com.

Tsar Nicholas would enjoy the cuisine here – with dishes like Ukrainian borscht, poached sturgeon and chicken Kiev, plus seven kinds of caviar on the menu. It's a fun place to eat with the pre-theater crowd before walking over to a Broadway show.

Gallagher's

$$$ Steakhouse
228 W. 52nd St. between Broadway & Eighth Ave., Midtown. 212-245-5336. www.gallaghersnysteak house.com.

Beef, beef and more beef—the finest quality and cuts—fill the menu at this Theater District steakhouse. From out front you can even spot the carcasses hanging in the restaurant's meat locker. Inside, the wood-paneled dining room has checkered tablecloths and pictures of Broadway stars.

Gotham Bar and Grill

$$$ American
12 E. 12th St. between Fifth Ave. & University Pl., Union Square. 212-260-4020. www.gothambarandgrill.com.

Gotham is consistently rated one of New York's finest restaurants, and Chef Alfred Portale fits New York to a T, creating towering "skyscraper" presentations that are a treat for the eye as well as the palate. Seafood salad is a high-rise concoction of lobster, scallops,

Gotham Bar and Grill
©Gotham Bar and Grill

octopus, squid and avocado, crowned with purple lettuce.

Keens Steakhouse

$$$ **Steakhouse**
72 W. 36th St. between Fifth & Sixth Aves., Garment District. 212-947-3636. www.keens.com.

A carnivore's delight, Keens serves up big slabs of prime rib, steaks and lamb in a historic setting. The restaurant opened in 1885, when Herald Square – which is around the corner – was still the city's Theater District. Hanging from the ceiling is a collection of churchwarden clay pipes.

Bluemoose Room, Keens Steakhouse
©Keens Steakhouse

Maloney & Porcelli

$$$ **American**
37 E. 50th St. between Madison & Park Aves., East Midtown. 212-750-2233. www.maloneyand porcelli.com.

Come with a big appetite (and a big wallet) to take on crackling pork shank, the house specialty. The hearty hunk of meat is deep-fried, then slow-roasted and served with jalapeño apple sauce.

Nobu Next Door

$$$ **Japanese**
105 Hudson St. at Franklin St., TriBeCa. Dinner only. 212-334-4445. www.myriadrestaurant group.com.

Although it's nearly impossible to get a table at the highly acclaimed Nobu, you can sample essentially the same food at Nobu Next Door. The Southeast Asian-inspired decor harmonizes with the sensual pleasures of clawless lobsters, sea urchins, seafood udon (noodles) and mochi ice-cream balls. Go early to avoid a long wait.

Park Avenue

$$$ **Contemporary**
100 E. 63rd St. at Park Ave., Upper East Side. 212-644-1900. www.parkavenyc.com.

The former Park Avenue Cafe, this cheery space gives you a different experience depending on when you go by transforming itself top to toe, front to back, each season. Decor, menu, even the restaurant's name changes in a quarterly reincarnation designed to showcase the finest ingredients in spring, summer, autumn and winter. Award-winning design firm AvroKO took inspiration from Captain Cook's expeditions to loosely frame the design references for each season. The restaurant was recognized among the best openings of the year by New York Times,

MUST EAT

Park Avenue

©Park Avenue

New York Magazine and New York Observer. Chef Craig Koketsu is one of the top up-and-coming chefs in New York City.

Perry Street

$$$ **Contemporary**
176 Perry St. at West St.,
West Village. 212-352-1900.
www.jean-georges.com.

Marked by impeccable service, sleek surroundings and flawlessly prepared food, Perry Street may well be Jean-Georges Vongerichten's most appealing restaurant. Sink deep into one of the snug chairs or banquettes and turn your eye to the menu. Seafood is a specialty, and the desserts are divine.

The Modern

$$$ **Contemporary**
9 W. 53rd St. between Fifth
& Sixth Aves., Central Midtown.
Closed Sun. 212-333-1212.
www.themodernnyc.com.

This upscale spot is as well known for its excellent cooking as for its unbeatable location edging the Museum of Modern Art's sculpture garden. You can order à la carte at lunch, but dinner is strictly prix-fixe ($88–$138), featuring creative fare

like licorice-poached East Coast halibut on a warm salad of haricots verts and chanterelles.

🍴 Union Square Cafe

$$$ **Italian**
21 E. 16th St. between Fifth Ave.
& Union Sq. W., Union Square.
212-243-4020. www.unionsquare
cafe.com.

Open since 1985, this popular bistro – restaurateur Danny Meyer's flagship – still packs in crowds every night. It's not hard to see why: the service is friendly and impeccable, the surroundings cool and comfortable, the food imaginative. Select from the list of entrées like creamy crab risotto, or cod with seasoned lentils—or one of the daily specials.

Union Square Cafe

©Union Square Café

MODERATE

Blue Ribbon Sushi

$$ **Japanese**
119 Sullivan St. between Prince
and Spring Sts., SoHo.
212-343-0404. www.blueribbon
restaurants.com.

A downtown sushi mainstay, Blue Ribbon Sushi has a vast menu of fresh and buttery raw fish, as well as a kids' menu of assorted yakimono and maki (there's even fried chicken and catfish fingers). Thanks to its no-reservations policy, the waits can be long.

Blue Water Grill

$$ Seafood
31 Union Sq. at E. 16th St., Union Square. 212-675-9500. www.brguestrestaurants.com.

Maine lobster, Maryland crab cakes and a selection of oysters from the raw bar draw seafood lovers to this lively restaurant overlooking Union Square. You can also order sushi and maki rolls. Jazz music bumps up the tempo even more.

Blue Water Grill dining room
©Blue Water Grill

The Boathouse

$$ Contemporary
In Central Park (E. 72nd St. & Park Dr. N.), Upper East Side. Lunch year-round. Dinner Apr–Nov only. 212-517-2233. www.the centralparkboathouse.com.

Nestled on the shore of the lake in the middle of Central Park, the Boathouse offers peaceful water views to go along with dishes like jumbo lump crab cakes served with cornichon and caper remoulade, or pan-roasted pork tenderloin. On sunny days, sit

out on the deck and watch the rowboats drift by.

Bread Tribeca

$$ Italian
301 Church St. at Walker St. 212-334-0200. www.breadtribeca.com.

Sandwiches are the specialty here, filled with the likes of Sicilian sardines, handmade mozzarella, and prosciutto di Parma stuffed between Italian ciabatta bread or crusty baguettes. Desserts like the caramelized banana tart are bound to please the most discriminating sweet tooth.

El Cid

$$ Spanish
322 W. 15th St. between Eighth & Ninth Aves., Chelsea. 12-929-9332.

This unpretentious Meatpacking District eatery is one of the best spots in the city for tapas (appetizer-size portions of Spanish dishes) and fresh sangria. The dozen tables are jammed together and the bar is crowded, so don't forget to reserve.

El Parador

$$ Mexican
325 E. 34th St. between First & Second Aves., East Midtown. 212-679-6812. www.elparador cafe.com.

Start your evening at this upbeat restaurant (don't be fooled by the windowless facade) with a stiff margarita, then settle in for mole poblano or bouillabaisse veracruzana, a succulent stew of lobster, shrimp, scallops, clams and mussels in broth.

MUST EAT

©William Brinson

Outdoor garden, Gascogne restaurant

Gascogne

$$ French
158 Eighth Ave. between W. 17th & W. 18th Sts., Chelsea. 212-675-6564. www.gascognenyc.com.

If you're craving rustic fare from the southwest of France, stop in here for the excellent cassoulet (a stew of white beans, duck confit and garlic sausage) or veal kidneys flamed with Armagnac. In summer, opt for the shady outdoor garden.

Gigino at Wagner Park

$$ Italian
20 Battery Pl. at Little West St., Downtown. 212-528-2228. www.gigino-wagnerpark.com.

On the vast back deck with harbor views, sample selections from the expansive menu like wood oven-fired pizzas or the house special, spaghetti de Padrino (made with beets and escarole). It'll be a hit with the whole famiglia.

Good Enough to Eat

$$ American
483 Amsterdam Ave. between W. 83rd & W. 84th Sts., Upper West Side. 212-496-0163. www.good enoughtoeat.com.

A white picket fence marks the entrance to this homey little place with its brick walls and folk art. Comfort food stars on the menu, which features perennial favorites like meatloaf, pumpkin pie and turkey dinner with all the trimmings.

Il Palazzo

$$ Italian
151 Mulberry St. between Grand & Hester Sts., Little Italy. 212-343-7000. www.littleitalynyc.com.

Right on Little Italy's main drag, Il Palazzo dishes up a generous selection of classics: veal saltimbocca, chicken cacciatore, rigatoni alla vodka, linguine with clam sauce, shrimp scampi. Head around the corner to Ferrara *(195 Grand St.)* bakery for espresso and gelato.

Les Halles Downtown

$$ French
15 John St. between Broadway & Nassau Sts., Financial District. 212-285-8585. www.leshalles.net.

Chef/author Anthony Bourdain opened this restaurant after the terrorist attack of September 11, 2001 – one of the first new restaurants to open in the Financial District at the time. Here he serves up such palate-pleasing French dishes as steak au poivre and coq au vin.

RESTAURANTS

Macelleria

$$　　**Italian**
*48 Gansevoort St. between
Greenwich & Washington Sts.,
Meatpacking District.
212-741-2555. www.macelleria
restaurant.com.*

Housed in a reconstructed butcher
shop, this engaging trattoria offers
an outstanding variety of salami,
homemade pastas, meat dishes
and Italian wines. Start with the
iceberg lettuce wedge with gor-
gonzola and peppercorn dressing,
then move on to a pasta dish such
as green and white tagliolini with
peas and prosciutto, or garganelli
with oxtail ragu.

Marseille

$$　　**Mediterranean**
*630 Ninth Ave. at W. 44th St.,
Theater District. 212-333-2323.
www.marseillenyc.com.*

Marseille is a terrific spot for pre-
and post-theater dining. Serving
French cuisine with Moroccan,
Turkish and Tunisian overtones,
Marseille's decor makes you think
you're on the set of *Casablanca*.
The menu runs the gamut from
bouillabaisse to lamb tagine.

Ocean Grill

$$　　**Seafood**
*384 Columbus Ave. between
W. 78th & W. 79th Sts, Upper
West Side. 212-579-2300.
www.brguestrestaurants.com.*

You'll think you've boarded an
ocean liner when you set foot
in this dining room, decked out
with photos of the seashore and
porthole windows. Try a plate of

oysters from the raw bar, simply
grilled fish or the house maki roll.

Odeon

$$　　**American**
*145 West Broadway between
Thomas & Duane Sts., TriBeCa.
212-233-0507. www.theodeon
restaurant.com.*

A TriBeCa hot spot since the early
1980s, Odeon has long been a
place where the glitterati come to
eat. You may still catch a glimpse
of the big names here, but the real
draw is the refined cuisine. If you're
interested in dining at odd hours,
Odeon serves a brasserie menu
of light fare daily from 3pm to
5:30pm, and from midnight until
2am every night.

The Red Cat

$$　　**Contemporary**
*227 10th Ave., Chelsea. 212-242-
1122. www.theredcat.com.*

New England-style decor (wood-
paneled walls, red and white color
scheme) highlights New American
dishes like grilled brook trout,
pan-roasted organic chicken and
sugarcane-roasted pork tenderloin.

Rocking Horse

$$　　**Mexican**
*182 Eighth Ave. between 19th &
20th Sts., Chelsea. 212-463-9511.*

Mexican folk art and bright colors
make a vibrant background for
authentic Mexican regional cuisine. Dinner selections range from
chiltepe-glazed tuna to mustard-
crusted lambchops. Save room for
the rich tres leches cake

MUST EAT

Schiller's Liquor Bar

$$ **American**
131 Rivington St. at Norfolk St. 212-260-4555. www.schillersny.com.

A great spot for a late-night meal, this Lower East Side mainstay offers macaroni and cheese with bacon, moules frites and lamb curry among other noshes. Open until 1am (3am Fri and Sat).

Spotted Pig

$$ **Gastropub**
314 W. 11th St. at Greenwich St., West Village. 212-620-0393. www.thespottedpig.com. No reservations.

The Spotted Pig sports a country-cute decor with rustic tables covered in butcher-block paper, pig paraphernalia and other bric-a-brac. Chef April Bloomfield turns out robust fare like fried calf livers and rabbit stew. Come early to avoid the horrendous line.

Tamarind

$$ **Indian**
41–43 E. 22nd St. between Broadway & Park Ave., Union Square. 212-674-7400. www.tamarinde22.com.

Flavors of India abound at Tamarind; cowbells hang in the alcoves of the gleaming-white dining room; a large, wrought-iron wall hanging from a maharaja's palace greets guests at the entrance. Bustling cooks prepare piquant regional Indian dishes in the glassed-in kitchen. For lighter, cheaper fare, go to the tea room next door.

INEXPENSIVE

Angelica Kitchen

$ **Vegan**
300 E. 12th St. between First & Second Aves., East Village. 212-228-2909. www.angelica kitchen.com.

Health-conscious New Yorkers love the creative vegan fare at this popular East Village eatery. Many dine on a wide assortment of simply prepared salads, grilled vegetables, tofu and breads.

Azuri Café

$ **Falafel**
465 W. 51st St. between Ninth & Tenth Aves., Midtown. 212-262-2920.

For fresh, savory Middle Eastern food, including some of the best falafel, tabouli and baba ghanoush you'll find in New York, Azuri can't be beat. Order one of the plates, which will give you an entrée (try the falafel) with an assortment of salads and bread.

Cafe Habana

$ **Cuban**
17 Prince St. at Elizabeth St., Nolita. 212-625-2001. www.ecoeatery.com.

Small, hip and always crowded, this corner diner serves up some of the best skirt steak and fried plantains this side of Havana; runners-up include the grilled corn and the egg burrito. For quicker service head to the take-out window next door.

RESTAURANTS

Candle Café

$ Vegetarian
*1307 Third Ave. between 74th &
75th Sts, Upper East Side. 212-472-
0970. www.candlecafe.com.*

Freshness and seasonality are the
watchwords at this no-frills vegetarian restaurant. Farmers market
entrees include chili with beans
and brown rice, and chipotle
grilled tofu; there's also a long list
of smoothies, elixirs and juices to
go with your meal.
Candle has a second location for
finer dining: **Candle 79** *(154 E.
79th St. near Lexington Ave. 212-
537-7179)*, voted Best Vegetarian
Restaurant 2007.

 Carnegie Delicatessen

$ Kosher
*854 Seventh Ave. between W. 54th
& W. 55th Sts., Midtown. 212-757-
2245. www.carnegiedeli.com.*

It's hard to tell what this kosher
deli is more famous for: salty
service or mile-high pastrami
sandwiches. It's best to endure the
former for the latter – split a sandwich if you want, to save room for
the delicious cheesecake.

Dim Sum Go Go

$ Chinese
*5 E. Broadway at Chatham Square,
Chinatown. 212-732-0797.*

New-wave dim sum is served
to order at this sleek restaurant.
Mushroom and pickled-vegetable
dumplings, duck skin and crab-
meat wrapped in spinach dough,
or chive and shrimp dumplings in
a ginger-vinegar dipping sauce are
just a few of the many choices.

Great N.Y. Noodletown

$ Chinese
*28 Bowery at Bayard St.,
Chinatown. 212-349-0923.*

This is a casual place. Noodles
dominate the menu—you can get
them pan-fried, Cantonese-style,
or in Hong Kong-style lo mein.

'inoteca

$ Italian
*98 Rivington St. at Ludlow St.,
Lower East Side. 212-614-0473.
www.inotecanyc.com.*

Magnet for the chic young Lower
East Side set, this clamorous restaurant offers a superb selection
of well-priced Italian wines from
every region of Italy. The menu
stars small plates and panini
(stuffed with the likes of fontina
and arugula, or roasted vegetables
and fresh ricotta).

Soba-Ya

$ Japanese
*229 E. Ninth St. between First
& Second Aves., East Village.
212-533-6966.*

On a cold day, nothing warms
you up like a steaming bowl of
housemade buckwheat noodles
swimming in broth and topped
with meat and vegetables. In
warm weather, try your noodles
cold with add-ons heaped on top.

RESTAURANTS BY THEME

Whether you're looking for just the right spot for a special occasion, a restaurant with a celebrity chef, the perfect place for brunch or a neighborhood gem, New York's got it. In the previous pages we've organized the restaurants by price category; here we've arranged them by theme to help you find the perfect place to eat. All restaurants listed below are in Manhattan.

Bring the Kids
Carnegie Delicatessen *(p 168)*
Dim Sum Go Go *(p 168)*
Great N.Y. Noodletown *(p 168)*
Rocking Horse *(p 166)*

Brunch Spots
Carnegie Delicatessen *(p 168)*
Good Enough to Eat *(p 165)*
Park Avenue *(p 162)*

Celebrity Chefs
Café Boulud (Daniel Boulud) *(p 160)*
Gotham Bar and Grill
   (Alfred Portale) *(p 161)*
Le Bernardin (Eric Ripert) *(p 160)*
Les Halles Downtown (Anthony
Bourdain) *(p 165)*
Nobu Next Door
   (Nobu Matsuhisa) *(p 162)*
Perry Street (Jean-Georges Vong-
erichten) *(p 163)*

Easy on the Budget
Angelica Kitchen *(p 167)*
Azuri Cafe *(p 167)*
Café Habana *(p 167)*
Dim Sum Go Go *(p 168)*
Great N.Y. Noodletown *(p 168)*
'inoteca *(p 168)*
Soba-Ya *(p 168)*

Vegetarian
Angelica Kitchen *(p 167)*
Candle Cafe *(p 168)*

Hip Scenes
'inoteca *(p 168)*
Nobu Next Door *(p 162)*
Odeon *(p 166)*
Gotham Bar and Grill *(p 161)*
Spotted Pig *(p 167)*
Union Square Café *(p 163)*

Neighborhood Favorites
Café Habana *(p 167)*
Carnegie Delicatessen *(p 168)*
Great N.Y. Noodletown *(p 168)*
Il Palazzo *(p 165)*
'inoteca *(p 168)*
Union Square Cafe *(p 163)*

Outdoor Seating (seasonal)
Boathouse at Central Park *(p 164)*
Gascogne *(p 165)*
Good Enough to Eat *(p 165)*

Pre-Theater Dining
Firebird *(p 161)*
Marseille *(p 166)*

Quick Bites
Azuri Cafe *(p 167)*
Soba-Ya *(p 168)*

Special-Occasion Restaurants
Boathouse at Central Park *(p 164)*
Cafe Boulud *(p 160)*
Chanterelle *(p 160)*
Gotham Bar and Grill *(p 161)*
Le Bernardin *(p 160)*

Steakhouses
Gallagher's *(p 161)*
Keens Steakhouse *(p 162)*

RESTAURANTS

HOTELS

The properties listed below were selected for their ambience, location and/or value for money. Prices reflect the average cost for a standard double room for two people in high season. Hotels in New York often offer special discount rates on weekends and off-season.

Quoted rates don't include New York City's hotel tax of 13.62% and the $3.50 per room per night surcharge. For a list of hotels by theme, see p. 179. A complete listing of hotels mentioned in this guide appears in the Index.

| Luxury | **$$$$$** | over $350 | Moderate | **$$$** | 175–$250 |
| Expensive | **$$$$** | 250–$350 | Inexpensive | **$$-$** | 100–$175 |

LUXURY

The Carlyle

$$$$$ 187 rooms
35 E. 76th St. at Madison Ave., Upper East Side. 212-744-1600 or 888-767-3966. www.thecarlyle.com.

Unequalled service, comfort and fine furnishings abound at this Upper East Side fixture. Guest rooms may be small compared to newer properties, but they are luxuriousy appointed with Louis XVI-style furnishings, plush carpets and marble baths. The location is superb, near Central Park.

City Club

$$$$$ 65 rooms
55 W. 44th St., Midtown. 212-921-5500. www.cityclubhotel.com.

Originally a gentlemen's club, the City Club has the feel of an exclusive apartment building, with a discreet lobby, modern decor and attentive service. Rooms are small but luxuriously appointed with marble bathrooms, supple linens and DVD players. The sleek **DB Bistro Moderne ($$$)** is renowned for serving the city's most decadent hamburger: it's stuffed with black truffles and foie gras.

Inn at Irving Place

$$$$$ 12 rooms
56 Irving Pl. between E. 17th & E. 18th Sts., Gramercy Park. 212-533-4600 or 800-685-1447. www.innatirving.com.

You won't find the name of the inn on these two 1834 brownstones; just look for the address. Within you will find stylish guest rooms appointed with 19C furnishings (four-poster beds, overstuffed chairs) as well as up-to-the-minute technology, including wireless Internet access. Afternoon tea, a real treat, is served in Lady Mendl's Victorian tea salon *(reservations required)*. Martinis and nibbles can be had in the downstairs lounge.

The Lucerne

$$$$ 184 rooms
201 W. 79th St. at Amsterdam Ave., Upper West Side. 212-875-1000 or 800-492-8122. www.newyorkhotel.com.

Set in an historic 1903 building in the heart of the Upper West Side, the Lucerne has been transformed into a modern, European-style boutique hotel with spacious guest rooms and a full slate of amenities, from in-room movies

©Cynthia Ochterbeck/MICHELIN

The Lucerne

to marble bathrooms and a fitness center. **Nice Matin ($$$)** features fine Mediterranean cuisine..

Mandarin Oriental

$$$$$ **251 rooms**
80 Columbus Circle at W. 60th St., Upper West Side. 212-805-8800 or 866-801-8880. www.mandarin oriental.com.

From its lofty perch on floors 35 to 54 of the Time Warner Center, the Mandarin Oriental boasts wide-angle views of the city and Central Park. Soaking tubs in the bathrooms sit in front of picture windows. There's also a full-service spa and fitness center with an indoor lap pool. With its panoramic vistas, the **Lobby Lounge** is an eye-catching spot for cocktails.

Millennium Hotel New York UN Plaza

$$$$$ **427 rooms**
One United Nations Plaza between First & Second Aves. 212-758-1234 or 866-866-8086. www1.millenniumhotels.com.

Sitting directly across from the UN, the Millennium offers convenient

access to the Midtown business district, as well as fashionable East Side restaurants and boutiques. The hotel's spacious and elegantly appointed guest rooms start on the 28th floor, and offer breathtaking views of the New York skyline and the East River. The Millennium has both an indoor tennis court and a glass-enclosed pool.

Muse Hotel

$$$$$ **200 rooms**
130 W. 46th St. between Sixth & Seventh Aves., Theater District. 212 -485-2400. www.themusehotel.com.

This 19-story hotel, recently refurbished, sports bright hallways and warmly inviting rooms. Guests enjoy feather beds, L'Occitane bath products, marble bathrooms and original artwork. It's a pet-friendly hotel too, with Wi-Fi access throughout.

New York Palace

$$$$$ **892 rooms**
455 Madison Ave., between E. 50th & E. 51st Sts., Midtown. 212-888-7000 or 800-804-7035. www.newyorkpalace.com.

©New York Palace Hotel

New York Palace Hotel

HOTELS

Enter this 55-story skyscraper through the 19C Villard Houses *(see Historic Sites)*. Just inside, note the mansion's original molded ceiling, before descending the staircase into the marble-columned lobby. Oversize guest rooms are decorated with gold-brocade bedspreads. A 7,000 sq ft fitness center gives guests good options for exercise.

The Regency

$$$$$ 266 rooms
540 Park Ave. at E. 61st St., Upper East Side. 212-759-4100 or 800-235-6397. www.loewshotels.com.

Recently treated to an extensive renovation, the Regency stands just two blocks east of Central Park on tony Park Ave. Guest quarters are luxurious, done in soft beiges with contemporary accents and outfitted with Frette linens. Singer Michael Feinstein is often on hand to entertain in his namesake lounge.

Ritz-Carlton Battery Park

$$$$$ 298 rooms
2 West St. at Battery Pl. 212-344-0800 or 800-241-3333. www.ritzcarlton.com.

Spring for a harbor-view room at this monolith of a hotel towering over Battery Park, and you'll have your own telescope to view New York Harbor and the Statue of Liberty. Guest rooms sport rich fabrics and fine bed linens; bathrooms are awash in marble. Enjoy a cocktail at the 14th-floor Rise Bar followed by dinner at the hotel's restaurant, **2 West ($$$$)**, specializing in Prime Angus Beef.

SoHo Grand Hotel

$$$$$ 363 rooms
310 W. Broadway at Grand St., SoHo. 212-965-3000. www.sohogrand.com.

The hotel sits at the southwest edge of SoHo, a short walk from trendy TriBeCa. Swathed in neutral tones, the rooms all have Bose Wave CD/radios, Egyptian cotton linens, flat-screen TVs, minibars and 24-hour room service. The SoHo Grand welcomes pets, and will even provide a goldfish for your room upon request.

Waldorf-Astoria Hotel

$$$$$ 1,425 rooms
301 Park Ave. between E. 49th & E. 50th Sts., Midtown. 212-355-3000 or 800-925-3673. www.waldorfastoria.com.

Having been recently renovated to the tune of $400 million, the 1931 Art Deco Waldorf-Astoria remains one of New York City's most enduring symbols of luxury. Casual dress (cutoff jeans, tank tops, T-shirts) is not permitted in the marble-floored lobby, where guests can tap into free wireless Internet service. Spacious units in the exclusive Waldorf Towers are

Boudoir Bathroom at the Waldorf-Astoria

©Boudoir Bathroom, Waldorf-Astoria

known for their exquisite European furnishings and butler service.

Wall Street Inn

$$$$$ 46 rooms
9 S. William St. at Broad St., Financial District. 212-747-1500. www.thewallstreetinn.com.

Business travelers especially will appreciate this boutique hotel near the New York Stock Exchange. Its business center and workout facility are added draws. The Jacuzzi tubs in the penthouse rooms invite relaxation after a busy day, and the hotel offers a time-saving complimentary continental breakfast.

Westin New York at Times Square

$$$$$ 863 rooms
270 W. 43rd St. at Eighth Ave., Midtown. 212-201-2700 or 866-837-4183. www.westinny.com.

The design firm Arquitectonica of Miami created this attention-grabber, a daring addition to the New York hotel scene. Guest rooms boast sleek furnishings and bold abstract art on muted wall coverings. The health club offers a panoramic view of the city. **Shula's Steak House ($$$$$)** specializes in serving the "biggest and best" cuts of certified Angus beef.

EXPENSIVE

Algonquin Hotel

$$$$ 174 rooms
59 W. 44th St., between Fifth & Sixth Aves., Midtown. 212-840-6800 or 800-304-2047. www.algonquinhotel.com.

Living Room Suite, Algonquin Hotel
©Algonquin Hotel

This quiet hotel was the site of Alexander Woollcott's famous Algonquin Round Table, a 1920s gathering place for a celebrated clique of writers, including Dorothy Parker and Robert Benchley. The Algonquin's popular cabaret bar, the Oak Room, hosts some of the country's top vocal jazz acts; the Roundtable Room has a moderately priced pre-theater menu, and the Blue Bar offers casual dining.

Bentley Hotel

$$$$ 197 rooms
500 E. 62nd St. at York Ave., Upper East Side. 212-644-6000 or 888-664-6835. www.nychotels.com.

The Bentley's rooftop restaurant lounge has views of the city, but then so do many rooms in this sleek yet reasonably priced hotel. Rooms have floor-to-ceiling windows, custom-designed contemporary furniture, CD players, on-demand movies and down comforters. Complimentary continental breakfast is served in the lobby, where there's also a 24-hour espresso bar.

HOTELS

The Carlton

$$$$ **316 rooms**
*88 Madison Ave. at E. 29th St.,
TriBeCa. 212-532-4100 or 800-601-
8500. www.carltonhotelny.com.*

This early 20C Beaux-Arts structure
was restored, inside and out,
in 2005. The lobby now has a
dramatic two-story waterfall; guest
rooms boast luxurious Scala-
mandre fabrics and Frette linens.
High-tech amenities include free
wireless Internet access and iPod
docking stations. The top-notch
restaurant, **Country ($$$$)** serves
French-influenced classics made
with seasonal ingredients.

Casablanca Hotel

$$$$ **48 rooms**
*147 W. 43rd St. between Ave.
of the Americas & Broadway,
Theater District. 212-869-1212.
www.casablancahotel.com.*

Surround yourself in a Moroccan-
style setting right in the middle of
Manhattan. The recently renovated
guest rooms feature comfortable
furnishings as well as high-tech
amenities. The hotel provides
a complimentary continental
breakfast and use of a nearby
fitness facility.

Hotel 41 at Times Square

$$$$ **47 rooms**
*206 W. 41st St. between Seventh &
Eighth Aves., Midtown. 212-703-
8600. www.hotel41.com.*

Opened in 2002, Hotel 41 is a
cozy, reasonably priced boutique
hotel that's just steps from Times
Square. All rooms come with a
private safe, bottled water, Belgian
linens, down pillows, Frette robes,

◦ *Hotel 41 at Times Square*

©Brigitta L. House/Michelin

CD/DVD players, daily newspaper
and high-speed Internet access.
Choose a movie or CD from the
lending library and enjoy a drink
on the house before going out
and painting the town red.

Hotel Chandler

$$$$ **123 rooms**
*12 E. 31st St. between Fifth &
Madison Aves, Murray Hill.
212-889-6363 or 866-627-7847.
www.hotelchandler.com.*

Close to the Empire State Building,
this sleek hotel offers understated
elegance. Photographs of New
York street scenes decorate the
guest rooms, which are outfitted in
Frette linens and Aveda toiletries.

Hotel Wales

$$$$ **87 rooms**
*1295 Madison Ave., at 92nd St.,
Upper East Side. 212-876-6000.
www.waleshotel.com.*

This nicely restored property lies in
a pleasant residential/commercial
neighborhood within walking distance of Museum Mile. Amenities
include a relaxing rooftop terrace,
down comforters on the beds and
fresh flowers in the rooms. There's
also a fitness room onsite.

On the Ave

$$$$ 267 rooms
2178 Broadway at 77th St.,
Upper West Side. 212-362-1100.
www.ontheave.com.

A recent renovation brought this early-20C hotel luxuriously up to date. In your room you'll find a flat-screen plasma TV and Frette robes; on your bed Italian sheets, down comforters and, on the pillow, Belgian chocolates. Rooms on the top three floors have views of the Hudson River or Central Park; a 16th-floor balcony is dotted with Adirondack chairs for relaxing.

Roger Smith

$$$$ 135 rooms
501 Lexington Ave. at 47th St.,
East Midtown. 212-755-1400.
http://rogersmith.com

In contrast to the hushed minimalism that defines most upscale hotels, the Roger Smith basks in eccentricity: it runs its own contemporary art gallery onsite and fills the lobby with original work; rooms are individually decorated, some with iron bed frames. Pets are welcome and the staff is warm and gracious.

MODERATE

Cosmopolitan Hotel

$$$ 150 rooms
95 West Broadway at Chambers St.,
TriBeCa. 212-566-1900.
www.cosmohotel.com.

The longest continuously operated hotel in New York City, dating back to 1850, the Cosmopolitan

is located in the heart of TriBeCa, within easy walking distance of the World Trade Center Site, City Hall, SoHo and Chinatown. Rooms are newly renovated, with private baths and color television.

Excelsior Hotel

$$$ 198 rooms
45 W. 81st St., between Central
Park West & Columbus Ave.,
Upper West Side. 212-362-9200.
www.excelsiorhotelny.com.

Overlooking the American Museum of Natural History, this newly renovated hotel excels at making guests feel at home. Ask the concierge for help with restaurant reservations and theater tickets. One- and two-bedroom suites, done up in country-French décor, contain plush bathrobes and in-room safes.

Hotel Pennsylvania

$$$ 1,700 rooms
401 Seventh Ave. between W. 32nd
& 33rd Sts., Garment District.
212-736-5000 or 800-223-8585.
www.hotelpenn.com.

Across the street from Madison Square Garden and Penn Station, the recently-renovated Pennsylvania is one of New York's largest hotels. The labyrinthine corridors in its 17 floors of guest rooms can be daunting, but the hotel is quite affordable by New York standards. There's a sightseeing and airport-transportation desk in the lobby and plenty of amenities for business travelers.

Hudson Hotel

$$$ **1,000 rooms**
356 W. 58th St., between Eighth
& Ninth Aves., Midtown.
212-554-6000 or 800-697-1791.
www.hudsonhotel.com.

Located a short walk from Lincoln
Center and the Theater District,
the super-stylish Hudson offers a
wide array of services and in-room
amenities to go with its diminu-
tive guest rooms. Its restaurant,
the Hudson Cafeteria, features
communal tables and the rooftop
garden boasts hot tubs.

Hudson Hotel
©Hudson Hotel

Mayfair New York

$$$ **78 rooms**
242 W. 49th St. (between Broadway
& Eighth Ave.), Midtown.
212-586-0300 or 800-556-2932.
www.mayfairnewyork.com.

One of the few family-run hotels
in Manhattan, the hospitable and
gently priced Mayfair is located in
the heart of the Theater District.
Guest rooms and common areas
showcase a collection of rare historic photos from the Museum of
the City of New York; double-pane
windows filter out street noise.

Off SoHo Suites Hotel

$$$ **38 rooms**
11 Rivington St. between Bowery
& Chrystie Sts., Lower East Side.
212-979-9808 or 800-633-7646.
www.offsoho.com.

If you'd rather not go out for meals
every day, consider staying at this
all-suite hotel located within an
easy walk of a Whole Foods Market.
Kitchens are fully equipped, and
newly renovated rooms all have
hardwood floors and flat-screen
TVs. Economy suites share a bath,
so be sure to ask for accommoda-
tions with private bath if that's
your preference.

Washington Square Hotel

$$$ **165 rooms**
103 Waverly Pl. at Washington
Square West, Greenwich Village.
212-777-9515 or 800-222-0418.
www.wshotel.com.

Across Washington Square Park in
Greenwich Village, this intimate
1902 property features guest-
rooms updated with a minimalist
décor of mustard-colored walls
and ebonized-wood night stands.
North Square ($$) restaurant
(lower level) is a secret neighbor-
hood find.

Washington Square Hotel
©Washington Square Hotel

MUST STAY

Wolcott Hotel

$$$ **169 rooms**
*4 W. 31st St. at Fifth Ave.,
Garment District. 212-268-2900.
www.wolcott.com.*

Just three blocks from the Empire
State Building, this 1904 hotel
offers elegance at a terrific price.
Rooms are relatively large and
well furnished, with air-condition-
ing, safes, WebTV, and Nintendo
games. Free coffee and muffins are
served every morning in the lobby.

INEXPENSIVE

Americana Inn

$ **50 rooms**
*69 W. 38th St., Midtown.
212-840-6700 or 888-468-3558.
www.theamericanainn.com.*

Catering to a budget-minded
clientele, the Americana is short
on amenites, but the price is
unbeatable for the location. The
small rooms are blissfully quiet and
spanking clean, as are the shared
bathrooms. All rooms have color
TVs, coffee makers and air con-
ditioning, and there's a well-kept
kitchenette on every floor.

Amsterdam Inn

$$ **28 rooms**
*340 Amsterdam Ave. at W. 76th St.,
Upper West Side. 212-579-7500.
www.amsterdaminn.com.*

For a simple quarters at a bargain
price, try the Amsterdam Inn,
formerly a residential building.
Some rooms share baths, some
have private facilities; all have color
TV, air conditioning, phones and
maid service. Some rooms have
kitchenettes. The hotel has four

floors and no elevator; a doorman
can assist you during the day.

Chelsea Lodge

$$ **22 rooms**
*318 W. 20th St., Chelsea.
212-243-4499 or 800-373-1116.
www.chelsealodge.com.*

Budget travelers rave about
the bargain-basement rates
and neighborhood feel at this
European-style hostelry in the
heart of Chelsea. The small, simple
rooms boast amenities not gener-
ally found in budget hotels, like
flat-screen TVs and free Wi-Fi. Each
room has a sink and shower; toilets
are down the hall.

East Village Bed and Coffee

$$ **10 rooms**
*110 Ave. C, between Seventh
& Eighth Aves. 212-533-4175.
www.bedandcoffee.com*

Rooms in this funky almost-bed-
and-breakfast (as the name says,
there's only coffee) are bright,
clean and individually decorated according to themes. All the
rooms share baths. There's a full
kitchen on every floor, bicycles for
your use and free Wi-Fi.

Gershwin Hotel

$$ **150 rooms**
*7 E. 27th St. between Madison
& Fifth Ave., Flatiron District.
212-545-8000. www.gershwin
hotel.com.*

Young international travelers, as
well as up-and-coming models
and families, are drawn to this
funky little hotel in the Flatiron
District. The décor recalls Andy
Warhol and his Pop Art brethren.

HOTELS

177

For families there are two creatively appointed suites, as well as baby-sitting services.

Hotel Belleclaire
$$　　**170 rooms**

250 W. 77th St. at Broadway, Upper West Side. 212-362-7700 or 877-468-3522. www.hotelbelle claire.com.

Built in 1903, this Upper West Side landmark features tasteful rooms. The staff is friendly and helpful, and the brand-new fitness center is free for guests. For breakfast, grab a homemade bagel from nearby 🦫**Zabar**'s *(see Must Shop)*.

Hotel Belleclaire
©Hotel Belleclaire

Hotel Grace
$$　　**139 rooms**
125 W. 45th St., Midtown. 212-354-2323. www.room-mate hotels.com.

Spare, modern furnishings outfit the tiny guest rooms at this budget find, but the beds are swathed in quality linens and there's a flat-screen TV and a CD/DVD player in every room. The Midtown location is excellent, just steps from Bryant Park. Continental breakfast is included.

Larchmont Hotel
$$　　**60 rooms**
27 W. 11th St., between Fifth & Sixth Aves., Greenwich Village. 212-989-9333. www.larchmon thotel.com.

You're smack in the middle of Greenwich Village when you stay at this trim, well-maintained property. Rooms are outfitted with blonde furnishings. Guests are provisioned with a robe and slippers – and a complimentary continental breakfast. Rooms come with a wash basin, but shared bathrooms are down the hall.

Pod Hotel
$$　　**156 rooms**
230 E. 51st. St. (between Second & Third Aves.), Midtown. 212-355-0300 or 800-742-5945. www.thepodhotel.com.

Admittedly spare and diminutive, the cheerfully decorated guest rooms ("pods") are nevertheless impeccably clean and plenty comfortable with all the basics in a space designed for maximum efficiency. Not all pods have bathrooms, but those without have an indicator to let you know when one of the nicely appointed shared baths opens up.

Lobby, Pod Hotel
© The Pod Hotel

MUST STAY

HOTELS BY THEME

Looking for a place that will welcome you and your two toddlers? How about one that will tolerate – nay, pamper – your darling chihuahua? In the previous pages we've organized the properties by price category; here we've arranged them by theme to help you find the perfect accommodations. All hotels listed below are in Manhattan.

HOTELS

MICHELIN GUIDE

The Michelin Guide provides a comprehensive selection and rating of hotels and restaurants in all categories of comfort and prices. As part of our meticulous and highly confidential evaluation process, Michelin's American inspectors conducted anonymous visits to restaurants and hotels in New York. The following is a selection to suit all wallets, taken from the current edition.   *Jean-Luc Naret, Director, Michelin Guides*

Restaurants

A number of things are judged when giving Michelin stars, including quality of ingredients, technical skill and flair in preparation, blend and clarity of flavors, the balance of the menu and the ability to produce excellent cooking time and again.

| Cuisine | ❀ to ❀❀❀ |
| Comfort | ❀ to ❀❀❀❀❀ |

DOWNTOWN

Babbo ❀❀
ITALIAN
110 Waverly Pl.
(bet. MacDougal St. & Sixth Ave.)
Subway: W 4 St. – Wash Sq.
Phone: 212-777-0303
Web: www.babbonyc.com
Prices: $$$

With an empire of New York City restaurants and an armful of cookbooks to his credit, pony-tailed star chef Mario Batali somehow finds time to man the kitchen at his flagship. Seasonal ingredients from the Union Square Greenmarket team up with products imported from Italy, in rustic, authentic dishes. The pasta tasting menu offers a small portion of all the highlights, and the Italian wine list is one of the most exhaustive in New York.

Del Posto ❀❀ ❊❊❊❊
ITALIAN
85 Tenth Ave.
(bet. 15th & 16th Sts.)
Subway: 14 St. – 8 Av.
Phone: 212-497-8090
Web: www.delposto.com
Prices: $$$$

A child of the partnership between Mario Batali and the Bastianich family, Del Posto garnered attention long before it opened. As it turns out, the praise is well deserved for lusciously delicate dishes like spaghetti with crabmeat, chive blossoms and habañero peppers, and young fried chicken cacciatore. Spacious balconies on three levels overlook the stunning first-floor dining room.

Fatty Crab ❀
MALAYSIAN
643 Hudson St.
(bet. Gansevoort & Horatio Sts.)
Subway: 14 St. – 8 Av.
Phone: 212-352-3590
Web: www.fattycrab.com
Prices: $$

Fatty Crab delivers bold Asian cooking just out of earshot of the Meatpacking District. The diminutive dining room is China-chic, with red lacquer accents and vases of chopsticks. Chef Zak Pellacio spent time in Malaysia, and the menu shows it. Go for any of the house specialties, especially the chili crab, a messy bowl of fun with large pieces of Dungeness crab in a spicy-sweet tomato chili sauce.

Kittichai XX
THAI
60 Thompson St.
(bet. Broome & Spring Sts.)
Subway: Spring St. (Sixth ave.)
Phone: 212-219-2000
Web: www.kittichairestaurant.com
Prices: $$$

Located in the fashionable Sixty Thompson Hotel (see hotel listing), this sensual SoHo newcomer offers toned-down Thai cooking, thanks to Chef Ian Chalermkittichai, who came to New York from the Four Seasons Hotel in Bangkok.
The food is as appealing as this exotic setting, where orchids float in bottles on lit shelves; lush silk fabrics and Thai artifacts adorn the walls; and a reflecting pool forms the centerpiece of the dining room. Appetizers and entrées are modern and approachable, balancing European technique with New York accents and Thai inflections.

Mesa Grill XX
SOUTHWESTERN
102 Fifth Ave. (bet. 15th & 16th Sts.)
Subway: 14 St. – Union Sq.
Phone: 212-807-7400
Web: www.mesagrill.com
Prices: $$$

A graduate of the French Culinary Institute, celebrity chef Bobby Flay gravitated not to foie gras, but to native American products like corn, chilies and black beans. While you wouldn't pick boisterous Mesa Grill for a quiet evening out, you would come for zesty Southwestern cuisine like yellow corn-crusted chile relleno, goat chees *queso fundido* and margaritas.

MIDTOWN

Anthos ✿ XXX
GREEK
36 W. 52nd St. (bet. Fifth & Sixth Aves.)
Subway: 47–50 Sts. – Rockefeller Ctr.
Phone: 212-582-6900
Web: www.anthosnyc.com
Prices: $$$

Michael Psilakis presides over this Midtown temple of upscale Greek cuisine like a culinary Greek god. Anthos (Greek for "to bloom") bursts with restrained elegance in its chocolate-brown chairs, and white- and pink-linen-topped tables. Distinctive dishes depend on the market, and the menu reads like a tribute to Greek haute cuisine. Main courses are seafood-heavy (olive-oil-poached halibut over yogurt manti and caviar), while desserts, like a trio of baklava, are Olympic in stature. Food this good is usually reserved for the expense-account crowd, but Anthos delights foodies on a tighter budget with its $28 prix-fixe lunch.

Felidia XX
ITALIAN
243 E. 58th St.
(bet. Second & Third Aves.)
Subway: Lexington Ave. – 59 St.
Phone: 212-758-1479
Web: www.lidiasitaly.com
Prices: $$$

The flagship restaurant of cook-book author and TV personality Lidia Bastianich features a bi-level dining room, sunny colors, towering flower arrangements and hardwood wine racks. Northern Italian specialties like whole-grilled Mediterranean sea bass and bitter chocolate pappardelle with wild boar ragu are just a sampling

RESTAURANTS

of what you might find on the seasonal menu. The award-winning wine list cites some 1,400 selections, most of them Italian.

The Four Seasons ✗✗✗✗
AMERICAN
99 E. 52nd St.
(bet. Lexington & Park Aves.)
Subway: 51 St
Phone: 212-754-9494
Web: www.fourseasons restaurant.com
Prices: $$$$

The moneyed and the powerful frequent the Four Seasons, where they blend right in with the opulent setting designed by Mies van der Rohe and Philip Johnson. You know you've really made it in New York when Julian assigns you a regular lunch table in the Grill Room. The kitchen updates classics (Chateaubriand, Dover sole), while respecting the traditional dishes patrons have been asking for since 1959.

Le Bernardin ✿✿✿ ✗✗✗✗
SEAFOOD
155 W. 51st St.
(bet. Sixth & Seventh Aves.)
Subway: 47–50 Sts. – Rockefeller Center
Phone: 212-554-1515
Web: www.le-bernardin.com
Prices: $$$$

In a city where chefs seem to change at the drop of a toque, it's remarkable that Le Bernardin has been under the same ownership since 1986, and that French-born chef Eric Ripert has helmed the kitchen since 1994. Ripert is a master in the treatment of fish. His exceptional and inventive cuisine incorporates the very freshest bounty of the sea as well

as a depth of flavor netted from ingredients imported from around the globe. On the prix-fixe menu you can choose among categories of "almost raw" (carpaccio of tuna), "barely touched" (grilled salt cod salad) and "lightly cooked" (black bass with masala spices).

Per Se ✿✿✿ ✗✗✗✗✗
CONTEMPORARY
10 Columbus Circle
(in Time Warner Center)
Subway: 59 St. – Columbus Cir.
Phone: 212-823-9335
Web: www.perseny.com.net
Prices: $$$$

Having built his reputation at the storied French Laundry in Napa Valley, Thomas Keller took his talents to New York with Per Se. Precision reigns, from the choreographed service to the superlative cuisine. Diners are treated to a parade of sublime small courses, and while the portions are diminutive, the tiny servings show astonishing attention to detail, amounting to modern art on the plate. Exceptional wine pairings are worth the splurge.

UPTOWN

Beyoglu ✗
TURKISH
1431 Third Ave. (at 81st St.)
Subway: 77 St
Phone: 212-650-0850
Web: N/A
Prices: $$

Small plates star at this meze house, where low prices and a casual, convivial atmosphere add to the appeal. The simple, bright dining room sets the scene for sharing meze, from tangy homemade yogurt with cucumber and garlic to smooth stuffed grape leaves. Most of the recipes—and some of the beer offerings—come from Turkey, though you'll detect Greek and Lebanese accents.

Daniel ✿✿ XXXXX
FRENCH
60 E. 65th St. (bet. Madison & Park Aves.)
Subway: 68 St. – Hunter College
Phone: 212-288-0033
Web: www.danielnyc.com
Prices: $$$$

Raised on a farm outside Lyon, Daniel Boulud worked with some of the best chefs in France before landing in the States as executive chef of Le Cirque. An arched colonnade defines the Italian Renaissance-style dining room, a palatial setting in which to dine on artful French cuisine created from the best domestic and imported products. The talented kitchen team adds a soupçon of American flair to the seasonal menus.

Jean Georges ✿✿✿ XXXX
CONTEMPORARY
1 Central Park West
(bet. 60th & 61st Sts.)
Subway: 59 St. – Columbus Cir.
Phone: 212-299-3900
Web: www.jean-georges.com
Prices: $$$$

Jean-Georges Vongerichten owns a galaxy of restaurants in New York but this one shines above the rest. The dining room's minimalist geometric decor is surrounded by huge window walls looking out on Columbus Circle. Dishes like tender squab with Asian pear, candied tamarind and orange jus marry flavors and textures in extraordinary ways, with sublime ingredients transformed by the hand of a master. For quality and

value, go for the prix-fixe lunch menu.

Maya XX
MEXICAN
1191 First Ave. (bet. 64th & 65th Sts.)
Subway: 68 St. – Hunter College
Phone: 212-585-1818
Web: www.modernmexican.com
Prices: $$

Maya defines casual elegance, expertly straddling the line between weeknight-informal and weekend-upscale. The spirited restaurant's pastel walls and vibrant artwork make it feel like an elegant private home. Far from the burrito-laden menus of the competition, Richard Sandoval's menu reads like a love letter to Mexico. Time-honored culinary traditions are updated with contemporary twists, and a seemingly limitless margarita menu complements the elegant and zesty creations that go well beyond fajita fare.

Picholine ✿✿ XXXX
MEDITERRANEAN
35 W. 64th St.
(bet. Broadway & Central Park West)
Subway: 66 St. – Lincoln Center
Phone: 212-724-8585
Web: www.picholinenyc.com
Prices: $$$

Picholine pulls in a cadre of smartly dressed regulars with a taste for chef Terrance Brennan's sophisticated Mediterranean cuisine. A recent facelift re-made the staid space in sleek tones of lilac, cream and gray. The updated menu still stars the best products of the season, striking gold with signatures like sea urchin panna cotta or wild mushroom risotto. Don't pass up the cheese course—it's one of the best in the city.

RESTAURANTS

Hotels

Accommodations in New York run the gamut from designer boutique hotels in trendy districts to historic neighborhood properties that now spike their traditional comforts with the latest technology. Wherever you stay, brace yourself for steep rates—even "inexpensive" seems to have a different definition in New York. The hotels listed here are from the most recent edition of the Michelin Guide to New York City.

Comfort to

DOWNTOWN

Bowery Hotel
117 Rooms/ 18 Suites
335 Bowery (at 3rd St.)
Subway: Astor Pl.
Phone: 212-505-9100,
866-726-9379
Web: www.theboweryhotel.com
Prices: $$$$$

This nondescript block of what was once known as Skid Row might seem an unlikely location for a trendy boutique hotel, but this East Village property is making its presence known. Though the block can be dicey late at night, it's within an easy walk of New York's coolest 'hoods (SoHo, Nolita, Lower East Side). From the outside, the redbrick facade towers above its neighbors. Step inside the lobby, where dark woods, velvet couches and mosaic mirrors create a distinctly Old World air. Huge, sound-proofed windows afford great city views, and make the rooms seem larger. A mix of period and contemporary pieces add to

the Art Deco-meets-21st-century design. 500-thread-count bed linens, HDTV and rainfall shower-heads add luxury.

Gansevoort
158 Rooms/ 20 Suites
18 Ninth Ave. (at 13th St.)
Subway: 14 St. – 8 Av
Phone: 212-206-6700,
877-462-7386
Web: www.hotelgansevoort.com
Prices: $$$$

Swank redefined, the upscale hotel in the Meatpacking District, the Gansevoort rises 14 stories above the burgeoning hip-dom of this once-gritty area. The lobby of this oh-so-cool property is outfitted in cherrywood paneling and Matisse-inspired carpet. Elegant guest rooms wear a dusky palette with touches of color, and huge windows overlook the Hudson River and surrounding city. Bathrooms are large and luxurious. But the coup de grace is the hotel's rooftop, complete with a popular bar and 45-foot-long heated pool with underwater music.

Gramercy Park Hotel
140 Rooms/ 44 Suites
2 Lexington Ave. (at 21st St.)
Subway: 23 St. (Park Ave. South)
Phone: 212-920-3300,
866-784-1300
Web: www.gramercyparkhotel.com
Prices: $$$$

The Gramercy Park has been hosting artists, writers and celebrities since 1925. With hip hotelier Ian Schrager and artist Julian Schnabel breathing new life into this property, the hotel is back and it's hot. Posh British-castle-meets-Gothic-Revival describes the dark lobby décor with its coffered ceiling and crystal chandeliers, red velvet draperies and tapestry-print fabrics. Thoughtful amenities range from a fully-loaded iPod (upon request) to a key to Gramercy Park (impossible to access unless you live on the square overlooking the gated greensward).

The Hotel on Rivington
89 Rooms/ 21 Suites 🏦
107 Rivington St.
(bet. Essex & Ludlow Sts.)
Subway: Delancy St
Phone: 212-475-2600,
800-915-1537
Web: www.hotelonrivington.com
Prices: $$$

The remarkable result of a collaboration of cutting-edge architects, designers, decorators and artists from around the world, this hotel combines sleek minimalist decor with ultramodern amenities, and, yes, comfort. If you notice anything but the glorious views of the surrounding cityscape, you'll appreciate the Tempur-pedic mattresses, Frette linens, and wake-up calls synchronized with motorized curtains. The deluxe Italian-tile bathrooms are equipped with heated floors, steam showers and Japanese-style soaking tubs.

Seaport Inn 🏦
72 Rooms
33 Peck Slip (at Front St.)
Subway: Fulton St
Phone: 212-766-6600,
800-937-8376
Web: www.seaportinn.com
Prices: $$$$$

Hard by the Brooklyn Bridge in Lower Manhattan, the Seaport Inn caters to both tourists and business travelers. The former enjoy the location in the South Street Seaport area; the latter like the proximity to the Financial District. Inside you'll find clean, well-kept rooms with country-style furnishings, floral prints, in-room safes and refrigerators. Some guestrooms have terraces and whirlpool tubs. Complimentary wireless Internet access is available. In the morning, wake up to a continental breakfast; in the afternoon, fresh-baked cookies are set out.

Tribeca Grand 🏦
196 Rooms/ 7 Suites
2 Sixth Ave. (at Church St.)
Subway: Canal St. (Sixth Av)
Phone: 212-519-6600,
877-519-6600
Web: www.tribecagrand.com
Prices: $$$$

Swanky, hip and Eurocentric, the Tribeca Grand fits its trendy neighborhood like a glove. Inside, the soaring atrium lends the lobby an airy feel; the Church Lounge here draws crowds in the evening for light fare and drinks. In warm weather, outdoor seating spills out onto Sixth Avenue. Guestrooms are large, comfortable, and well-equipped for both business and leisure travelers. The desk, accompanied by an ergonomic chair, is actually big enough to work on, and there's Wi-FI access in every room. You'll also find a flat-screen TV, a DVD player (the hotel owns a vast library of movies), and a Bose Wave radio in your room. Children and pets are welcome.

MIDTOWN

The Vincci Avalon 🏦
80 Rooms/ 20 Suites
16 E. 32nd St.
(bet. Fifth & Madison Aves.)

HOTELS

Subway: 33 St
Phone: 212-299-7000,
888-442-8256
Web: www.theavalonny.com
Prices: $$$$

A classic European-style boutique property, the Avalon appeals to business travelers whose work takes them to the nearby Gramercy Park, lower Madison, Flatiron and Murray Hill areas. In addition to its superior rooms, the hotel has suites that are particularly well outfitted for professionals, with two-line telephones and T1 lines for internet access. Many rooms boast a view of the Empire State Building. Jacuzzi tubs, bidets and double sinks furnish the Italian-marble baths in the larger suites. Guests enjoy access to Bally's Sports Club and health spa.

Elysée 🏛🏛

89 Rooms/ 12 Suites

60 E. 54th St.(bet. Madison & Park Aves.)
Subway: 5 Av. – 53 St.
Phone: 212-753-1066,
800-535-9733
Web: www.elyseehotel.com
Prices: $$$$

Since the 1920s the Elysée has harbored writers, actors and musicians like Vladimir Horowitz, Tennessee Williams and Marlon Brando. The period atmosphere lingers in the Neoclassical-style furnishings, careful service and recently redecorated rooms—some with terraces, kitchenettes or solariums. Lovely bathrooms are clad in marble. Modern conveniences include Wi-Fi access, iPod docking stations, and two-line phones. Complimentary breakfast and evening wine and hors d'œuvres are served in the second-floor Club Room. Guests are offered

complimentary use of the nearby NY Sports Club.

Metro 🏛🏛

179 Rooms/ 3 Suites

45 W. 35th St. (bet. Fifth & Sixth Aves.)
Subway: 34 St. – Herald Sq.
Phone: 212-947-2500,
800-356-3870
Web: www.hotelmetronyc.com
Prices: $$$

Though not hip or stylish, the Hotel Metro is nonetheless a good stay for the money. Located in the heart of the Garment District, near noisy Penn Station, the building was constructed in 1901. An Art Deco-inspired lobby leads to a spacious lounge where complimentary breakfasts are served each morning, and tea and coffee are available during the day. Guest rooms have been recently refurbished and are equipped with mini-bars and plush-top mattresses. The hotel offers Wi-Fi access as well as a small business center. Rates include a complimentary continental breakfast. From the large rooftop bar, you'll have stunning views of the Empire State Building and the neighborhood, including Macy's.

W – The Tuscany 🏛🏛

113 Rooms/ 7 Suites

120 E. 39th St.
(bet. Lexington & Park Aves.)
Subway: Grand Central – 42 St.
Phone: 212-686-1600,
888-627-7189
Web: www.whotels.com
Prices: $$$$

Tucked away on a tree-lined street not far from Grand Central Station, The Tuscany cultivates a sensual, relaxed atmosphere. It begins in the cozy lobby, done up in luxuriant purples, greens and browns. Velvets and satins, leather and rich woods add to the lush feel of the place. Spacious guestrooms feature original contemporary furnishings, and comforts like pillow-top mattresses, goose-down duvets and spa robes. Bathrooms are on the small side. In-room electronics include access to a CD/DVD library; high-speed Internet access is available for a fee. Need a workout? Try Sweat, the on-site fitness facility.

Washington Jefferson Hotel 🏛

135 Rooms
318 W. 51st St.
(bet. Eighth & Ninth Aves.)
Subway: 50 St. (Eighth Av.)
Phone: 212-246-7550,
888-567-7550
Web: www.wjhotel.com
Prices: $$$

Located near the Theater District in the up-and-coming Hell's Kitchen neighborhood, this hotel delivers contemporary style without a high price tag. Rooms are somewhat spartan, with platform beds dressed in crisp white linens, yet provide all the necessary amenities (TV with premium channels, radio/CD player. Bathrooms are outfitted with slate flooring and slate-tiled tubs. Guests have 24-hour access to a fitness room on-site, or you can take advantage of a reduced-price pass to nearby Gold's Gym.

UPTOWN

The London NYC 🏨
549 Rooms / 13 Suites
151 W. 54th St.
(bet. Sixth & Seventh Aves.)

Subway: 57 St.
Phone: 212-307-5000,
866-690-2029
Web: www.thelondonnyc.com
Prices: $$$$

The London NYC is like a hop across the Pond without the guilt of those pesky carbon emissions. Formerly the Righa Royal Hotel, The London with its ivy-covered façade rises 54 stories above Midtown. Guest suites epitomize modern sophistication with Italian linens, limed oak flooring, sectional sofas, and embossed-leather desks. Tones of soft gray, plum, sky-blue, and crisp white dominate. Styled by Waterworks, bathrooms have the last word in luxury, with white marble mosaic-tile floors, double rain showerheads and sumptuous robes.

The Lowell 🏨
23 Rooms/ 47 Suites
28 E. 63rd St.
(bet. Madison & Park Aves.)
Subway: Lexington Av. – 63rd St.
Phone: 212-838-1400,
800-221-4444
Web: www.lowellhotel.com
Prices: $$$$$

A block from Central Park and close to Madison Avenue boutiques, the Lowell occupies a landmark 1928 building on a tree-lined Upper East Side street. The hotel's intimate size, discreet staff and sumptuous ambience will draw you back time after time. As a guest here you'll be cosseted in lavish suites, most with working fireplaces and private terraces. A recent renovation added new marble-clad baths—complete with mini TVs and Bulgari toiletries—king size half-canopy beds and upgraded kitchens to all rooms.

NEW YORK

The following abbreviations may appear in this Index: NHS National Historic Site; NM National Monument; NMem National Memorial; NP National Park; NHP National Historical Park; NRA National Recreational Area; NWR National Wildlife Refuge; SP State Park; SHP State Historical Park; SHS State Historic Site.

INDEX

List of Maps

INDEX

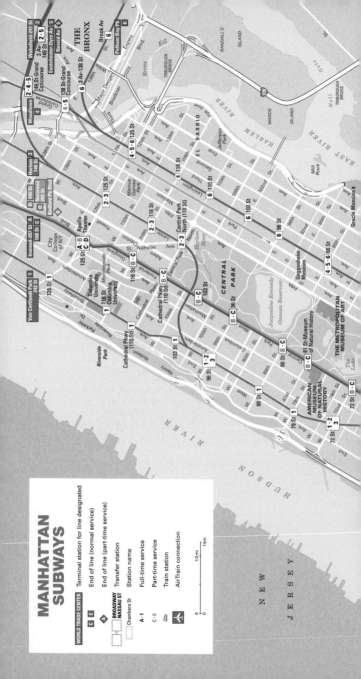